KU-717-502

OCCASIONAL PAPERS

BY

HIS EMINENCE CARDINAL MORAN,

ARCHBISHOP OF SYDNEY, N.S.W.

BROWNE & NOLAN,

NASSAU STREET, DUBLIN,

Printers and Publishers,

1890.

CONTENTS.

PAGE

I. The Church and Social Progress . . . 1

II. The Emperor Julian the Apostate . . 38

III. The Destiny of Christian Rome 67

IV. The Civilization of Ireland before the Anglo-Norman Invasion 119

V. Joan of Arc 156

VI. The St. Bartholomew Massacre in France . . 173

VII. Catholics and Irishmen 232

VIII. Religion in Education 240

IX. Ireland and Australia 252

X. The Fruits of Self-Culture 258

I.

THE CHURCH AND SOCIAL PROGRESS.

(*Lecture in St. Patrick's Hall, Perth, Wednesday, 3rd February*, 1887.)

THE statesmen and philosophers of the old centres of civilization in Europe, though they may differ among themselves on many points, are all agreed in asserting that they and their friends are the promoters and true champions of Social Progress. But many of them are not content with this. They will go farther; and, whilst at home and abroad the motto, "Social Progress," is emblazoned on their banners, they will proclaim that the Catholic Church is their great obstacle in the paths of civilization—the one common enemy of human progress, whom all should conspire to overthrow.

We, who are the children of the Catholic Church, know full well how groundless this accusation is. We believe that the diadem of truth is hers; that her mission is divine; the light of heaven is on her brow, the seal of wisdom upon her lips, and the blessings of redemption are the inheritance of her children; and we are convinced that, though proud men may ignore the Church, and wicked men may cast aside her salutary influence, yet, even in matters which do not come within her immediate sphere, her influence cannot be but for good.

I will ask you this evening to consider this question in

the light of facts. For 1800 years the Church has exercised a paramount influence on society. What has been the result of her influence? Does the witness of history justify the accusation made by the Church's enemies? Far from it. The voice of history attests and loudly proclaims that amid the growth and decay of nations, the changes of dynasties, and the overthrow of empires, at every stage of the world's history, the Church has proved herself the devoted friend of true progress; she is at all times to be found among the foremost in her patronage of everything that could adorn social life and ennoble man—of everything that could elevate, purify, and perfect his noblest faculties, advance his interests, or promote his welfare.

When the Church went forth from Jerusalem on her beneficent career, the pagan civilization of imperial Rome was in the zenith of its triumphs. But no matter how perfect that civilization might appear to be, there was corruption at the core, and its gold was mere glittering dross. I need name but three conditions of society in those days to justify this statement. Poverty was branded as a crime; more than this, slavery was the very corner-stone of the social fabric; and, above all, despotism, unchecked and uncontrolled, ruled supreme. All this was changed through the influence of the Catholic Church; but it was not by a wrench of society, or by stirring up commotion in the existing order of things, that she achieved so happy a result. She was content to announce the teachings of divine truth, and to repeat those sacred principles which, in due time, were destined to renew society, and to leaven the whole order of civilization. "The spirit of Christianity," writes Mr. Lecky, in his *History of Rationalism*, "moved over the chaotic society of paganism, and not merely alleviated the evils that convulsed it, but also reorganised it on a new basis. It did this in three ways: it abolished slavery, it created charity, it inculcated self-sacrifice."

The Church proclaimed that all men are equal before God; all have the one Father who is in heaven, kneel at the same altar, are sanctified by the same sacraments, walk in the same paths of piety, and aspire to the same heavenly destiny. Hear the golden words of Lactantius: "God has imposed on all the same condition of living: He has formed all to wisdom: He has promised immortality to all: no one is cut off from His heavenly gifts. For, as He distributes to all alike His one light, to all sends forth His fountains, supplies food, and gives the most refreshing rest of sleep; so He bestows on all equity and virtue. In His sight no one is a slave, no one a master; for, if all have the same Father, by equal right we are all His children. No one is poor in the sight of God, but he who is without justice; no one is rich, but he who is full of virtue . . . Some one will say: Are there not among you some poor and others rich; some servants and others masters? Is there not some difference between individuals? There is none; nor is there any other cause why we mutually bestow upon each other the name of brethren, except that we believe ourselves to be equal. Riches do not render men illustrious, except that they are able to make them more conspicuous by good works; for men are rich, not because they possess riches, but because they employ them on works of justice." It is, in a certain way, like the vine and the elm-tree in the vineyard that the poor and the rich are both alike necessary for the well-being of society. The vineyard elm has of itself neither beauty nor fruitfulness to commend it. The vine, without the elm to support it, will produce but little fruit. But entwine them together and the vineyard becomes arrayed in all its full richness and comeliness.

Let us see how this teaching of the Church was carried into practice. St. Lawrence was led before the Prefect of Rome, and commanded to surrender the riches of the Church entrusted to his care. At his request, three days were granted him that he might gather to an appointed place all his treasures. At the fixed time, the Prefect sees marshalled before him the widows and orphans, the helpless, the poor, the aged, and the infirm : "These," cried out St. Lawrence, "these are our riches, these our jewels, these the treasures that we prize." Again, we read of a Christian empress, in those days, who went about visiting the sick and the poor, and with her own hands ministered to their wants and relieved their distress. Some would remonstrate with her: "It was enough," they said, "that the emperor should bestow alms." She replied: "To give silver or gold is the part of the emperor; but it is mine to serve the poor, in order that heaven may bless the empire." I will mention but one other fact. A Christian prince, whilst hunting in the forest, found a blind man who had lost his way, and cried aloud for help. Without making himself known, the prince, heedless of the excitement of the chase, dismounted, and, taking the poor man by the hand, led him to the beaten path. The blind man, exhausted through anxiety and fatigue, asked for a drink of water. The prince went in search of a spring, and, when he had found it, gave him to drink. The blind man no sooner tasted the water, and bathed his eyes with it, than his sight was restored. Such was the blessing of heaven upon the true charity of that Christian prince.

As regards slavery, let us take the instance of St. Paulinus. He was of Pretorian rank, and had held the office of Imperial Prefect of Rome. Nevertheless, he sold out all his possessions and distributed the price among the poor. In after years, a widow's son, her only support, was carried off and sold as a slave. Having no other means at his command, Paulinus, to purchase the freedom of the slave, gave himself as a substitute into slavery, that thus the slave might be set free, to bring consolation to his sorrowing mother. Of this heroism of charity there have been many examples in the Church; and even a religious order was established whose brethren bound themselves by vow to devote their labour, and to sacrifice their liberty, if necessary, to procure the liberation of Christian slaves.

When St. Martin, the great patron of Gaul, was as yet in the army and a Catechumen, passing by the gate of the city of Amiens, he met a beggar, almost naked through extreme poverty. Full of compassion, he drew his sword, and cutting his military mantle in twain, gave half of it to the poor man. The bystanders jeered and laughed; but that night St. Martin saw in a vision our Saviour seated on His throne, surrounded by the hosts of heaven, and wearing the half mantle which He had received from the hands of Martin, and which now beamed with light brighter than the sun. In after years, St. Martin chose for the site of his monastery Marmoutier, a lovely spot on the banks of the Loire, shut in by sandstone cliffs and by the forest, and only to be reached by a narrow path. Rich and poor flocked to him thither to be his disciples, were enrolled among the brethren, and had all things in common. Whilst the saint sojourned there, the Count Avitianus dragged to Tours a long chain of captives, who the following day were to suffer torture or death. St. Martin hastened to the city, and, though the night was far advanced, proceeded to the palace door, which he besieged with his prayers and cries. The attendants paid no heed to his clamour; but the count, who had heard those cries, and was impatient at his servants' carelessness, hurried to the door himself, and found the venerable bishop, with bare head, and prostrate at the threshold, and his hands stretched out in supplication. The count recognized St. Martin, and said to him: "Do not even speak; I know thy request. Every prisoner shall be spared. For thy sake I grant them their lives and liberty."

To remove the stain of slavery, and to lessen the hardships which it involved, has ever been the aim of the

Catholic Church. "Since the Saviour and Creator of the world,"—thus writes Pope Gregory I.—"wished to become man, in order, by grace and liberty, to break the chains of our slavery, it is right and good to bestow again upon man, whom nature has permitted to be born free, but whom the law of nations has brought under yoke of slavery, the blessing of their original liberty." These golden words were repeated from age to age, till at length, in the thirteenth century, another Pontiff, Pope Pius II., could say: "Thanks to God and the Apostolic See, the yoke of slavery does no longer disgrace any European nation."

The same spirit of Christian charity that loosed the bonds of slavery, provided abundantly for the wants of the poor. In mediæval times the poor were not despised, but were treated with respect, reverence, and honour.

Men, foremost in every walk of life, made themselves familiar with the most repulsive forms of misery, that they might bring consolation to the aching heart, and alleviate the burden of those who were in distress. Animated by the divine spirit of charity, innumerable maidens of noble birth and high estate forsook the gay attractions of the world to dry the tears of the poor, and to minister to the sick. Charity, indeed, was the never-failing fountain of happiness in the ages of faith. The poor were seen by the rich, were served by them, and loved by them. The wealthy and the powerful did not distain to live among the poor—nay, they recognized in the poverty of those around them a golden opportunity which Providence placed within their reach, enabling them to fulfil the most solemn duties of religion. The alms which they bestowed were a voluntary tribute paid for our Saviour's sake. If liberality, and kindness, and tender feeling controlled the whole system of alms-giving, it was purified and perfected by genuine charity. Thus poverty was not branded as a crime, nor were the destitute crushed and humiliated; but those who were in distress became reconciled to their lot, and loved their benefactors. Political economists of our own days would adopt another course. Having flung aside ths Catholic traditions of the past, they would fain condemn the mediæval system of dealing with poverty, and revive, in all its harshness, the pagan system. What are the poorhouses now-a-days, and the official benevolent asylums, but dreary prisons for the poor? In the press and on the platform the maxim is dinned into our ears: "If a man will not work, neither shall he eat." But why should these words of the apostle be applied only to the poor? Must they not hold equally for the rich drones who pass their years in idleness, amidst the surfeits of luxury and vanity, and never make a day's return in the field of labour for the wages received from the providence of God? It was not so with true Christian charity. None were exempt from labour save those who by infirmity or age were unfitted for it. Almsgiving itself, and the relief of those who were in distress, became for the wealthy a field of meritorious toil, and the exercise of charity conferred far more blessing on those that gave than on those who received.

What shall I say of the Church's attitude towards despotism? The great doctor, St. Ambrose, expressed the sentiments of all the bishops when he wrote: "It is the glory of our ministry that the power of him, whom the orphan and the widow cannot resist, is checked and awed by the authority of the Church." His actions correspond to his words. The Emperor Theodosius, in a fit of anger, had ordered the citizens of Thessalonica to be put to the sword. A few days later, accompanied by his guards, he presented himself at the Church of Milan; but St. Ambrose met him at the threshold, and, with grave and stern countenance, forbade him to enter. "Did not David sin, and yet find pardon?" cried out the emperor. "Thou hast imitated David in his guilt," replied Ambrose; "imitate him also in his repentance." The emperor acknowledged his fault, and humbly asked forgiveness; and religion and humanity gained an immortal triumph. But I must invite your attention to other phases of the benign influence of religion.

Before the close of the sixth century the victory of the Church was complete. The cross—the symbol of her triumph—was everywhere planted over the ruins of paganism; and the wisdom and refinement of the ancient civilization, acknowledging the power of divine faith, bowed down before the majesty of religion. It was at this moment that the barbarians, rushing forth from their northern fastnesses and their eastern steppes, fell like an avalanche upon affrighted Europe. They did not propose to themselves merely to defeat and to subdue; they came to conquer and destroy, to stamp out the civilization of the old world, and to overthrow every monument which it had raised. Everywhere ruin and desolation marked their course; and, amid the universal shipwreck, the Church alone survived.

We are not to wonder that Providence should permit such vicissitudes in the history of the world. The revolutions in social life, which the world presents, would seem to reflect the changes which, each recurring year, we witness in the material order of things. When autumn's fruits have been gathered, winter comes, with its storms and biting cold, and all that was rich and comely in nature withers at its approach. Time goes on, and the furrows again are opened and the seed is cast into the ground, and, with the returning smiles of spring-time, all the earth is clothed with the freshness of a new life. Then summer's sunshine comes, with its genial heat, and once more autumn's fruits and harvest repay the labour of the husbandman.

Amid the chaos which followed in the footsteps of the barbarians, the Church never for a moment faltered. Conscious of her divine mission, she took the rude barbarians to herself as her inheritance. She led them to the altar, ennobled and sanctified them. Thus the blessings of civilization were renewed, and the benign influences of the Church moulded these rough children of the forest into the most polished nations of the modern world.

Even in the material way the mantle of the Church more than once averted impending ruin, and served to shelter a remnant of the overthrown empire. The barbarians could not but admire the heroism of Christian virtue, and they could not but feel the irresistible influence of heavenly truth. When Attila, the scourge of God, threatened to destroy Rome, Pope Leo, accompanied only by his deacons, fearlessly went forth to confront him on the banks of the Mincio, near Ravenna, and presented himself before him. The haughty barbarian showed due honour to the Pontiff, granted him his prayer, and Rome was saved. When the soldiers asked why he had thus been submissive to an unarmed old man, Attila, replied that while the Pontiff spoke there appeared to him in the heavens two men of venerable mien, who, with drawn swords, menaced death, if he did not comply with the Pontiff's request. In like manner the Bishop St. Lupus, arrayed in his episcopal robes, checked the barbarian hordes at the gates of Troyes. So, too, St. Aignan rescued Orleans from destruction, and Paris itself owed its safety to the prayers of St. Genevieve no less than to its material bulwarks. When Gondebaud, King of the Borguignons, led away 6,000 captives who were doomed to death or slavery, the King of Italy, Thedoric, commissioned St. Epiphanius to procure their freedom. "What ransom shall I offer?" asked the venerable bishop. "Your own presence shall be their ransom," was the king's reply. At his prayer the captives were set free, and as they returned to their homes, their tears of joy and canticles of thanksgiving proclaimed the triumph of religion.

In later ages the Moslem power threatened once again to

inundate the world with barbarism. But the voice of religion stirred up the chivalry of Europe and sent forth the Christian knights to smite the enemy in his far distant home in the East. The decisive blow was struck when the Christian fleet, accompanied by the prayers and the blessing of St. Pius V., achieved the glorious victory of Lepanto.

In the incomparable work of building up anew the civilization of Europe, the monasteries were one of the chief means made use of by the Church. "Monasteries," writes the Protestant historian of the dark ages, "were beyond all price in those days of misrule and turbulence, as central points whence agriculture was to spread over bleak hills and barren downs and marshy plains, and deal bread to millions perishing with hunger and its pestilential train: as repositories of the learning which was to be; as nurseries of art and science, giving the stimulus, the means, and the reward to invention, and aggregating around them every head that could devise and every hand that could execute; as the nucleus of the city which, in after days of pride, should crown its palaces and bulwarks with the crowning cross of its cathedral."—(Dr. Maitland, *The Dark Ages*, Pref.) In the monasteries labour was honoured as an act of prayer. We read of the great Abbot St. Columbanus, that in his monastery of Fontaines, he used to kiss the hands of his religious brethren as they returned from their daily labour. Through the unceasing toil of the monks, the arid plains and dense forests were changed into rich gardens, fertile valleys, and well-cultivated fields. But it was not agriculture alone that was attended to. The various trades were taught, chronicles were compiled, manuscripts were copied, and the higher paths of science and art were eagerly pursued: at the same time the virtues of the brethren shone brightly in the light of heaven, and the example of their lives told with even greater force than their words on the hearts of the barbarians. Thus the monastery was a hive of piety and industry, wherein the monks gathered in abundance the richest honey of religion, literature and science, to be freely dispensed to those around them.

Let us take an instance from the life of one of those holy men. St. Eloi, better known by his Latin name—Eligius—was skilled beyond all his contemporaries in the working of silver and gold. Being summoned to the Court of Clothaire, riches and gifts were lavished upon him. All that he received, however, was again bestowed in acts of charity, for he loved the poor, so much so, that whenever a stranger came to visit him, the ordinary answer was, "Go into such a quarter, and where you see a crowd of poor people you will find him." One of his special works of mercy was to procure the release of captives. When he heard of a sale of slaves, he set off at once and bought sometimes as many as a hundred at a time, and when he had got them he led them before the king that they might be set free with all the forms of law. One day he asked the king to bestow a holding on him that he might there build a ladder by which they might both get to heaven. By this heavenly ladder he meant a monastery. The king granted him the site which he desired. He spent on it "all that he had, all that he could get from the king, all that he could honestly come by in any way, and all that the great were willing to give." The contemporary writer adds, "There is now a great company there, adorned with all the flowers of various graces. There are also many artificers skilled in divers art, who being perfected in the fear of Christ, are always prepared to yield ready obedience. No man there claims anything as his own, but all things are in all respects common. And the place is so fertile and so beautiful, that anybody going there, amidst its wide orchards and pleasant gardens, might well exclaim, 'How lovely are thy tents, O Jacob, and thy tabernacles, O Israel! like shady woods, as cedar trees beside the waters, as gardens by the river side.'" His biographer then goes on to describe how the enclosed grounds were a mile and a quarter in circumference, and how the fruitfulness of the place, combined with the varied beauties of wood and water, together with the order of the monastery, might almost make one fancy that Paradise was revived before him. The like results were everywhere witnessed in the monastic institutions. Vast districts, the most wild and uncultivated, were as a rule, allotted to them, but every difficulty was overcome; abundant harvests gradually repaid the toil of the religious brethren, whilst bridges and roads, comfortable homes and prosperous towns, served as lasting proofs of their unwearied and watchful benevolence.

It was not only, however, in a material way that the monks thus became the restorers of civilization and the benefactors of society. They were the teachers of the ignorant, the friends, the guides, the fathers of the people. "They were," as Kemble writes, "permanent mediators between the rich and the poor, between the strong and the weak; and it must be said to their eternal honour that they understood and fulfilled in a marvellous way the duties of this noble mission. They alone had the right and the means of arresting the rough hand of power, of mitigating the just severity of the law, of showing a gleam of hope to the eye of the slave, and of finding, even in this world, a place and means of existence for all those forsaken ones whose existence was ignored by the State."—(Kemble's *Saxons in England*, vol. ii., page 375.) Throughout all France these great centres of civilization rapidly multiplied. They sprang up along the banks of the Rhine and of the Rhone; they spread out to the shores of the Adriatic. The monks climbed the rugged hills of Switzerland, they penetrated far into the Saxon territory, they were to be found in the depths of the German forests, and wherever these devoted sons of the Church were to be met they were the pioneers of a new social order, the heralds of virtue and religion.

And to illustrate what I have been saying, may I not take an instance from an institution which I have been visiting during the past few days, an institution of which this colony of Western Australia is justly proud, I mean the Benedictine Monastery of Nuova Norcia. Forty years ago the Victoria Plains were nothing better than a desert waste, which the hand of man had as yet made no attempt to cultivate. The Aboriginals in these plains, and, indeed, throughout the whole colony, were described as the lowest type of the Negro race, men to whom there could be no hope of bringing home the blessings of religion and civilization. Thanks to the spirit of sacrifice, the unwearied patience, the indomitable energy, the untiring perseverance of the venerable Abbot of Nuova Norcia and his Brother Benedictines, a great monastery has arisen as if by magic in those plains. In the literal as well as in the spiritual meaning of the words, the desert has been transformed into a smiling garden, which has put forth its blossoms, and been clothed with comeliness, and in fragrance and fruitfulness now yields to few of the grand monasteries that are the pride of the old Christian nations. And yet it is not of the material monastery that I would wish to speak. Neither is it the spirit of discipline and the exemplary life of its religious brethren that I desire to commend. I would refer rather to the moral triumph which those good Benedictines have achieved by imparting the blessings of religion and civilization to the Aboriginals, and by realizing not in mere fanciful theory, but in stern fact, that there is no instruction, no mental development, no virtue, no moral improvement of which the white race is capable, which the Aboriginals also are not capable of receiving. I could hardly have given credence to such wonderful results had I not myself been privileged to witness them. But instead of giving you my own impressions, permit me rather to cite the words with which the amiable lady of the present worthy Governor of this Colony has described the joy which her visit to Nuova Norcia gave her in 1883 : " It is impossible," she writes, "to imagine anything more devoted and beautiful than the life the good Benedictine Fathers lead, or more encouraging than the results of their mission work of about thirty-five years. You can imagine how hard it must have been at first to catch the Aboriginal savages, and to teach them anything at all ; and knowing this made it more wonderful to see all these civilized, comfortable, industrious people, whose parents were very little better than beasts of the fields in habits and customs. But perseverance and kindness and infinite patience have worked a change like a miracle. One saw the result of it all during the long, pleasant day spent in visiting schools and workshops, going into the neat, comfortable cottages, and finally sitting down to watch a capital game of cricket. Do you know what Benedictines are? Well, these good Fathers belong to that Order; I don't understand much about it myself, but I can only say that any Order, or any creed, or any country, may well be proud of such excellent, devoted men, and of the results of their life's work,"—(*Letters to Guy*. By Lady Barker. London, 1885, page 93.) But I must resume my subject of the Middle Ages from which I have diverged.

It often happened, as was to be expected in those times of turbulence, that men armed with sovereign and irresponsible power would attempt to violate justice, or to substitute their own passions for law, and to trample on the rights of their subjects. The Church, and the Church alone, could interpose her authority to check the hand of tyranny, to protect the weak, and to shelter the oppressed. This was her heavenly mission, and fearlessly and faithfully did she correspond to it. Towards the close of the sixth century the Lombards spread havoc and ruin throughout the fairest regions of Italy, and gathered like a tempest around Rome. The Pope, St. Gregory the Great, appealed to the emperor to protect his subjects; but the Court at Constantinople was too much engaged in the pursuits of pleasure to heed the Pontiff's appeal. "Disappointed in his hopes," writes Gibbon, "Pope Gregory presumed to save his country without the consent of the emperor or the exarch. The sword of the enemy was suspended over Rome; it was averted by the mild eloquence and seasonable gifts of the Pontiff, who commanded the respect of heretics and barbarians. The merits of Gregory were treated by the Byzantine Court with reproach and insult, but in the attachment of a grateful people he found the purest reward of a citizen and the best right of a sovereign."

There was scarcely a century in which the Pontiffs were not compelled to use their spiritual sword to correct the vices of princes, and to recall them to the paths of justice and morality. Leibnitz attests that the exercise of this authority was fruitful of blessings to society: "It is beyond question," he writes, "that the Popes checked many disorders by their efforts in season and out of season, remonstrating with princes, as their authority enabled them to do, and threatening them with ecclesiastical censures." Philip I. of France, to the scandal of his subjects, dismissed his lawful wife and lived in a state of open adultery. The Pope punished his crime with excommunication. The prince acknowledged his fault, and presented himself in bare feet before an assembly of bishops, asking to be reconciled to the Church, and promising on the Gospels to give scandal no more. Hallam remarks that, "the submission of such a prince, not feebly superstitious, nor vexed with seditions, but brave, firm, and victorious, is, perhaps, the proudest trophy in the scutcheon of Rome."—(*Middle Ages*, chap. 7.) Another French sovereign, Philip Augustus, separated from his queen, Ingelburga, and took to himself another wife in her place. Ingelburga was a Danish princess, and had no one to befriend her in France, but though she was thus friendless in a foreign land, her voice could reach her spiritual father. Fierce indeed was the struggle made by the passions of the prince, but at length the authority of the Pontiff triumphed, and after sixteen years she was recalled from banishment and restored to her royal rights. In Germany, Henry IV. sought to enslave religion by intruding unworthy men into the sanctuary, whilst he wantonly shed the blood of his subjects, and laid an intolerable burden on the necks of a free people. He, too, felt the spiritual sword, and acknowledging his fault, came as an humble applicant to seek the Pontiff's forgiveness at Canossa. What did not Henry VIII. of England promise if only it were permitted him to violate the rights of his queen and be married to Anne Boleyn? Terrible was the ruin which his uncontrollable passion brought upon his kingdom; but thanks to the Sovereign Pontiff, the cause of the weak was sheltered, the moral law was upheld, and justice was avenged. In later times Pope Pius VII. hurled the thunders of the Church against another European despot. The haughty emperor asked in derision had the muskets fallen from the hands of his soldiers; but soon afterwards in the Russian campaign his frozen troops let fall their arms, and he who had so long been the terror of Europe was cast down from his pride of place, and was led a prisoner to fret away his closing years in captivity and exile.

The sublime perfection attained by the sciences and arts is another trophy of religion. Under the patronage of the Church the noblest works of Grecian architecture were rivalled and surpassed. So also the Gothic style was gradually arrayed in all its comeliness, and with those mediæval towers, the emblem of enduring strength, those arches that lift up our thoughts to heaven, those pillars that appear to be not the work of men, but of angels, it attained its full development. What shall I say of the mosaics and the stained-glass windows, and the illuminated MSS., all of which we owe to the patronage and protection of religion in those times, and which for richness of colouring, and delicacy of tracery, and accuracy of outline, and an incomparable minuteness and perfection of detail, are the admiration and the wonder of those best skilled in art at the present day.

It was religion that gave inspiration to the illustrious men who revived the art of painting in the Middle Ages, and it is to the munificence of the Sovereign Pontiffs we owe the noble progress which was made in that art before the close of the sixteenth century. It is in the churches of Italy, and in the monasteries of the Franciscans and Dominicans, that we must seek for the master-pieces of Cimabue, and Giotto, and Beato Angelico da Fiesole. The last-named, the greatest painter of his age, would never engage at any work of art till first he had knelt in prayer.

So full of angelic sweetness were the countenances which he depicted, that some one complained they were not like to the countenances which we see around us every day. He replied: "I endeavour to paint nature not as it is, but as it should have been, were it not for our fallen state. John Forbes Robertson, one of the latest of our English writers on the great painters of Christendom, thus pronounces his eulogy: "Those inspired ideals of Angelico, so tender in modelling and in outline, so dignified and noble in the fall of every fold of their robes, and so divinely gentle in expression—in spite of all that art has since achieved, and the devious ways into which she has wandered, still possess for us a wonderful charm; and when the modern artist would make palpable on the canvas the beauty of holiness, he but reproduces the religious type first created for him by Angelico, whose art remains for all time something ultimate and apart."

Raphael, whom the world, by common consent, has declared to be the prince of painters, found in Julius II. and Leo X. generous patrons, who knew how to appreciate his genius and to remunerate his labour. One of the noblest series of his works adorns the rooms, now known as the Stanze of Raphael, at the Vatican. Robertson thus describes them: "He filled the apportioned spaces with representations of subjects, secular and sacred, pagan and Christian, of an excellence which has never been equalled. These compositions form a magnificent epic, in which are strikingly interwoven the endowments of human intellect, the doctrines of Catholic faith, and the incidents of ecclesiastical history, all as conducing to the triumphs of the Christian Church" (page 88). The same writer adds, that Raphael, during the twelve last years of his life spent in Rome, "created the grandest of all the Italian schools of painting, and gave concrete reality to the aspirations and longings of his predecessors, by carrying art to a height all but ultimate; and he made his own works not less the expression and measure of all the knowledge, philosophy, and poetry of the time, than witnesses to his genius, and vouchers for what we call the immortality of his fame. During these years he lived like a prince, and achieved the labours of a demigod."

In our own days, the German Overbeck, the great reviver of Christian art, chose Rome for his residence. He was as yet a Protestant, when a prized order was given him to paint a Madonna. Again and again he applied himself to the task; but each attempt was made in vain. There was nothing in his Lutheran teaching that could inspire his genius for such a subject; and he turned instinctively to seek that inspiration in Catholic truth. This led him to the Church; and, during the half-century that he toiled with unrivalled success in the Eternal City, he gathered around him a school of religious art whose works rival the masterpieces of mediæval times, and have spread his name and fame throughout the civilized world.

In sculpture, Canova, at the beginning of the present

century, renewed in Rome the glory of Phidias and Praxiteles. Byron used to say, "Italy has great names still; Europe, the world, has but one Canova." The Emperor Napoleon I. wished to detain this great sculptor in Paris. "I could not pursue my art except in Rome," was his reply. "But I will transfer to Paris," said the emperor, "all the great models of antiquity that are in Rome." "Sire," replied Canova, "for my purpose, you should transfer Rome itself."

The name of Michael Angelo Buonarotti also leads our thoughts to Rome. Though he lived in an age when Christian art had reached its zenith, it has been justly said of him that he stood almost unrivalled as a painter, sculptor, and architect. Of him Robertson writes: "He was the intensest and grandest artist Christendom has produced. In presence of his achievements, the boldest genius of our day must stand humbled and abashed, and acknowledge that Michael Angelo is one of the few creative geniuses belonging to all time" (page 68). The fresco of the Last Judgment is his masterpiece in painting. A prelate of the Vatican household who, while the work was in progress, had given some annoyance to the painter, found himself unmistakably depicted among the sufferers in the lower regions, and complained to His Holiness, asking to have at least this part of the painting altered or removed. The Pope replied: "If you had been put in purgatory there would be some grounds for your asking me to help you; but, as you have been put elsewhere, I cannot interfere." Michael Angelo's gigantic work in sculpture, representing Moses holding the Tables of the Law, is so perfect in every detail that it seems to live. It is said that the artist himself, when the work was complete, was so struck by its living attitude that he flung the chisel at it, and cried out: "Speak, Moses, speak." St. Peter's Church owes its present noble architecture to Michael Angelo. When his friends discoursed with him about the beauty of the Pantheon, the most perfect architectural monument of Imperial Rome, he promised that he would place it as a trophy to crown the shrine of the Prince of the Apostles. His prediction was verified in St. Peter's wondrous dome, of which Byron has so justly sung:—

> "Majesty,
> Power, Glory, Strength, and Beauty, all are aisled
> In this eternal ark of worship undefiled."

Even Voltaire could not restrain his meed of admiration for this noblest work of human genius, and for the enlightened patronage that enabled the artist to achieve it: "All nations," he says, "acknowledge that nothing was ever comparable to the chief temple of modern Rome, the most beautiful, vast, and bold that ever existed in the universe. . . . Ten Popes successfully contributed, almost without interruption, to the completion of the Basilica of St. Peter's, and encouraged the arts generally. Nothing of the kind was seen throughout the rest of Europe at that period. The glory of genius at that time belonged to Italy alone, as it had been formerly distinctive of Greece." It is characteristic of Michael Angelo that he refused all remuneration for his labour at St. Peter's, regarding it as a service to the glory of God. This great monument, that enshrines the relics of the Prince of the Apostles, is as old as Protestantism. It has seen the thousand varying sects of that heresy arise, have their excitement for a day, and then die away; but itself remains unchanged. Ever firm as the rock, ever fresh in unchanging beauty, like the Catholic Church, of which it is the fit emblem, it is to-day, as it was three hundred years ago, the admiration of Christendom.

As the fine arts grew to perfection, under the fostering care of religion, so, too, was it with literature and every branch of human knowledge. It was during those ages of faith that the languages of Europe were formed and attained full growth—the Italian, with all its sweetness; the French, with its elegance; the Spanish, with its gravity; the German, with its vigour; the English, with its force and richness. Universities were more numerous in those days than they are in the present age of boasted progress and enlightenment. Nor were they empty names. Ten thousand students flocked to the halls of Bologna, and eighteen thousand were enrolled on the registers of Padua. As early as the beginning of the fourteenth century, Pope Clement V. ordained that Greek, Hebrew, Arabic, and Chaldean should be taught at Rome, at Paris, Oxford, Bologna, and Salamanca. The name of St. Thomas Aquinas suffices to recall to mind all the triumphs that were achieved in the paths of science in those days. This one great doctor has done more to illustrate the truths of religion, and to develop the study of philosophy, and to harmonize the maxims of human science with the teaching of divine faith, than all the united aspirants to literary fame who have sprung up in the ranks of the so-called philosophers during the past three centuries.

It is now universally admitted that Italy took the lead in the revival of literature. It guarded the lamp of knowledge with religious care, and the other nations of Europe bent thither their steps to kindle their torch of science. In the words of an American Protestant writer, "Italy, in the Middle Ages, was like Mount Ararat in the Deluge—the last reached by the flood, and the first left. The remains of the Roman social world were either never utterly dispersed in that country, or far later than anywhere else. . . . The great ascendency of the Papal power, and the influence of Italian genius on the literature and the fine arts of all countries, made Italy essentially the centre of light, the sovereign of thought, the capital of civilization." Macaulay's testimony is not less explicit: "During the gloomy and disastrous centuries which followed the downfall of the Roman Empire, Italy had preserved, in a far greater degree than any other part of Western Europe, the traces of ancient civilization. The night which descended upon her was the night of an Arctic summer: the dawn began to re-appear before the last reflection of the preceding sunset had faded from the horizon. . . . Rome, protected by the sacred character of its Pontiffs, enjoyed at least comparative security and repose. Even in those regions where the sanguinary Lombards had fixed their monarchy, there was incomparably more of wealth, of information, of physical comfort, and of social order, than could be found in Gaul, Britain, or Germany." Dante and Petrarch were the morning stars of modern literature. Throughout the brilliant era which ensued in Italy, the laurel crown, from the hands of the Sovereign Pontiff, was the highest reward, and the most ambitioned prize, which men of genius sought, whose applause was on the lips of Europe; and so many were the Poets Laureate who were successively appointed to the high post of Pontifical Secretary, that, for a time, that office was regarded as a sort of appendage of the laurel wreath.

Nor were the claims of music forgotten. The Irish monk, Marcellus, kept alive its traditions in the monasteries of St. Gaul. His disciple, Totilo—a name which appears to me to faintly conceal the Celtic Tuathal—was worthy of his master's fame. His character is sketched for us by the ancient chronicler of St. Gall's Monastery, and you will probably say that it is worthy of the Irish monks at home in those days of old: "Totilo," he says, "was a good and useful man; as to his arms and all his limbs, such as Fabius teaches us to choose for a wrestler. He was eloquent, with a fine voice; he was skilful in carving, and a painter. He was a musician, like his companions; but in all kinds of stringed and wind instruments he surpassed everybody, and, in a place appointed by the abbot, he taught the children of the nobility to play on stringed instruments. In building and other arts he was eminent. He was, by nature, powerful, and ready at singing in either language; cheerful, whether in jest or in earnest. But with all this, what was of more consequence, he was most useful in the choir; and in secret given to tears, and very skilful in making verses and melodies." When Guido of Arezzo invented the gamut, in the eleventh century, the Pope summoned him to Rome that he might teach the clergy, and wished himself to become his disciple. Thus, in every branch of literature and the arts, Italy, under the patronage of the Pontiffs, took the lead—

> "Italia! too, Italia! looking on thee,
> Full flashes on the soul the light of ages;
> ——— still
> The fount at which the panting mind assuages
> Her thirst of knowledge, quaffing there her fill,
> Flows from the eternal source of Rome's imperial hill."

Was the Church the enemy of patriotism? Let us ask Spain, so proud of her national traditions. She replies that it was the voice of the Church that kept alive the national spirit of her people throughout the six hundred years of Moslem oppression, and at length rallied together all her sons to cast off the hated yoke. France attests that it was at the altar the heroic Maid of Orleans plighted her vow to hurl back the invaders of her country—a vow which, with the blessing of the Church, she faithfully fulfilled. Switzerland will point to the little chapel of William Tell, on the banks of Lake Lucerne, as the cherished sanctuary whither pilgrims from her hills and valleys hasten, year after year, to renew in their hearts the holy fire of love of country. In Italy, the free cities chose Pope Alexander for their leader, and they decreed that the memorial of their triumph should bear his name. In England we see a stately bishop leading on the barons of the kingdom to extort from a worthless monarch the *Magna Charta* of the nation's freedom. In Ireland, shall not the name of St. Laurence O'Toole be for ever revered alike as patriot and saint? And in the era of the

Confederation of Kilkenny, when ruin seemed impending on the national cause, did not the bishops assemble in the city of Kilkenny, and there organize a form of government which gave consistency to the efforts of the people, and, so long as union lasted, assured victory to their arms, and won the applause of Christendom? Throughout the long night of unparalleled misery and persecution, which fell upon Ireland under the penal laws, patriotism and religion were inseparably blended; while the Sovereign Pontiff, and he alone of the sovereigns of Europe, proved himself the faithful, generous, and constant friend of the Irish people.

It will be said, however, that the Church is at least opposed to scientific research. Writers are not wanting, at the present day, who tell us to look back to the case of Galileo, and to the attitude of the Church in the beginning of the seventeenth century; and men appeal to this as a sufficient proof that it was the Church's aim and endeavour to bar the progress of the human mind. This accusation has been so persistently repeated from year to year, in newspapers, pamphlets, and periodicals, that by many it is regarded as a sort of first principle, not to be called in question, in the philosophy of the history of those times. And yet it would be difficult to devise another accusation so groundless, so devoid of proof, so repugnant to the facts which the whole course of the Church's history presents.

It would be passing strange, indeed, were the Church to be found among the enemies of scientific research; for true science is the handmaid of religion, and the paths of research which she pursues all lead to the very threshold of divine truth. The Church condemns only false science; that is to say, the spirit of ignorance and error that would assume the mask of science. So long as knowledge is imperfectly developed, it may appear to be in collision with divine truth; but no sooner is our knowledge perfected, and the mists of error removed, than each discovery of science is found to be in perfect harmony with the Church's teaching, and human research but adds new lustre to the triumphs of religion.

As, however, the enemies of the Church appeal to the beginning of the sixteenth century, it may be well to interrogate the history of that time, that we may see who, in those days, were the opponents, and who the friends and the promoters of scientific research. To me it seems unquestionable that the Church was then, as she is to-day, the generous champion of every true progress in human knowledge, and that she most freely and most generously extended her patronage and support to those whose genius was devoted to the pursuit of science, and whose researches gave promise of adding to the domain of truth. But first let us see what was achieved in this noble cause by the Protestant governments of those times.

Tycho Brahé, one of the most distinguished names of which astronomical science can boast, may be justly reckoned among the illustrious contemporaries of Galileo. Descended from a noble Swedish family, he was educated in Denmark, and was from infancy imbued with Protestantism. By his genius and wonderful conquests in the domain of knowledge, he made the name of Denmark honoured throughout Europe. The island of Huen, situated six miles from the coast of Zealand, was chosen for his observatory. The island, which seemed like a mountain gradually rising from the beach, and ending in a vast plain, was rich in deer and partridge, and afforded excellent pasturage for cattle. Here Tycho expended £40,000 in the erection of an observatory, the most complete of which Europe could then boast. This observatory was surrounded by a semicircular rampart, the inner diameter of which was ninety feet, and by shrubberies with three hundred varieties of trees. To the north and south fronts were attached two round towers, whose inner diameter was about thirty feet. Those towers formed the observatories, and had windows in their roofs that could be opened towards any part of the sky that the astronomer might wish to scan. Nothing was left undone to make the arrangements perfect; and Tycho called the island Uraniburg, or *The City of the Heavens*. For a short time everything seemed to prosper; but the puritanical spirit of the Danish court was not slow in giving proof that it extended only an unwilling toleration to the scientific pursuits of Uraniburg. A committee was appointed to report to the government on the nature and utility of Tycho's studies. They visited the place, and reported that "his studies were of no value, and they were not only useless, but noxious." (Brewster, page 138.) Following on this report, prohibitory orders were issued; and Tycho resolved to remain no longer in an ungrateful country. He packed up his instruments, and his barque, "freighted with the glory of Denmark" (*ibid.* page 138), brought him safely to Rostock. In Rudolph, the Catholic Emperor of Austria, he found a munificent patron. Wealth and honours were lavished on him; and, in return, he wished to hand down to posterity the name and fame of the Catholic sovereign, and gave to the important astronomical calculations, of which the publication was only begun at the time of his demise, the title which they still retain—*The Rudolphian Tables*. A few years later, some pilgrims of science visited the island of Huen. Of the observatory not a trace was to be found; desolation reigned supreme, and, as the result of Danish bigotry, a shapeless mound was all that remained of the short-lived glory of Uraniburg.

John Kepler, one of the greatest astronomers of all ages, though a German Protestant, found also at the Court of Rudolph the patronage which the Lutheran princes denied him. Of him, Menzel, the historian of Germany, relates that "his (astronomical) discovery was condemned by the Protestant Tübingen University as contrary to the Bible.

He was about to destroy his work when an asylum was granted to him at Graz, which he afterward quitted for the Catholic Imperial Court. He was, notwithstanding his Lutheran principles, tolerated by the Jesuits who knew how to value scientific knowledge. He was persecuted solely in his native country, where he with difficulty saved his mother from being burned as a witch."—(*Hist. of Germany*, vol. ii., page 308.) When the religious wars threatened to exhaust the Austrian treasury, the English Ambassador, Sir Henry Wotton, in the name of James I., invited him to make England his home. This, Kepler persistently refused, for he well knew that penury and starvation would await him in Protestant England. Do not say that I exaggerate the case. Hear the statement of Sir David Brewster, in his sketch of the Life of Kepler: "During the two centuries which have elapsed since the invitation was given to Kepler, there has been no reign during which the most illustrious foreigner could hope for pecuniary support either from the Sovereign or the Government of England. What English science has never been able to command for her indigenous talent was not likely to be proffered to foreign merit. The generous hearts of individual Englishmen, indeed, are always open to the claims of intellectual pre-eminence, ever ready to welcome the stranger whom it adorns; but through the frozen life-blood of a British minister, such sympathies have seldom vibrated; and amid the struggles of faction, and the anxieties of personal and family ambition, he has turned a deaf ear to the demands of genius, whether she appeared in the humble posture of a suppliant, or in the prouder attitude of a national benefactor. If the Imperial Mathematician (Kepler) had no other assurance of a comfortable home in England than that of Sir Henry Wotton, he acted a wise part in distrusting it; and we rejoice that the sacred name of Kepler was thus withheld from the long list of distinguished characters whom England has starved and dishonoured."—(Brewster, page 200.)

Such was the fate of the two most illustrious Protestant Astronomers, the contemporaries of Galileo. We must admire the bright genius with which nature endowed them, but it is lamentable to reflect on the many errors, even in scientific matters, of which they were the dupes. Suffice it to say that both were adepts and promoters of Astrology, and that Kepler, in his *System of Harmonies*, states his firm belief this earth of ours is an enormous living animal; he regards the tides as waves produced by the spouting out of water through its gills, and he explains their relation to the solar and lunar motions by supposing that the terrene monster has, like other animals, its daily and nightly alterations of sleeping and waking. Those Protestant governments, in rejecting the claims of science, were faithful to the traditions of Luther himself, who would fain make his followers believe that the teaching of Copernicus was contrary to the Word of God. Michelet, in his *Life of Luther*, relates that he branded Copernicus as "a silly fellow who wants to upset the whole established astronomy; but [he added] according to Scripture, Joshua commanded the sun to stand still and not the earth."—(Book iv., chap. 4.)

And now we may ask, what was the attitude of the Sovereign Pontiffs towards the astronomical theories which are linked with the name of Galileo? The first among the learned men of the Middle Ages, who in a scientific way propounded the earth's motion around the sun, was Nicholas of Cusa. Was an anathema fulminated against him for his scientific pursuits? No; but as a mark of approval he was promoted to the Roman Purple in the year 1448. A century later came Copernicus, who, by his wonderful researches, gave his name to this solar system. Was he condemned by the Catholic Church? No; but he was made professor of astronomy in Rome, received rich ecclesiastical preferment in Germany to enable him to pursue his studies, and his famous work on the *Motion of the Planets*, the fruit of his life's toil, was dedicated to, and published under the auspices of Pope Paul III. In the seventeenth century Galileo won the applause of the learned men of Europe by his scientific discoveries; but his resources were after a time exhausted, and he became overwhelmed with debt. Who was it that stretched out a helping hand to him, and by a pension secured to him the means and the leisure to apply his genius to astronomical pursuits? It was the Sovereign Pontiff; and to enhance the gift, a similar pension was accorded to his son, who gave proof of a desire to pursue the same paths of science. And here allow me to add the remarkable words of Sir David Brewster: "The pension," he says, "thus given by Pope Urban was not the remuneration which Sovereigns award to the services of their subjects. Galileo (a Florentine) was a foreigner at Rome. The Sovereign of the Papal States owed him no obligation; and we must, therefore, regard the pension of Galileo as a donation from the Roman Pontiff to science itself, and as a declaration to the Christian world that religion was not jealous of philosophy"—(page 63). Science was not the fault of Galileo in the eyes of the Pontiff. But Galileo was not content like the other great astronomers of his time, to demonstrate the Copernican system as an hypothesis astronomically true; he would insist on its physical certainty, although many of the arguments on which he mainly relied were far from being faultless. For instance, he derived his chief argument from the flux and reflux of the tides, which, however, no astronomer now-a-days holds to be a proof of the earth's motion. There were also many physical difficulties in the way, for the specific gravity of the air was not as yet determined; and it was not till fifty years after Galileo's time that the law of gravitation was discovered by the genius of Newton. Add to this that Galileo dragged the Sacred Scriptures into the controversy, and contended that his interpretation, which oftentimes was more fanciful than accurate, was alone to be accepted. Cardinal Bellarmine, who was one of the most prominent Counsellors of the Holy See, at this period set the matter in its true light when he wrote as follows to Galileo: "We cannot so bend the interpretation of the Scriptures as to suit your system of astronomy; but this I tell you, when the demonstration shall be found to establish the earth's motion, it will be proper then to interpret the Holy Scriptures otherwise than they have hitherto been in those passages which mention the moving of the heavens and the stability of the world."

Moreover, Galileo attacked in a most unmeasured way the whole system of the Aristotelic philosophy, and thus stirred up the wildest passions of a rival school, whose champions vowed vengeance against him. It would be a serious blunder for us to endeavour to form a judgment of the controversies of the seventeenth century by the standard of our ideas at the present time. Everyone now admits the Copernican theory, but in the beginning of the seventeenth century it was not so. Prescinding entirely from religion, some of the foremost men of the age rejected the Copernican theory as fanciful, groundless, and contrary to the sound principles of scientific inquiry. Take, for instance, Francis Bacon, Baron Verulam, Lord Chancellor of England under James I. He was renowned in his day for his researches in the field of physical science, and some writers still assign him an honourable place among the most distinguished scientific men to whom England has given birth. Ben Jonson writes of him: "My conceit of his person was never increased towards him by his place or honours; but I have and do reverence him for the greatness that was only proper to himself; in that he seemed to me ever, by his work, one of the greatest men, and most worthy of admiration, that had been in many ages." Lord Macaulay in his *Essays*, adds, that "from the day of Bacon's death his fame has been constantly and steadily progressive; and we have no doubt that his name will be named with reverence to the latest ages, and to the remotest ends of the civilized world." Lord Bacon's principal work, the *Novum Organum*, was published in 1620. In it he shows himself well acquainted with Galileo's discoveries; nevertheless, he ridicules "Copernicus and his followers," and declares that the Copernican system is contrary alike to scientific principles and to fact. Thus in Book ii., chap. 36, he lays down that "the diurnal motion should certainly be considered as real in the heavens, and that of the earth must be rejected; for it will be evident that the motion from east to west is part of the system of the world and universal, since it is most rapid in the height of the heavens, and gradually grows weaker, till it stops and is extinguished in rest in the earth." Elsewhere, after rejecting some false notions regarding the firmament, he adds, "the absurdity of these notions has thrown men upon the extravagant idea of the diurnal motion of the earth, an opinion which we can demonstrate to be most false." When scientific men were so determined in their hostility to the earth's motion, we can readily appreciate the prudence of the theologians of Rome in their unwillingness to commit themselves to Galileo's theories. That hostility served also to strengthen the hand of the champions of the Aristotelic philosophy in their attacks upon the Florentine astronomer, whilst his own intemperate language and violent invectives deprived him of the sympathy of his best friends. At length, sentence was pronounced against Galileo by one of the tribunals of Rome in the year 1616. The assailants of the Holy See would fain persuade us that this sentence is a blot on the teaching of the Sovereign Pontiff. But be the sentence in error as you please, it is no more a blot on the teaching of the Sovereign Pontiff than an erroneous decision of a county magistrate would be a blot on the common law of the kingdom. Even after this condemnation many of the leading Cardinals and other members of the Papal Court continued to extend their patronage to the popular champion of science. Cardinal Barberini, afterwards Pope Urban IV., even published poems in his praise. When this illustrious Cardinal was raised to the Pontificate in 1623, Galileo proceeded from Florence to Rome to convey to him in person his enthusiastic congratulations. The astronomer was welcomed with the greatest applause in Rome. Six times he was allowed the privilege of special audience of the Pope, and he was fêted and publicly honoured by the literary men and the most distinguished ecclesiastics of the Eternal City. When Galileo was returning to Florence, the Pontiff, wishing to give further proof of his favour, addressed a letter to the Grand Duke of Tuscany, which fortunately has been preserved. It is dated the 7th of June, 1624, that is to say, eight years after his condemnation. In it Pope Urban refers briefly to Galileo's astronomical discoveries, "the fame of which, he says, will shine on earth so long as Jupiter and his satellites shine in heaven;" and then, after declaring that he felt a true fatherly affection for so great a man, thus continues: "When he came to congratulate us on our accession, we embraced him affectionately and listened with pleasure to his learned demonstrations, which add fresh renown to Florentine eloquence. We desire that he should not return to his native country without having received, by our generosity, manifold proofs of our Papal favour. That you may fully understand to what extent he is dear to us, we wish to give this brilliant testimony to his virtues and piety. We are anxious to assure you that we will thank you for all the kindness that you shall show him, by rivalling or even surpassing our fatherly generosity."

Assuredly there was nothing in all this to discountenance the pursuit of astronomical studies. However, Galileo again allowed himself to be deceived by false friends. Relying on the Pontiff's patronage he resumed with greater violence his old mistaken attacks on the adherents of the rival school: once more the Sacred Scripture was dragged into the controversy: again the physical certainty of his theories was affirmed: in a word, Galileo's promises were broken, and all his faults repeated, and in consequence he was a second time condemned. Some English writers have been accustomed to conjure up dismal visions of dreary dungeons and torture, and violent punishment after sentence, but as Von Gebler, the latest German historian of Galileo's life, has fully proved, in all this there is not a single particle of truth. According to the legal procedure of those times he was sentenced to imprisonment. But let us see what that imprisonment meant. At first, apartments were assigned him in the Holy Office, which are described by the historian just referred to as the private apartments of the official of that congregation, "large, light, and cheerful rooms: on one side you enjoy the prospect of the majestic dome of St. Peter's, and on the other of the beautiful gardens of the Vatican." —(Von Gebler, page 210.) A few days later more splendid apartments were allotted him, the same in which sixty years before the greatest astronomers of Italy had met at the invitation of Pope Gregory XIII. to deliberate on the reform of the Julian Calendar, and which in our own time have been allotted as the residence of the Private Archivist of the Vatican. Some years ago, when I was residing in Rome, I conducted an Irish Protestant gentleman to inspect these apartments. He admired beyond measure the frescoes and decorations of the rooms, the gardens which the windows overlook, and the noble prospect of the surrounding country which they command. Before leaving I told him that it was in these rooms Galileo was imprisoned: "I wish to heaven somebody would imprison me here," was at the instant his emphatic exclamation. There is some analogy between the fate of Galileo and that which befel Lord Bacon, the Chancellor of England. This nobleman was sentenced to imprisonment and to a heavy fine, not indeed for his scientific opinions, but for corruption in the administration of justice. Through the royal clemency the fine was remitted, and the imprisonment was limited to a few days in the tower. Galileo was also punished, not for his astronomical researches, but, among other heads, of guilt for the crime known in English law as contempt of Court. Men of the present day may not accept the tribunal, but its authority was admitted by Galileo, and nevertheless in a most unmeasured way he set himself to vilify and ridicule the sentence of the Court which he professed to most reverently accept. Some writers gravely affirm that Galileo was detained at the Vatican for six years. Even Sir David Brewster considers he is very moderate when he states that Galileo was kept in prison there only for one year. However, the now published letters of Galileo dispel these myths, and prove that the whole time he spent at the Vatican, and that in the gorgeous apartments of which I have spoken, was twenty days. From the Vatican he was transferred to the Villa Medici, which, unrivalled in its position and crowning the Pincian hill, was the centre of fashion in those times, as it is at the present day one of the loveliest villas of the Eternal City. Thence he proceeded to the City of Siena, where he took up his abode in the palace of the bishop of that see, who had for many years proved himself the devoted friend and patron of Galileo. After a time he returned to his own home near Florence, and as a contemporary record attests, there went out to visit him a host of relatives and noble friends, amongst the latter being no less a personage than the Grand Duke himself. Such was the much-talked-of imprisonment of Galileo. Throughout all this period of turmoil, and to the day of his death, he continued to enjoy the pension which years before had been munificently assigned to him by the Sovereign Pontiff. From all this it seems to me to result that in the case of

Galileo we have a further unquestionable proof of the princely patronage with which the Popes promoted study in those days, and encouraged literary men in their pursuits of science. At the very time that Galileo, through his own recklessness and indiscretion, was beset with trouble, Castelli and Cavalieri, and other distinguished astronomers, publicly taught the Corpernican theory in the Papal States and elsewhere throughout Italy. Men, worthy heirs of their renown, have continued to hand on the traditions of science, and there have been no brighter names among the scientific men of our own times than Vico and Secchi, illustrious Italian Jesuits, who have won immortal fame by perfecting Galileo's theories, and whom it was my privilege in different classes to have had for professors during my collegiate years. Among the Protestant writers who have formed a just appreciation of the whole question regarding Galileo, I may mention the name of Dr. Whewell, who in his *History of the Inductive Sciences* attests that it was Galileo's own behaviour that provoked the interference of the ecclesiastical authorities; "and," he adds, "that the controversy must be looked upon rather as a question of decorum than a struggle in which the interests of truth and free inquiry were deeply concerned. The general acceptance of the Copernican system was no longer a matter of doubt. Several persons in the highest positions, including the Pope himself, looked upon the doctrine with favourable eyes, and had showed their interest in Galileo and his discoveries."

I have incidently referred to the reform of the Julian Calendar, but I must mention it again, as it plainly illustrates how the Church has invariably taken the lead in promoting everything connected with scientific progress. The Julian style of reckoning time, though comparatively perfect, was found to differ a few seconds from the true solar year; this difference in the course of centuries had grown into days, and in the year 1582 the vernal equinox coincided with the

11th of March instead of the 21st of March, on which day it fell at the time of the Council of Nice, in the year 325. Pope Gregory XIII. had an enlightened mind to understand the many inconveniences that had arisen and should continue to arise from this ever-increasing irregularity. His generous patronage gathered around him the ablest scientific men of Europe to devise the necessary remedy, and before the close of the year 1582 the Calendar, which bears this great Pontiff's name, and which is now almost universally used throughout Christendom, was published to the world, regulating the exact computation of time, restoring harmony between the civil and the solar year, and conferring an inestimable boon on the civilized world. Spain and Portugal readily accepted the new Gregorian Calendar; France followed after a few months. As Hallam remarks, "the Protestant countries came much more slowly into the alteration, truth being no longer truth when promulgated by the Pope."—(*Hist. of Litt.*, vol. ii., chap. 8.) Will it be believed that it was not till the year 1700 that this triumph of scientific calculation and of Catholic genius was accepted by the Lutherans of Germany, Switzerland, and the Low Countries: England did not bow to it till the year 1752: Sweden followed her example in 1753, and now Russia is the only country that refuses to receive scientific light "because it proceeds from Rome." Thus it is that religion led the way in matters of social progress, and the nations of the civilized world tardily, perhaps reluctantly and grudgingly, yet effectually, and despite their religious prejudices, were compelled by the universal assent to award the meed of praise to the enlightened wisdom of the Sovereign Pontiff.

It is time I should bring this lecture to a close. I feel fully conscious of how far I have been from doing justice to the important subject on which I have addressed you. Nevertheless, the facts, no matter how rudely and roughly they may have been set before you, must speak for themselves, and they more than suffice to justify my statement that the Church has not been, as her enemies misrepresent her, the enemy of social progress, but on the contrary, has ever proved herself to be the devoted friend and patron of whatever promotes civilization and advances the welfare and happiness of man.

II.

THE EMPEROR JULIAN, THE APOSTATE.

(*Lecture in St. Patrick's Hall, Sydney, 4th March*, 1889.)

THE Emperor Julian holds, in some respects, a unique place in the history of the Christian world. There were other persecutors who, no less than he, had wielded the whole power of Imperial Rome, whilst they vowed the destruction of the Church; but he alone, amongst them all, is known by the epithet of *The Apostate*. The others had grown up in a pagan atmosphere, and unsheathed the sword of persecution, that they might uphold the traditions of the empire and the superstitions of their fathers. Julian was by birth a Christian, and he deliberately proposed to himself to outstrip the glory of his uncle, the Emperor Constantine, by reversing his policy, overthrowing the Christian Church, and replacing paganism on the pedestal of imperial splendour from which it had fallen.

He was yet a child when Constantius, to remove all competitors of his throne, pronounced sentence of death against the representatives of the indirect branches of the imperial family. Julian was concealed within the sanctuary by an ecclesiastic named Marcus, whom we shall hereafter meet as Bishop of Arethusa; and, when the storm had passed, his life was spared, partly as a matter of policy, and partly through compassion for his tender years.

Exiled from the court, his youth was spent in the schools

of Nicomedia and Greece. The ablest rhetoricians of those times were assigned to him as tutors; men nominally Christians, but whose pride and passions yearned for the revival of paganism. His religious training was left in the hands of the Arian flatterers of the court, whose empty declamation and heretical teachings gave no vigour to his soul; and the more effectully to remove his thoughts from the imperial diadem, he was enrolled as Lector among the Arian clergy of Nicomedia. St. Gregory, of Nazianzum, and St. Basil, were his fellow-students in the halls of Athens, and they attest that he was even then fierce in his passions and restless in his pride; so much so, that he was regarded as a monster of impiety, and men foretold that he would one day prove the scourge of the empire. "What a plague the Roman empire is breeding!" cried out St. Gregory, one day. "God grant I may be a false prophet."

Nicocles, a celebrated Grecian sophist, was chief among the tutors of Julian. He was nominally a Christian; but he used religion as a mask to win court favour. He was at heart a heathen; and he left nothing undone to imbue his pupil with hatred of the Christian name. In Constantinople, and again at Nicomedia, and Bithynia and Athens, Julian, captivated by the flattery of the sophists, became secretly initiated in the rites of Mithras, which may justly be styled the anti-Christian freemasonry of those days; and thenceforth the study of magic and the art of divination had a resistless attraction for him.

It is related that on one occasion, amid the pagan orgies, Julian, struck with terror, instinctively made the sign of the cross, when at once all the phantasms which encompassed him disappeared. His tutor explained to him that the gods thus retired in order to manifest their displeasure at his cowardice, and warned him never again to use the Christian symbol.

Men who studied the signs of the times, could easily

foretell that a violent reaction against the Christian name would have the sympathy of the world in those days. The edicts of the Emperor Constantine were not forgotten. In opposition to the holiest and wisest bishops of the Church, he had adopted violent measures to suppress the pagan worship and to exalt the cross. There were many who, in consequence of these decrees, had assumed the mask of Christianity to secure the imperial favour; whilst others clung to it lest they might be deprived of the rich emoluments and high dignities which they enjoyed. Some of the patrician families in Rome, and many of the wealthy leaders of society in Greece, were longing for the return of those days when there were no restraints on their luxurious feasts, or on the amusements and entertainments of the circus and amphitheatre. It was so, also, with many of the sophists and rhetoricians of the imperial schools. They made no secret of their hostility to Christian truth. The cross of our Blessed Lord had not ceased to be a matter of foolishness to their wisdom, and a stumbling-block in the path of their pride and ambition. They now hailed with delight the prospect of their cherished project being at length realised, and of paganism being once more enthroned in the palace of the Cæsars.

In the year 355, entering on his twenty-fifth year, Julian was elevated to the purple by the Emperor Constantius, and deputed, with the title of Cæsar, to reign over the countries beyond the Alps. During the six years of his rule in Gaul, he displayed a marvellous activity, which won the applause alike of the army and of the citizens. The whole day was spent in the administration of public affairs. He was indefatigable alike in the palace and in the camp. He showed his genius in choosing Paris, then a small village, to be the capital of Gaul; and, through his care, so skilfully was it fortified, and so rapid was its growth, that, a few years later, partly by its strength, and partly by the prayers of St. Genevieve, it was able to repel all the hosts of Attila. Julian very soon became the idol of his soldiers, whom he led from victory to victory, and enriched with the spoils of the Franks and the Allemanni. All this time the pagan rites, and incantations, and orgies were hidden from the public gaze; but, by means of the rhetoricians and other intimate friends, his real sentiments became known; so that all who desired the revival of paganism throughout the empire, centred their hopes in him, and availed of every opportunity to magnify his fame.

The death of Constantius left Julian without a rival; thenceforward Gaul, Italy, and the East, were blended into one, and he wielded, with firm and undisputed sway, all the power of Imperial Rome.

He no sooner entered Constantinople in triumph, than he laid aside the mask of religion, and proclaimed to the world his resolve to revive, with all possible splendour, the worship of the gods. From the very first day of his imperial rule, he gave proof that the title of *Pontifex Maximus* was no less dear to him than that of emperor. He erected in his own palace a temple to the sun, which he invoked as his tutelar deity. His apartments and gardens were adorned with altars to all the gods and goddesses. Every morning at sunrise he saluted the sun by offering a bull in sacrifice, and he slaughtered another every evening as a farewell offering. The moon, the stars, and the genii of the day and of the night, had, at stated hours, their special honours. Oftentimes he immolated a hundred oxen in one sacrifice, distributing the carcases to his soldiers. Immense herds of all sorts of cattle were constantly led to the temples; and even birds, the rarest that could be found in the remotest parts of the empire, were sacrificed as victims pleasing to the gods. There was no special sacrificial rite observed in the obscurest districts of Greece which was not patronised by Julian during his short reign. Nor was such patronage a matter of mere empty name. He made it his duty to slay the victim with his own hands; he carried the wood to the altar, kindled the sacrificial fire, and searched the entrails to learn the augury of the gods.

From the day that Julian was proclaimed emperor, it was the one ambition of his life to overthrow Christianity, and to revive the fortunes of fallen paganism. But he aimed at something more than a crude revival of the pagan worship of former times. He would simplify its teaching, elevate the character of its priesthood, and reform its practices. He would not admit a divine life or a divine power in Christianity. It had been crowned by success; but he would explain its success by the enlightenment of its teachers, the perfection of its organization, the charity of its members. He felt that, after the benign influence exercised by the Church upon the social and public life of the world, it would be impossible to induce society, all at once, to relapse into the gross excesses of earlier paganism. He would therefore engraft upon it the enlightenment, and organization, and benevolence of the Christian Church, thus to ensure its fruitfulness. For instance, he endeavoured to introduce something like refinement among the attendants at the altars of Isis, and Hermes, and Venus. He required them to absent themselves from the public theatres and other pleasurable resorts. He established schools for them; so that their intellectual training and moral character might, in some way, correspond to their sacrificial character. The pagan ritual was, as far as possible, conformed to the Christian discipline. A system of preaching was established for the pagan priests. They were dressed in purple robes; and, wearing wreaths and other ornaments, they were to popularize the worship of the gods. The use of sacrificial chant was also introduced. For this purpose a school was opened at Alexandria, where the aspirants were trained at the emperor's expense. He went so far as to institute pagan monasteries, in imitation of the Christian monasteries, whose fruitfulness of piety none could gainsay. We find him even publicly commending the fraternal love and charity of which the Christians gave constant proof, as if he felt himself unwillingly constrained to say to his followers, "Go you and do likewise." Thus, writing to the pagan high-priest of Galatia, he declares that nothing so contributed to spread Galilean impiety (it was always by some such name that he designated the Christian Church) as "philanthropy towards strangers, care for the burial of the dead, and an affected dignity of life." In another document he lays down that the Galileans (*i.e.*, the Christians) "have taken care to pay special attention to the poor, and have thus enticed men to their ruin." And then he writes: "Since nothing has contributed more to the spread of the Galilean impiety than their attention to the poor and friendless, let us immediately establish hospitals and other asylums for indigence and infirmity in every city; for it is no small ground for reproach that we should be so glaringly deficient in these things, whilst they cherish and receive not only the wretched of their own community, but ours likewise." And again: "I have given you 30,000 bushels of wheat a-year, to be given to the poor. Imitate the charity and humanity of the Galileans."

The Christians had soon an opportunity to avenge the insults that were offered them. All the evils that had hitherto prevailed were imputed to them; henceforth all those evils were to cease. Nevertheless, a terrible famine set in in some parts of the East, followed by pestilence. The Christians gave proof of their boundless charity towards the pagan persecutors, as well as their own brethren; spending themselves, and all that they had, in ministering to the wants of the suffering and the poor.

Julian was not content with restoring to paganism all the splendour of the imperial State religion; he endeavoured, moreover, by disabilities and countless petty hardships to harass and destroy the Christian Church. He hesitated, indeed, to publicly unsheathe the sword of persecution, for he feared lest the heroism of the martyrs would, as of old, win fresh laurels for the faith, and put to shame the persecutors; but—

1. He cancelled all the municipal and other public grants hitherto sanctioned for the support of the clergy and Church.

2. The immunity enjoyed by the clergy in regard to the military service, and other burdens of the State, was withdrawn.

3. The temples, with the lands and properties attached to them, were restored to pagan worship.

4. Wherever a temple had been destroyed, it was to be rebuilt at the expense of the Christians.

5. Wherever the property had been transferred to the Church, and the Christian clergy had been permitted to enjoy the revenues originally attached to pagan temples, they were now compelled to restore, not only the capital, but also all the revenue which had been received. This edict, in particular, was the source of many hardships; and a great number of the clergy were in a moment despoiled of everything that they had, and reduced to the most abject indigence.

The fate of Marcus, Bishop of Arethusa, on Mount Lebanon, will illustrate the working of these decrees. He it was who, many years before, had saved the life of Julian, concealing him within the sanctuary; and now, in his old age, he was honoured and revered throughout the East for his zeal and charity. He had made many converts, however, and a magnificent temple in his episcopal see had been reduced to ruin. He had neither the means, nor the will, to rebuild the temple. He, at first, betook himself to flight; but finding that some of his flock were endangered, he voluntarily presented himself before his enemies. A ferocious mob fell upon him, dragged him through the streets, and subjected him to every sort of indignity. "They inhumanly scourged him," writes Gibbon, "they tore his beard; and his naked body, anointed with honey, was suspended in a net, between heaven and earth, and exposed to the stings of the insects and the rays of a Syrian sun." Marcus shamed his cruel enemies by his fortitude; and, when at length he was set free, he everywhere received, at the hands of the Christians, the honours of a triumph.

So annoyed were the courtiers by the result of the sufferings of Marcus, that they would fain hold the hands of the agents of heathenism. Libanius, the confidant and panegyrist of Julian, writes to one of the governors regarding another distinguished prisoner who had been treated with the like cruelty: "If he is to die in his chains, look well before you, and see what will be the result. Take heed lest you bring upon us many others like Marcus. This Marcus was hung up, scourged, plucked in the beard; but bore all with constancy He is now honoured as the gods are honoured, and wherever he appears everybody is eager to take him by the hand. As the emperor is aware of this, he has not allowed the man to be executed. Let the preservation of Marcus be a law to us." There can be no higher eulogy of the constancy of Marcus than that which these words present; whilst they record, at the same time, the complete discomfiture of his enemies.

Notwithstanding the assumed attitude of the courtiers no less terrible scenes of disorder and bloodshed were enacted by the heathens, jubilant of their triumph, in other parts of the empire. Libanius was again compelled to complain of the cruel treatment of a Christian citizen of Bostra, named Orion, who had distinguished himself by his moderation towards the pagans in a former reign: "Orion," he says, "proved himself to be a mild and generous man; he did not imitate those who made a bad use of their power, but, on the contrary, blamed them. He neither made war against our worship, nor persecuted our priests, and he saved many from misery by the mild administration of his office. This man I have now seen cast down and full of distress; and, shedding a flood of tears before he could give utterance to his words, he said, 'I have but just escaped from the hands of those to whom I have shown kindness; though I have done evil to no man when I had the power to do so, I have, notwithstanding, been almost torn to pieces.'"

But instead of dwelling on individual instances of persecution, it may suffice to cite the words of the infidel historian, Gibbon, a writer no less friendly to Julian than he is hostile to the Christian name. He thus writes: "When the father of his country [Julian] declares himself the leader of a faction, the license of popular fury cannot easily be restrained, nor consistently punished. Julian, in a public discourse, applauds the devotion and loyalty of the holy cities of Syria, whose pious inhabitants had destroyed, at the first signal, the sepulchres of the Galileans (*i.e.*, the shrines of the martyrs); and faintly complains that they had revenged the injuries of the gods with less moderation than he should have recommended. This imperfect and reluctant confession may appear to confirm the ecclesiastical narratives; that in the cities of Gaza, Ascalon, Caesarea, Heliopolis, and elsewhere, the pagans abused, without prudence or remorse, the moment of their prosperity; that as the mangled bodies were dragged through the streets, they were pierced with the spit of cooks, and the distaffs of enraged women; and that the entrails of Christian priests and virgins, after they had been tasted by those bloody fanatics, were mixed with barley, and contemptuously thrown to the unclean animals."

There were not a few, particularly among those connected

with the administration of the State, who assumed the mask of apostacy the better to secure the favour of the emperor, and the more lucrative posts of dignity which were denied to the Christians. "How many abandoned the Church and ran to the temples [writes one of the contemporary Fathers]? How many allowed themselves to be enticed to apostacy by the bait of honourable offices? Branded with disgrace, and despised, they now wander about the cities, and are pointed out by the finger of scorn, as those who again have betrayed Christ for a few pieces of silver."

Special art and artifices were employed to engage the soldiers in the service of the gods. For instance, when seated on his throne, surrounded by images of Jupiter, Mars, Mercury, and other gods, he would summon the soldiers before him to receive a donation from his hands. He took care, however, to have a censer placed beside him, with a plate of incense. Whosoever would receive the donation should first cast some of the incense into the censer; and all who did so were proclaimed to have sacrificed to the gods.

One of the most remarkable decrees of Julian in his war against religion regarded education, for in this, as in so many other respects, the Apostate is the model of the enemies of the Church of our days. His first step was to reserve to himself the approval of all who would aspire to the rank of teachers. Throughout the empire the public education was entrusted to teachers maintained at the public expense, and distinguished by many lucrative and honourable privileges. Henceforward none should be chosen save those whose worship of the gods would receive his approval. He was next armed with authority to set aside all such persons actually engaged in the work of teaching whose enmity to the gods merited his censure; and then came the further decree which even the pagan sophists proclaimed to be "intolerable and intemperate, to be consigned to eternal oblivion" (*inclemens, perenni obruendum silentio*) a decree which interdicted the chairs of literature to Christian teachers, and enjoined on all the public masters to inculcate the worship of the gods. Some of the most distinguished rhetoricians and literary men of the age, such as Prohaerasius and Victorinus, at once withdrew from the public schools, but Julian heedlessly pursued his irreligious course, contenting himself with the sarcastic remark: "If they do not believe in the gods of Homer, and Plato, and Demosthenes, why should they read those books?" Christian children were invited to resort to those schools as heretofore, but it was in the same way that they were invited to the pagan temples, in the hope that at the threshold they would lay aside their Faith.

Julian had recourse to another stratagem, the better to weaken the Church which he so mercilessly assailed. Many of the orthodox bishops had been banished from their sees in the preceding reigns, and others intruded in their stead. Several champions of Arianism and of other forms of heresy, had also been sent into exile. A decree was now published, inviting all to return, in the hope that the various factions would be encouraged to assail each other, and that the rage of the conflicting sects being stirred up, the Catholic Church might be the more easily destroyed.

One of those, who, relying on this edict, returned to the flock that yearned for his presence, was St. Athanasius. He was universally regarded as the pillar of orthodoxy throughout the East. In season and out of season he had upheld the doctrines of divine truth, and in consequence he had been repeatedly subjected to imprisonment and banishment and hardships of every sort. He was now welcomed back with enthusiasm by his devoted Catholic flock. For a few weeks he pursued the work of his sacred ministry in peace, and preached and toiled with incomparable zeal. A special decree was soon issued, banishing him anew from the whole province of Egypt; but in its words of censure it pronounced his greatest eulogy, that is, that "through his influence the gods were despised." It was on this occasion that when he had entered a little boat to seek concealment in the neighbourhood of Alexandria, some soldiers were sent in pursuit. Athanasius, finding that he was pursued, turned his boat towards the city. The soldiers, mistaking him for a poor boatman, asked had he seen the old bishop to pass that way. "Go on, go on, quickly," he replied, "you are close to him." They went on their way with increased speed, and before they could discover their mistake, the saint was safely concealed among his devoted flock.

In many respects there was nothing new in the terrors of the persecution thus raging against the bishops and clergy and faithful children of the Church. Such things had been before, and the cruelty exercised against the Christians had its counterpart in the persecutions of Diocletian and Nero. Julian would use other weapons also to attain his end. He would discredit the traditions of the Christian Faith, for thus he hoped to undermine the hated edifice of the Catholic Church.

Our Saviour had made to His Apostles the prophetic announcement regarding the buildings of the temple of Jerusalem: "There shall not be left here one stone upon another that shall not be thrown down." (*Matt.* xxiv., 2.) Again, he had declared to the Jews that their "temple would be desolate" (*Matt.* xxiii., 38), and that their city would be "trodden down till the times of the Gentiles would be fulfilled." (*Luc.* xxi., 24.) So, too, the Prophet Daniel had foretold that their city and sanctuary would be destroyed, "and in the temple there shall be the abomination of desolation, and the desolation shall continue even to the consummation and to the end." (*Dan.* ix., 27.) Julian resolved to falsify these prophesies. He would rebuild the temple in all its splendour, and he would restore the Jewish sacrifices as of old in all the pomp of their religious ceremonial.

Severe laws hitherto prohibited the Jews from dwelling in Jerusalem. Many of the more zealous had clung to the neighbouring cities of Palestine, fondly cherishing the hope that they would see the promised land restored to them, but, from the days of the Emperor Adrian, it was forbidden them to come near to Jerusalem, and it was only from afar that they could gaze upon the hills that marked the site of the holy city. Julian, by imperial edict, removed all the disabilities to which the Jews were subjected. He pitied, he said, the misfortunes of their chosen race; he eulogised their constancy, condemned their oppressors, and proclaimed himself their champion and protector. Moreover, he invited them to return to Jerusalem, and encouraged them to rebuild the temple, declaring that their holy city should evermore belong to them; and the better to stimulate them in their undertaking, he avowed his intention of offering in the renewed temple rich spoils and gifts of thanksgiving upon his return in triumph from the Persian war.

It may be well to recall to mind the condition of Jerusalem at this period. In the midst of a barren and mountainous country, the walls of the city enclosed two hills. That to the south was crowned by the ruins of the fortress of David, whilst the northern hill or elevated plateau was Mount Moriah, where stood of old the temple erected and adorned by Solomon, Zorobabel, and Herod. The Roman army under Titus had demolished the temple, and so complete was its destruction that the ploughshare had passed over its ruins. On some of the hallowed spots, held sacred by the Christians as being sanctified by the sufferings, death, or entombment of our Saviour, the pagan emperors had erected profane monuments thus to desecrate the Christian sanctuaries, and to deter the faithful from frequenting them. For instance, over the holy sepulchre, a temple in honour of the goddess Venus was built; but this was demolished by order of Constantine, and through his munificence a magnificent church was erected in its stead.

At the summons of Julian, whom they saluted as their great deliverer, the Jews hastened from all the provinces of the empire to the Holy Land. Thousands of families gathered together their wealth, and with their servants and chattels journeyed in companies towards the city on which the hearts of all were centred. Orders were given by Julian to the governors of Judea, to spare no expense and to promote with all their energies the rebuilding of the temple. The ablest workmen and the most skilful architects were employed in the work, and the emperor sent Alypius, one of his most trusted confidants, who had held the high post of Vice-Prefect of Britain, to carry on the work and to ensure its success.

The enthusiasm of the Jews, now assembled from all quarters, knew no bounds, and each one claimed as a privilege some share in the pious labour. Many of the wealthiest Jews donned their richest dresses. Pickaxes and spades of silver were frequently seen and freely used in the work, and wealthy matrons did not hesitate to remove the rubbish in their mantles of silk and purple. The *débris* was quickly cleared away. Pillars of precious marble were being prepared on the spot. Huge blocks of stone were in readiness for the foundations, and the joy of the assembled multitudes was at its highest, when at length the signal was given, and the laying of the foundation stone was begun.

All this time the Christian citizens of Jerusalem were harassed in every possible manner, but the Bishop, St. Cyril, cheered them by his eloquent exhortations and saintly predictions. His memorable words are recorded—"Fear not this vain attempt of the enemies of Christ. All their efforts shall only complete the fulfilment of the Redeemer's prophecy, and destroy whatever remained of the foundations of the temple which they are endeavouring to erect." Facts soon began to verify his words.

To prepare the way for the new edifice every stone was carefully removed from the old foundations. And now, humanly speaking, there was nothing that could check the progress of the work. The resources of the empire, combined with the energy and wealth of a devoted people, were a sure guarantee that success would crown their efforts. On the day appointed for commencing the work of the foundations, thousands of Jews assembled, full of enthusiasm and delight, to witness what was for them the inauguration of a national enterprise. A terrible shock of earthquake cut short their rejoicings. The earthquake was again and again repeated, causing many of the surrounding edifices to crumble, and bringing death to many who were engaged in the work. The earthquake was followed by a hurricane, which swept over the city, adding to the confusion and completing the work of destruction. No sooner did the hurricane cease than the multitudes again assembled, gathering together the scattered materials, and vowing their determination to overcome every obstacle till their great design was accomplished. It was then, however, they began to realise that there was a higher power which they could not control. As evening approached globes of fire burst forth from the ground along the line of the foundations. Everything was soon involved in flames, and a great part of the implements and materials were reduced to cinders. Each time that the workmen attempted to resume their task the balls of fire again appeared, and what filled them with supernatural terror, a flaming cross, like a seal of fire, remained impressed on the garments of those who approached the foundations. At night a brilliant cross appeared in the heavens, resplendent with glory, over Jerusalem. None dared any longer to question the will of Heaven, and the workmen fled in terror, not daring to face the manifest judgment that awaited them. Many of the assembled Jews asked to be baptized; the rest, in sadness and sorrow, hastened away to the various cities of the East. No further attempt was made to resume the work, and Alypius conveyed to the emperor the unpleasant tidings that desolotion once more reigned supreme over the site of the ancient temple.

The facts connected with this marvellous interposition of heaven have never been questioned. They were published to the world by St. Gregory of Nazianzum in the very year in which they occurred. A little later they were attested by St. John Chrysostom and St. Ambrose. What is very remarkable they were attested by Ammianus Marcellinus, the pagan companion and panegyrist of Julian, who writes that "Julian desired to bequeath to posterity a monument worthy of his genius and his power, and with this intent resolved to rebuild the temple of Jerusalem, destroyed by Titus after a famous siege." And then, he adds, that "whilst Alypius, assisted by the governor of the province, urged with vigour and diligence the execution of the work, horrible balls of fire breaking out near the foundations, with frequent and reiterated attacks, rendered the place from time to time inaccessible to the scorched and blasted workmen; and the victorious element continuing in this manner obstinately and resolutely bent, as it were, to drive them to a distance, the undertaking was abandoned."

Julian, with prudent foresight, marked out the city of Antioch as the headquarters of his pagan revival. Beautifully situated on an island of the Orontes, with villas and gardens spreading out on the southern banks of the river, and thence stretching on to the slopes of the adjoining hills, Antioch had long been without a rival among the cities of the East. Every resource of art and of nature had been availed for centuries to embellish the city, and make it a pleasurable resort for the wealth and fashion of the empire.

The river connected it with the Mediterranean, which was only three miles distant, and served as a channel through which the richest merchandise from all parts of the world was poured into its favoured marts. A fresh-water lake, a few miles above the city, yielded fish in great abundance, and supplied crystal waters for its countless fountains. The prevailing westerly breezes were delicately cool and refreshing during the summer months, and a high mountain range sheltered the city from the storms of winter. Beautiful gardens and public baths added to its attractions. It was adorned with statues, monumental columns, colonnades, and marble porticoes; and each succeeding emperor, the better to inaugurate himself with his eastern subjects, made it a duty to contribute something to its many attractions. The cathedral, known as "the Great Church," was commenced by Constantine, and completed by Constantius. Immense sums were lavished upon the sacred structure; rich in its polished marbles, its golden dome, its religious paintings, its altars glistening with precious stones, it was justly reckoned among the distinctive ornaments of Antioch.

A few miles to the south-west of the city was the famous grove of Daphne, the favourite resort of all the devotees of pleasure. In its centre stood the Temple of Apollo, which in pagan times was famed as an oracle throughout the East. The temple was surrounded by cypresses, myrtles and bays, in whose refreshing shade were alleys impenetrable to the sun, with gardens of richest flowers, and fountains innumerable. The grove was ten miles in circumference, and contained everything that could gratify and charm the senses. All this told with enervating effect upon the morals of a people otherwise disposed to indulgence in luxurious pleasures. The temple itself was a gem of art. Its walls were encrusted with alabaster and varied marbles, and a colossal statue of Apollo, reaching almost to the roof, was enriched with plates of gold and other priceless ornaments.

Since the accession of the Christian emperors, Daphne and its temple had been allowed to fall into decay. It continued, however, to be frequented by the votaries of paganism from all parts of the East; and at length, in order to check the scenes of superstition and impiety often witnessed there, it was found necessary to erect an oratory in the grove adjoining the temple; and beneath its altar were enshrined the relics of St. Babylas, the martyred Bishop of Antioch, and his companions. When this religious oratory was erected, the pagan oracle ceased to give response to its votaries, and, instead of the orgies of former times, pious pilgrims, on the feast of St. Babylas, flocked thither to pay the tributes of their piety to God.

A few months after his accession to the purple, Julian took up his abode in Antioch. The work of spoliation of the Christian churches at once began. The chalices and silver lamps, and other precious ornaments of the "Great Church" were seized for the imperial exchequer. At the same time, large sums were applied to rebuild and adorn the pagan temple, and to supply hecatombs of victims for the sacrifices. All the emperor's efforts, however, to revive the worship of the false gods only served to quicken the piety of the faithful of Antioch. In one of his solemn processions through the city, with the pagan insignia borne in triumph before him, the psalmist's words resounded from a neighbouring monastery of Christian virgins: "The gods of the heathen are silver and gold, the work of men's hands: let those that make them be like unto them, and so also all they that put their trust in them." Julian sent at once an officer with a command to the nuns to cease to disturb the citizens by their seditious chant. When, a little later in the day, he was returning by the same route, he again heard the sacred words intoned: "Let God arise, and let His enemies be scattered." He could not contain his rage, and, sending a band of soldiers, he ordered the leader of the choir to be seized and scourged.

Special care was given by Julian to restore Daphne and its temple to their pristine splendour. He offered a whole hecatomb of oxen in sacrifice, and poured out rivers of wine as a libation to secure the friendship of Apollo. The other temples were honoured in a somewhat similar manner. It was Julian's pleasure to act as high-priest; to lead the victims to the altar, and himself to sacrifice them, and then to distribute the slaughtered cattle and other viands to the idle crowd that was sure to follow him. Even his panegyrist, Ammianus Marcellinus, was forced to complain that through the dissipation attendant on those sacrificial banquets, rioting and drunkenness were spread among the soldiers and citizens. Julian, however, would allow no obstacle to stand in the way of promoting the worship of the gods. Wherever there was a ruined temple in the suburbs, or the surrounding hills, he made a pilgrimage thither, no matter how steep or rugged the path, and brought his courtiers with him, to be witnesses of his gifts and sacrifice.

He had hoped that the people of Antioch would gradually be fired with some of his own enthusiam. Vast crowds, indeed, assembled at times to take part in the public games, and to witness the pageant of the solemn processions, but they always greeted him with "Long live the Emperor;" none but a few flatterers could be induced to join in the cry which he had himself dictated, "Long live the gods." He relates that he felt particularly aggrieved on one occasion. He had revived the ancient games, and restored the Temple of Apollo, and he invited the citizens to unite with him in manifesting their joy and celebrating with all possible pageant and splendour the renewal of the sacrifices at Daphne. He tells us how the citizens corresponded to his invitation: "Not an individual brought oil to kindle a lamp to the god; not one brought incense; not one a libation." Only one solitary individual appeared, bringing a victim, and that was a goose, for a sacrifice. Julian took occasion from this to address a bitter reprimand to the people of Antioch, and, unwittingly, he bestowed a grand eulogy on the Galileans (that is to say, the Christians) who, he complains, celebrated their festivals with great splendour, and lavishly poured out their wealth in deeds of charity.

Before setting out on his Persian expedition, Julian, confident in the protection of Apollo, ordered the aruspices to consult the oracle, but there was no answer. Again and again new treasure was expended and new sacrifices offered. At length, the offended deity, with muzzled sound, deigned to explain his silence. He was disturbed by the proximity of the relics of St. Babylas. "Break open the sepulchre, take up the bones, remove them hence," was the oracular reply. Julian ordered the saint's relics to be removed without delay from the adjoining oratory. The whole body of the citizens, young and old, rich and poor, full of reverence for the holy martyr, assembled on the occasion, and in solemn procession bore away the sacred relics to another oratory a few miles distant. The whole way along they chanted psalms, proclaiming the triumph of the Most High, and the vanity of idols, and in joyous acclaim they joined in the anthem, "Let all those be confounded who adore vain idols, and who glory in them." This processional triumph was regarded by the emperor as an insult alike to himself and to the gods, and he commanded the prefect of the city, Sallustius, to search out the most prominent actors in this scene, and to punish them with exemplary severity. A number of the citizens were thrown into prison. One in particular, a youth named Theodore, was for a whole day suspended on the rack, but no word of regret or of pain could be extorted from him. He continually intoned anew, "Let all those be confounded who adore vain idols;" and when he was at length taken from the rack, he declared that throughout his suffering an angel stood by him, bathing him with refreshing water, and wiping his limbs with a pure white cloth, so that, instead of pain, he felt pleasure and delight. The prefect, Sallustius, represented to Julian that such examples of heroism and constancy served to strengthen the Christian cause, and that it was vain to hope to overcome such men by punishment. Thus the other prisoners were released.

A greater humiliation awaited the patrons of paganism, when a few days later heaven itself seemed to avenge the insult offered to the relics of the saint. Whilst the votaries of Apollo prepared special sacrifices in his honour at Daphne, a violent thunderstorm broke over the temple. In an instant the lightning consumed the cedar roof of the building and reduced to ashes the gigantic statue of the god. Twenty years later St. John Chrysostom delivered, in Antioch, a panegyric of St. Babylas. He tells us that the oratory of the saint at Daphne was once more arrayed in beauty and stateliness, and enriched with his relics, and that crowds of pilgrims hastened thither to obtain the blessings of Heaven through his intercession, whilst the pagan temple, mournful in its ruins, and forsaken, presented a striking emblem of the overthrow of paganism. The idols were crumbling away and vanishing, despite every effort of man to sustain them, but the Christian Church, guarded by heaven, continued to triumph over all the assaults of wicked men, and to shelter the chosen children of God.

Julian, so far as in him lay, resolved to be avenged upon the Christians. At a given signal, he caused all the oratories around Antioch, which enshrined the relics of saints, to be destroyed, and on quitting the city on his Persian expedition, appointed a courtier, named Alexander, a man odious to the citizen for his violence and cruelty, to complete the work of destruction which he had begun. When some of his friends remonstrated with him on this appointment, he replied that Alexander was just the man whom the impious citizens (that is, the Christians) deserved to have for governor; and he added the remarkable confession that, were it not for the unconquerable heroism of the women of Antioch, paganism would have been triumphant.

Alexander spared no pains to induce the Christians to deny their faith. Promises, persuasions, and threats, were in turn employed, and those who refused to sacrifice to the idols, were branded as enemies of the emperor, and traitors to the State. In this persecution several citizens of Antioch, and in particular a priest named Theodoret, and two of Julian's guards, named Juventin and Maximin, attained the martyr's crown.

We now come to the closing stage of Julian's career. He had not as yet received the honours of a triumph. Such a public tribute had been for centuries the great aim and ambition of the military leaders of Rome. He might, indeed, long ago have mounted the capitol in triumph, had he been so pleased, after the splendid victories which he achieved in Gaul and Germany, but the Christian standard had not been as yet flung aside when he won his laurels on those battle-fields. He would appeal to the pagan deities as the arbiters of victory, and under their protection he would achieve some singular success which hitherto had never graced the imperial banners. He would vanquish the Persian enemy, and his glorious victories over such a redoubtable foe would, at the same time, redound to his glory and to the triumph of the pagan cause which he had so much at heart. Libanius, the leader of the pagan sophists, had prophesied that "the gods themselves would smite the Persians" at Julian's approach, and he had solemnly declared that the "emperor who had rebuilt the temples and the altars, who had forgotten no god and no goddess, and who had sacrificed upon the altars whole herds and hecatombs of sheep and oxen, would conquer, even without any mighty force, through the power of the gods." The oracles of Delos and Delphi also sent their greetings and auguries of success, and so confident was the emperor of victory that he vowed to mark his triumphant return by erecting in Jerusalem, an amphitheatre, to be dedicated with the blood of Christians, the most acceptable offering which could be made to the immortal gods. The Christians, on their part, redoubled their prayers and alms-deeds, that God would vouchsafe to restore peace to His Church, and many holy men, full of confidence, comforted the faithful by the assurance that the triumph of the Cross was at hand. When Julian had won some brilliant victory in the beginning of the campaign, one of the pagan leaders cried out insultingly to a priest of Antioch, "What is the son of the carpenter doing now?" The priest humbly replied, "He is preparing a coffin for the archenemy of Holy Church."

Early in the spring Julian set out on his expedition at the head of a formidable army, composed of the united veteran troops of the West and the East. On the third day he halted at Beroea, the modern Aleppo. Here the Senators were for the most part Christians, and Julian fiercely reprimanded them in that when welcoming him to their city, they disregarded his instructions, and no public sacrifice was offered to the gods. His reception at Batna, a few days later, was far more in accordance with his wishes. The town was pleasantly situated in a grove of cypresses, and as he approached, the odour of incense breathed upon him, and he beheld sacrifices offered up on every side. But here, too, there were many devoted Christians, and he complained that the smoke from the altars was the incense of flattery rather than of piety, and that the tumult of applause gave but little pleasure to the gods. Hierapolis was the rendezvous of the imperial troops, and there a bridge of boats opened the way for their advance. Here 30,000 men, under the emperor's kinsman, Procopius, and an experienced general named Sebastian, were detached from the main army to proceed by Nisibis, as well to punish the Christians of that city, renowned for its piety, as to unite with the troops of Arsaces, King of Armenia, and after ravaging Media with fire and sword, to rejoin the emperor under the walls of Ctesiphon, the Persian capital. The main body of the army, under the immediate command of Julian, marched along the left bank of the Euphrates through the rich plains of Mesopotamia, while the Roman fleet, consisting of 50 armed galleys and 1,100 transport ships descended the river, keeping pace with the troops, and supplying them with stores in abundance. At Charres, where stood a famous temple of the Moon, the emperor, with his own hand, immolated a Christian maiden in sacrifice to the gods. In the neighbouring desert of Cyrestica he found a hermit, famed for sanctity, named Dometius, to whose cell crowds of sick, lame, and blind, hastened from all parts in hope of being relieved from their infirmities. Julian summoned the hermit before him and said: "Have you not come to the desert in search of solitude? why, then, do you allow this crowd to disturb your retreat?" The hermit replied, that it was his earnest desire to commune in the silence of his heart with God, but that charity forbade him to repel those whose piety led them to ask his prayers, and to implore the mercy of God. Julian said to his officers in derision: "We must help him to keep his solitude," and ordered the hermit's cell to be walled up in every part, so that Dometius attained the martyr's crown.

At Callinicum new hecatombs were offered in thanksgiving, when the Arab tribes presented to the emperor a golden wreath in token of homage, and placed at his disposal several thousand light horsemen, for whom the Parthian plains and the deserts of Assyria had no terrors. On the 1st of April this army reached Circessium, the modern Carchemish, the frontier fortress of the empire. Here the river Chabora, a tributary of the Euphrates, formed the boundary between Persia and Rome. A bridge of boats led the army into hostile territory, and as soon as they had crossed over, the bridge was cut down to remind the soldiers that there was no alternative but victory or death. The campaign now began in earnest. In Julian's army there were 65,000 veterans, besides a countless array of Scythian auxiliaries and Arab cavalry, solely intent on rapine and plunder. When the army was drawn up in battle array on the enemy's territory, Julian addressed the veterans in an eloquent harangue, and distributed to each of them 130 pieces of silver. The vanguard had no sooner begun its march than a lion rushed into the ranks, and was at once despatched. The aruspices fiercely debated the meaning of this omen, but Julian cut short the controversy, declaring that the lion was a symbol of the Persian king, on whom the gods were about to inflict vengeance through his hands. Julian now laid aside the pomp and state of his imperial dignity, that he might the more effectually discharge the duties of commander, and accompanied by a chosen body of cavalry, he was to be found on all occasions at the post of duty or danger. The arid waste that stretches from the Chabora to the fertile plains of Assyria was pretty much the same as when it was traversed seven hundred years before by the younger Cyrus. "The country," as Xenophon relates, "was a plain throughout, as even as the sea, and full of wormwood; and if any other kind of shrubs or weeds grew there, they had all an aromatic smell; but no trees could be seen. Bustards and ostriches, antelopes and wild asses were the only inhabitants of the desert; and the fatigues of the march were alleviated by the amusements of the chase." The towns and fortresses situate on the banks of the Euphrates fell an easy prey to the Roman army, and for three hundred miles the march was little more than a triumphant progress. The fertile provinces of Assyria, laden with golden harvests, and the rich plains interspersed with groves of palm trees were next reached. Julian ordered the whole country to be ravaged, but this reckless destruction was quickly avenged. For purposes of cultivation the vast plain was intersected by a network of canals and water-courses, communicating on one side with the Euphrates and on the other with the Tigris, for, the two great rivers were not fifty miles apart. The Assyrians saw their opportunity, and cutting the canals, poured in a flood of waters upon the plain. Even the camp of the Roman army was inundated, and for several days the soldiers had to deal with an enemy whom their arms or discipline could not conquer. The fortress of Maogamalcha, eleven miles from Ctesiphon, threatened a long delay to the invaders, for its solid walls of brick and bitumen, and its sixteen massive towers, defied every assault. A mine, however, was skilfully carried under the fortifications, into the very heart of the city, and whilst the feint of a general assault drew off the garrison to the outer towers, a chosen cohort of veterans took possession of the citadel. An indiscriminate massacre followed; the governor was sentenced to be burnt alive; the walls were levelled to the ground, and in a few days not a vestige remained of the city and fortress of Maogamalcha.

The Persian capital, however, was deemed impregnable. It could only be reached by crossing the Tigris, and a large army intrenched on the left bank of the river made the approach impracticable, for the fleet, which hitherto had kept pace with them on the Euphrates, could be of no avail for crossing the Tigris. Roman energy and genius overcame the difficulty. It was known that the Babylonian monarchs in olden times had connected the two rivers by a channel, a few miles above Ctesiphon. The bed of this channel could still be traced. Julian set his army to work, and in a few weeks the waters of the Euphrates were once more flowing into the Tigris. The fleet passed through the channel in safety, and the Roman army, crossing the Tigris by night, had a secure footing on the left bank before the astonished Persians had begun seriously to realize their approach. A fierce battle ensued. The Persians fought the whole day with obstinacy, but at length Roman valour and discipline achieved a brilliant victory. Numerous deserters now flocked into the camp of Julian. They represented the country as abounding with provisions of every sort, whilst the only Persian army that now remained was demoralised and ready to seek safety in flight at the approach of the Romans. Julian listened to the insidious statements so flattering to his vanity. He resolved to go in pursuit of the Persian army, confident that the capital would open its gates to his victorious troops on their return. The fleet was considered to be no longer of much use, as the ships sailing against the rapid current of the Tigris could not keep pace with the army. It was, moreover, a stratagem, often made use of by the Roman leaders, to stir up the martial ardour of the troops, by removing all hope of safety, except in the success of their arms. For these reasons Julian gave orders for the fleet to be destroyed, and in a few hours the imposing array of galleys and other vessels were a prey to the flames.

Full of enthusiasm, the troops set out in search of the enemy, who were known to be at no great distance under the immediate command of Sapor, the Persian king. A few days' march opened the eyes of the Roman generals to the dangers that surrounded them. The plains, hitherto smiling with cultivation, were reduced to a wilderness; no provisions could be had at any price, and at every step a double barrier of fire and steel confronted the astonished soldiers of Julian. The emperor began to look anxiously towards the north for the concerted signal of the approach of the army from Nisibis, but he looked for such a signal in vain. The king of Armenia, offended by the imperious mandate of Julian, refused to aid the Roman generals, and beset their advance with difficulties, declared that Julian cherished greater hatred against the Christian religion than against the enemies of Rome. The rival commanders, too, had disagreed among themselves, and they were a thousand miles from Ctesiphon, whilst Julian was anxiously awaiting the signal of their approach.

The soldiers, full of ardour, continued to march onward in search of the Persian army, but at length further advance became impracticable, and the order was given to retrace their steps to the banks of the Tigris. On the third day of their retreat, about mid-day, whilst the soldiers pitched their tents, the sky was darkened with thunderclouds, and a hurricane, with its usual accompaniments of rain and dust and whirlwind fell upon the Roman camp. This was the opportunity which Sapor had been long awaiting. Under cover of the darkness, and sheltered by the clouds of dust, the Persian cavalry, almost unperceived, fell upon the Roman army, and soon a general battle ensued. Julian, who in the heat of the day had laid aside his heavy armour, seized his shield, and flung himself into the thickest of the fight. Nothwithstanding the disadvantages under which they fought, Roman valour and discipline once more proved invincible, and the shouts of victory ran along the lines. At length a large body of Persian cavalry took to flight, and Julian engaged eagerly in the pursuit. A veteran general, experienced in Eastern warfare, cried to him to desist, lest it might prove a mere feint of the enemy. Julian, confident of victory, was heedless of such counsel. At that moment a javelin, glancing from his shield, pierced the side of Julian. He made an effort to pluck it out, but in vain, and, fainting, fell from his horse. Recovering himself, he took a handful of the blood that flowed from the wound, and flinging it towards heaven, cried aloud with his last words: "Thou hast conquered, O Galilean."

The Romans remained masters of the battlefield, but the momentary victory only served to prolong the humiliation and the hardships of their retreat, and a mere handful of the veteran army made good the return to the frontiers of the empire. With Julian perished the last hopes of paganism, and his assaults, which aimed at the destruction of the Christian name, became a means, in the way of Providence, to ensure to holy Church an era of sunshine and peace, and to achieve its permanent triumph in Imperial Rome.

In the anti-Christian warfare, stirred up by the apostate emperor, all the agencies that this world could command were marshalled against the Church. In face of such all-powerful enemies, the Church, humanly speaking, was weakness itself. In the overthrow of those enemies, and in the triumph of Christian truth, we cannot but recognize the fulfilment of the Redeemer's words: "Behold, I am with you;" and, in unison with the early heroes of the Faith, we, too, must exclaim: "Why do the nations rage and the peoples devise vain things? He who ruleth in the heavens shall mock them, the Lord shall deride them."

III.

THE DESTINY OF CHRISTIAN ROME.

(Two Papers read in Dublin, in 1868 *and* 1871.)

I.

> "O ROME! my country! city of the soul!
> The orphans of the heart must turn to thee."

How many glories of the past rush to mind, how many endearing memories are awakened in the soul by the magic name of Rome! Pagan orators and poets saluted her as the Eternal City, Queen of the Universe, whose origin is divine, whose laws are everlasting, whose power embraces a world-wide range.

> "Omnia Romanae cedant miracula terrae."

This was an empty dream in the city of the Cæsars; but how is it realized in Christian Rome! The home of the Vicar of Christ, the throne of the fisherman of Galilee, its spiritual rule extends from shore to shore; the See of Peter—its line of sainted Pontiffs, as if by a golden chain, binds the faithful of to-day with the Redeemer's cross on Calvary; it has become, indeed, the centre of civilization, the mother of arts, the fountain-source, whence flow the streams of science and salvation to distant lands. Yes, it is not its palace of the Cæsars, its forum, its triumphal arches, its Capitol, its amphitheatre, that I would seek in Rome: it is the hallowed sanctuaries of the saints, the trophies of the martyrs' triumphs, the city of God, the new Jerusalem of Christ:—

> "Peter's See, the source of pastoral power,
> The world's capital:
> What realms she does not hold by arms
> She rules by religion."

For three hundred years Rome was the battle-field of Christian faith; it was purpled with the blood of martyrs from every distant land; and yet, even then, a pagan emperor declared that he was ready to exchange the imperial diadem for the sceptre of the Pope of Rome. But, from the day when the heralds of Constantine proclaimed the triumph of the Cross, the imperial rulers ceased to make Rome their capital: "It is not meet," says an ancient writer, "that the emperor of the earth should hold his sway in that city which heaven's Eternal Emperor has made the capital of the Christian religion." The city of the Cæsars became henceforth the inheritance of Christ, the common country of all the faithful, and that mysterious course of Providence began, which, after three centuries, forced the successors of St. Peter to assume the temporal sovereignty of Rome.

It is true, indeed, that it was only in the eighth century that the successors of Constantine finally surrendered the dominion of Rome; but long before that period the Sovereign Pontiffs had been its only protectors and fathers; they were, so to say, its uncrowned monarchs, and their rule, almost in spite of themselves, was supreme in the territory of the Seven Hills.

When, in the fifth century, barbarian hordes, like surge after surge in the storm, rushed over Italy, laying waste its fertile plains, it was the Popes that preserved a remnant of its people for Rome. In the year 409, Alaric led on his two hundred thousand Goths against the devoted city. To a holy monk, who on the way sought to appease his fury

Alaric replied: "It is not of myself that I advance towards Rome; there is one who urges me on, and daily torments me, saying: 'Go, plunder Rome.'" The wealth and opulence of the world's capital were soon the prey of the barbarian hordes. For three days the city was one continued scene of massacre and plunder; those alone who took shelter in the churches of St. Peter and St. Paul were saved; the rest of the inhabitants, hitherto the masters of nations, were now led away to slavery.

For forty years the Pontiffs laboured to heal the wounds thus made by the sword of Alaric. Then Attila, *the scourge of God*, crossed the Jura mountains, and, with his countless Huns, rushed down as an avalanche upon Milan, Aquileia, Pavia, and Verona. It was his boast that the grass should cease to grow where his legions passed. No power could resist his fury, and destruction everywhere marked his onward course. The Emperor Valentinian III., with his court, fled in terror from Ravenna. One man alone was found not disheartened amid the terrors of this dread crisis. He had grown old in the service of the poor and guardianship of the flock of Christ. He had already crushed the Eutychian heresy, and restored peace to the Church by the Council of Chalcedon; now he fearlessly goes forth to confront the advancing foe. On the 11th of June, 452, Pope Leo the Great, robed in the sacred vestments, and accompanied by his deacons, presented himself before Attila, on the banks of the Mincio, where now stands the little town of Governolo. At his words the surging torrent was rolled back, and Attila declared to his angry chiefs that, as the Pontiff prayed him to desist from his enterprise, one venerable in mien, appearing in the heavens, commanded him to obey. Thus Rome was saved.

Scarce have the citizens ceased their grateful acclamations to their deliverer, when another storm from the south bursts upon the Seven Hills. Genseric, with his Vandal fleet, setting sail from Africa, poured his well-trained troops upon the plains of Italy. At the city walls Pope Leo met the barbaric devastator; and, though for fourteen days all that Vandal rage could reach was devoted to destruction, yet, at his prayers, the chief basilicas at least were saved, and, from their walls, when Genseric retired, 80,000 citizens came forth, the sole remnant of a population which, a century before, was reckoned at 3,000,000.

Another while, and Totila advanced to enrich his followers with the spoils of their former masters; and now the anathema of Babylon is repeated by the finger of God in the dust of Rome. *Urbem reliquit vacuam*, is the concise narrative of Procopius; whilst another contemporary annalist assures us that "for sixty days Rome was so desolate that no human being could be found there, and no living thing but the wild beasts that flocked to it from the surrounding country."

Yet did not the Pontiffs cease to watch over the deserted walls; and for two hundred years they continued to be the temporal fathers, as they were the spiritual pastors of Rome. The Greek emperors had still their ministers there; "yet," as Muratori remarks, "the chief authority was vested in the Pontiffs, who, by the force and majesty of their station, and by that escort of virtues which surrounded them, wielded a placid sway over the city and its territory." Indeed, had it not been for the wonderful vigilance of the Popes, Rome would soon have ceased to exist. As Pestum, with its noble temples; as Pompeii, arising from the ashes of Vesuvius; as Memphis, amidst the sands of Africa—so now Rome would have nothing but its marble wilderness to attract the gaze of the distant traveller.

As years went on, the Greek emperors scarce deigned a commiserating look towards the ruined city. To use the words of Gibbon: "The lofty tree was deprived of its leaves and branches, and the sapless trunk was left to wither on the ground. . . . . Like Thebes, or Babylon, or Carthage, the name of Rome might have been erased from the earth, if the city had not been animated by a vital principle which again restored her to honour and dominion." St. Gregory the Great, in his letter to the emperor, complained that everything was given up to the mercy of the barbarians: "The cities are destroyed," he says, "the fortresses dismantled, the open country, stripped of its inhabitants, is become a wilderness for want of cultivation, and the servants of Christ are as daily victims immolated by the sanguinary superstition of these idolaters." Elsewhere he laments that the provisioning of the city, the appointment of consuls and officers, the enrolling of troops, the defence of the walls, the maintenance of public order, all devolved upon the shoulders of the Vicar of Christ. Well, indeed, does the infidel historian add: "Gregory might justly be styled the father of his country."

It cannot surprise us that Rome should be thus abandoned by the Greek emperors. It had no longer aught to attract their avarice or to repay their guardianship. There were other cares, moreover, to engross their thoughts. Hordes of Tartars precipitated themselves, in quick succession, on the defenceless frontiers of the East. The cloud-like cavalry bands of these barbarians, clothed in the skins of wild beasts, and armed with rude lances, could not be checked by courtier soldiers, brilliant in their armour, but cowards in their hearts; and it was necessary to summon away the veteran troops of the west to defend the imperilled throne of their master. Then it was that the Lombards descended into Italy; no longer as a passing wave of barbarians, but settling down on the deserted lands, and snatching city after city from the enfeebled grasp of the imperial deputies. Pope Stephen II., in the name of the Roman people, wrote to the emperor, earnestly imploring aid against the destruction that menaced them. But, as the Romans of old had abandoned Britain, so now the Greek emperors abandon Rome, a prey to the storm that encompassed it. Then it was that, through the necessity of self-preservation, and to save the city and its people from utter destruction, began the temporal sovereignty of the Pope in Rome.

The Britains, in their distress, invoked Saxon aid, and in their allies soon found new masters. The Sovereign Pontiffs were happier in their choice. Abandoned by the imperial power, the first thought of Pope Stephen was to seek to avert by treaty the menacing invasion. A treaty, indeed, was made; but only to be violated by the perfidious Lombards. The Pontiff exhorted the people to appease the anger of God by public prayers and penitential deeds. In one of the penitential processions the Pope himself was seen moving barefooted around the walls, and bearing upon his shoulders a large wooden cross, to which was attached the violated treaty of the Lombards. The next day the aged Pontiff, despite the Alpine storms of mid-winter, set out, in disguise, through the enemy's territory, to supplicate the assistance of the French king. Soon the troops of Pepin restore peace to the beleaguered city, and thenceforward the sword of the chivalrous Franks guarded the gates of Rome. Pepin and Charlemagne made it their boast to avenge every insult offered to the Vicar of Christ; and whilst they repelled invasion from the approach of Rome, they proclaimed to the world, in their capitulars, that that city should remain for ever inviolable as the home of the Spiritual Ruler of the Christian Church, and the patrimony of the successors of St. Peter.

How glorious was the Christmas Day of the year 800, when Charlemagne, having come for the fourth time to Rome as defender of its freedom, knelt at the threshold of St. Peter! The barons, clergy, and people were assembled there to pay him honour; and, whilst with universal acclaim they hailed him as champion of the Holy See and deliverer of Rome, the Pontiff poured the sacred chrism upon his brow, and crowned him with the imperial diadem of the West.

I have thus endeavoured to briefly sketch for you the origin of the temporal sovereignty of the Popes. It arose from the necessities of society and the free choice of a grateful people; and the rights of the Pontiffs, confirmed from age to age by the sanction of Christian nations, now stand before us with a prescription of eleven centuries. Assailed solely by the reckless theories of communism and revolution, these rights are confirmed by every principle of social justice and morality. Let the government of Europe be produced that can boast of like titles in its dynasty; but till then may the agents of socialism rage in vain around the time-honoured throne of the successors of St. Peter.

It would be tedious to mention in detail the many benefits which, in the exercise of their temporal sovereignty, were conferred by the Popes on the territory of Rome, on Italy, on all Europe. I can only refer briefly to a few of them, and yet they should be treated of in full, to do justice to the claims of the papal sovereignty.

From the first moment that this charge devolved upon the Popes they laboured incessantly to restore society in Italy, to reorganize its scattered members, to consolidate its strength. As an instance, I may name Leo IV., of whom Voltaire thus writes: "Leo IV., in his defence of Rome, proved himself worthy of its princedom; he fortified the city, armed the militia, and guarded against every attack; he was a native of Rome, and, like some stately column that stands erect though encompassed on every side by ruins, he alone, in that vile age of barbarism, seemed to retain the full genius and ardour of the early republican age." (*Essai sur les Mœurs*, ii. 28.)

Will I speak of the Pontiffs as men of learning and

science? Suffice it to mention Pope Sylvester II. Gioberti was no friend of the Holy See; still, writing of this great Pope, he is forced to cry out: "The primacy in science is a characteristic glory of Rome and its Pontiffs. The most surprising man that stands before us in the varied range of human science throughout the middle ages belongs to that illustrious See; and as individual genius is placed in bolder relief by the disproportion of its age, I know of no one to be compared in point of science with Gerbert, Pope Sylvester II." It is not without some natural pride that I have chosen the name of this great Pontiff, for he came forth from the Irish school of Bobbio, where in the tenth century still lived the traditions and the science of SS. Virgilius and Columbanus. And allow me to add that no century in the annals of Christendom presents more cheering scenes than the age that bears the name of Pope Sylvester. St. Henry II. ruled in Germany, and with his holy spouse, St. Cunegunda, diffused amongst his people the blessings of peace and piety. The Hungarians, with their king, St. Stephen, renounced their paganism and assumed the banner of the Cross. In Denmark another sainted monarch died martyr to his zeal. Norway was governed by St. Olaus; Scotland by the good St. Margaret. We had at home the bright example of the bishop-king, St. Cormac. England enjoyed the laws of Edward the Confessor; whilst in France the pious son of Hugh Capet strenuously laboured to lessen the evils of feudal anarchy. What a blessing it had been for mankind if some century of modern times had reckoned so many saints among its sovereigns!

I would also wish to speak of the patronage of literature for which the world is indebted to the Popes. Suffice it to name Nicholas V., who prepared a home for the Grecian muses exiled from the East. He loved to be styled the friend of Poggio, Marsilio Ficino, and Bessarion, and by the encouragement which he gave to the blessed Angelico da

Fiesole he laid the foundations of that school of painting which has ever since held the post of honour and pre-eminence in Europe.

Will I refer to their efforts to maintain the liberty of the Church during feudal times, and to preserve a spotless ministry within the sanctuary of God? In the iron age of feudal despotism ecclesiastical functions and benefices became the spoil and traffic of princes. Bishops were chosen, not called by God, but forced by the secular power upon the Church: they were selected, not for their virtues and spirit of religion, but for the attainment of wordly ends. Holy men had to blush for the desolation of the sanctuary, and it seemed that if the ark of salvation was about to be submerged amid the surging vices of a wicked world.

It is thus the divine Redeemer permits at intervals His holy Church to be imperilled. At one time it is corruption that assails it; at another it is heresy or schism. Sometimes the smile of the powers that be, sometimes open persecution, promises to achieve the work of Satan. But the Redeemer's words are our guarantee that *His* presence cannot fail in Holy Church. He may slumber for awhile, as in the storm of Genesareth, to teach His Apostles not to place too much reliance on human power or human genius—for the salvation of His earthly spouse must come from His divine hand alone—but in His own good time He shall hush the winds and waves, and calm and sunshine shall once more shine on His mystic bark.

It was Hildebrand, Pope Gregory VII., that was raised up by God to break the shackles that bound the milk-white hind, and restore to her her freedom. In the silence of the cloister he had wept over the evils of the Church, and when raised to the chair of Peter it was his first resolve to remedy them. Henry IV., with all the power of Germany and all that was wicked in Italy and France, was leagued against him; yet the genius of Hildebrand triumphed over them all.

He died, indeed, in exile, a victim of persecution, but even then his victory was secure, and his name is embalmed in the memory of Holy Church as the faithful guardian of her sanctuary. One of the greatest men of modern times was heard to exclaim: "Were I not Napoleon, I would wish to be Hildebrand;" and historical research in our own days has proved that whilst Henry IV. was the Nero of Germany, Gregory VII. was the unflinching defender of social order and religion in Europe, thus verifying the dying words of the great Pontiff: "I have loved justice and hated iniquity, therefore is it that I die in exile."

Need I do more than mention the efforts of the Popes to preserve inviolable the sanctity of Christian marriage? Yes, they braved every peril in enforcing it; and often, too, it was their glory to suffer in that holy cause. The names of Lothaire, King of Lorraine, and Philip Augustus of France, at once recur to mind; and yet there is another monarch nearer home to whom I will rather refer. When Henry VIII. in shameless passion would divorce his lawful queen, he wrote to the Pontiff: "Grant the favour which I ask, and England shall be with you; if you refuse it, you shall feel my wrath." Clement VII. well knew the stubborn heart of Henry, but above all the law of God should be maintained, and sooner than favour the passion of the monarch, he allowed the fair jewel of England's kingdom to be snatched from his tiara, or rather from the crown of Christ.

The Popes never ceased to exercise their power for the suppression of slavery, and from the days of Gregory the Great, who so beautifully laid down the duties of Christian masters, to the Encyclical of Pope Gregory XVI., in 1840, there was not one in the long line of Pontiffs but laboured strenuously to promote emancipation and to lessen the evils of slavery. At the same time they have never been prevented by human regards from rebuking despotism and assisting those who were oppressed. During the long dreary period in which our own dear country suffered all the woes of irreligious persecution, the Popes were the only friends of our fathers. A little later, when the hydra of revolution raged in France, towards the close of the last century, and when it was the boast of England to welcome some of its victims to her shores, the Sovereign Pontiff, with the limited resources at his command, was able to support no fewer than 24,000 refugees. In our own times, when each effort of Poland to regain her independence was crushed by brute force, and provoked the most vexatious enactments and the direst excesses of cruelty, the powers of Europe looked on in sullen silence. The voice of the Pontiff alone was heard, and the Encyclical in reproof of tyranny and in support of the just claims of that Catholic people, shall be cherished as one of the most glorious monuments of the reign of the present immortal Pontiff.

I should also commemorate the untiring zeal of the Popes in propagating the faith of Christ, and extending to the remotest regions the blessings of the Cross.

> "How beauteous on the hills the feet of Him
> ('T is thus Isaias sings)
> Who preaches heavenly peace, and brings to man
> The tidings of good things!
> Christ first, His Vicar now to us fulfils
> This gracious work of God;
> No land by seas or mountains so concealed,
> But Peter there hath trod."

There is, however, one great benefit for which Rome and Italy and Europe are indebted to the Sovereign Pontiffs, and which merits more than a passing mention in the matter of which I treat: this is their preservation from Moslem barbarism. See the results of Mahommedan conquest in Africa and the East. The shores of Morocco were once renowned as the home of industry and science; now the wild beasts of the forest dispute there the mastery with pirates: Egypt, despite all its natural resources, is a wilderness: Arabia has relapsed into barbarism: Syria and Palestine present nothing but ruins and desolation: and the same ruin and barbarism would reign over all Europe at the present day, were it not for the influence and exertions of the Sovereign Pontiffs.

From the first moment that the Mussulman cloud began to gather on the horizon, the Popes sounded the alarm, and never did they cease their vigilance till the half-moon set for ever in the reddening waters of Lepanto.

When all Spain had been well nigh subjugated by the Moors, and when the Saracen leaders looked down from the slopes of the Pyrenees upon the rich plains of central Europe, meditating new conquests and vowing to exterminate the Christian name, it was a Roman Pontiff, St. Gregory III., that aroused the martial ardour of the Franks. Medals blessed by the Pope on the altar of St. Peter's were distributed to the army of Charles Martel, and on the plains of Poitiers the myriad Mahommedan hosts were humbled to the dust by the soldiers of religion. Europe was saved, and, after God, it owed its preservation to the vigilance of Pope Gregory.

I pass over the almost uninterrupted struggles of the ninth and tenth centuries. In the beginning of the eleventh, a Saracen fleet landed a large army in the north of Italy; they ravaged the coast of Tuscany, but were driven to their ships by the courageous troops of Pope Benedict VIII. Before setting sail, the emir sent to the Pontiff a sack full of nuts, with the message that as many as were these nuts, so many legions would he bring back next year to raze the very foundations of Rome. Pope Benedict was not idle. The Normans who hitherto had vied with the Saracens in the plunder of North Italy, were invited to his standard. He even journeyed on to Germany, and at Bamberg prayed the emperor Henry II. to defend the interests of Christian Europe. A powerful army soon crossed the Alps to aid the pontifical troops, and when the emir returned with a numberless fleet, he again was driven back with slaughter from the coast of Italy.

And as I have mentioned the Normans, allow me to refer to another incident which is characteristic of those times, and explains to us how it was that the Popes were able to enlist peoples and armies, otherwise conflicting, in the one common cause of the defence of the Christian name. In the year 1049, Leo IX. ascended the throne of St. Peter. The Normans renewed their irruptions into central Italy; at Dragonara the papal army was defeated, and the victors rushed on to Civitella, where the Pope then resided. There the Normans knelt before Leo, offering themselves to take the place of his valiant soldiers. The Pope, in tears, returned with them to the battle-field. For two days the Normans by fasting and prayer sought to expiate their fault, but Pope Leo felt that his end was at hand. Three days before his death, summoning his clergy to his bedside, he said to them: "The time has come for me to leave this world. Last night I was shown the land of Heaven, and whilst I marvelled at what I beheld, all the brethren who died in Apuleia fighting for the Church, came before me. Their garments shone like gold; each held in his hand a palm of unfading beauty; they all called to me aloud: 'Come and dwell with us, for it is by thee that we have gained this glory:' and I heard another voice which said: 'In three days thou shalt rejoin us; this is thy place; thy throne is prepared and awaits thee.'" Thus eight hundred years ago was anticipated the glorious scene of Castelfidardo, when once more the soldiers of Rome became martyrs of faith. There was this difference: the modern Saracens continued their career of reckless plunder, whilst the Norman troops became the champions of civilization and liege soldiers of the Cross.

It was to defend Europe against the tide of Saracenic

barbarism that the Crusaders marched to the Holy Land. The master-minds of Sylvester II. and Gregory VII. had already resolved on this line of warfare, but it was reserved for Urban II. and the Council of Clermont to carry it into effect. The great Carthaginian leader immortalized his name by transferring the seat of war into the rich territories of his assailants. Such was the course which the Pontiffs now judged to be the only defence of Europe against the Saracens. After the fall of the Carlovingian dynasty, Europe was split up into innumerable independent princedoms, rivals in their aspirations and their interests. Too weak to resist separately the Saracen assault, and too jealous to combine against the common foe, they must inevitably have fallen one by one before the ever-increasing power of the crescent, were it not that the common father of all combined their energies under the banner of faith, and moulded them into one compact whole. Abelard, indeed, like the modern rationalists, derided the crusades, but the *folly of the Cross* ever triumphs over the vain wisdom of false philosophy; by the crusades Europe was saved, society was re-constructed, and the feudal dissensions, and jealousies, and rival ambitions of petty princes were forgotten amid the cries of "Dieu le veut," as the Crusaders, bearing the banner of the Cross, marched to the rescue of the sepulchre of Christ.

The exertions of the Pontiffs against the Mahommedan foe were not confined to exhortations. They themselves were foremost in every enterprise in defence of Christian Europe. In the celebrated defence of Belgrade, 60,000 men, equipped by Pope Callixtus III., fought under the renowned Hunyad, and the Papal legates, John de Carvayal and St. John Capistran, were there to encourage the troops. The Turkish camp soon became a prey to the Christian army, and 40,000 of the Saracen slain attested the fury of the combat.

Seven years later, Pius II., though well-nigh weighed down by years and infirmities, when he saw the Turkish armies again mustering all their strength on the banks of the Danube, thus addressed the assembled Cardinals:—"Let our words to the princes of Europe no longer be: *Ite*, go to the combat against the enemy of Christianity; but let us say: *Venite*, come with us to combat your own foe: when they see the Vicar of Christ, aged and infirm, assuming the Crusader's staff and sailing for the Holy Land, they will be ashamed not to share his perils. As for me," he added, "I will take my place in the foremost ship, and from its prow I will raise my hands in prayer to implore on their arms the blessing of the God of victories."

And again he said: "No doubt war is unsuitable to the weakness of old men and to the character of Pontiffs, but when religion is ready to succumb, what can detain us? We shall march with our standard of the Cross unfolded, we shall bear with us the relics of the saints, we shall have with us Jesus Christ Himself in the Holy Eucharist."

Grand, indeed, would have been the spectacle of the venerable Pontiff thus appearing before the walls of Constantinople; but God had not willed it so. At the appointed day the Pope arrived at Ancona, where 30,000 Crusaders were assembled, but as the Venetian galleys entered the port to receive his army the Pontiff expired, turning a last fond look towards the land of his desires.

His successor, Paul II., continued his efforts to combine the powers of Europe against the Saracens. It was at the Shrine of the Apostles, and under the protection of the Pontiff, that the Albanian hero, Scanderbeg, derived the resistless ardour which achieved for him twenty-two victories over the armies of the Sultan. When Mahomet II. heard of this hero's death, he is said to have danced with joy, and exclaimed: "Now that the Albanian lion is no more, I shall exterminate the Christians." Albania, indeed, was soon overrun with Turkish troops, and the inhabitants were everywhere put to the most cruel torture and death. The letters, however, and prayers of the Pope aroused Europe from its lethargy. Once more an army of 200,000 men was mustered from France, Germany, and Italy; and though the Pontiff, like his predecessor, expired at the moment that success seemed to smile upon his enterprise, the terror alone of such an armament checked the victorious Moslem in his career. Moreover, the enthusiasm which it awakened in Europe produced another happy fruit: it led to the conjunction of the armies of Ferdinand and Isabella in Spain, which was the signal of triumph of the Christian cause, and soon banished for ever the Mahommedan rule from the peninsula.

For St. Pius V., however, was reserved the crowning glory of that great work which had so long engaged the thoughts of the Sovereign Pontiffs. The Sultan Soliman was accustomed to say of this great Pope: "I fear the tears of the old man more than all the arms of Europe:" he might have added that he feared his prayers. St. Pius, under the tiara, wore the humble habit and loved the religious cloister of St. Dominic, and the pilgrim may still visit the silent cell at St. Sabina's on the Aventine, where, shedding tears and with arms extended, he stood entranced for hours in prayer, looking towards the East on the memorable day of Lepanto. At length he exclaimed: "Thy cause, O Lord, has triumphed;" and hastening to the altar, he there with joy invited his astonished companions to intone with him in thanksgiving, *Te Deum laudamus*. That joyous hymn was soon reechoed throughout Europe: the efforts of the holy Pontiff to combine all the energies of Christian princes, and still more his tears and prayers, had merited at length the blessing for which all Christendom had so long sighed—the Saracen power was for ever discomfited, and Europe was again saved from the horrors of barbarism. Well may we apply to this great Pontiff the words used by a Protestant historian in regard to an earlier Pope: "He might now give his blessing to all the emperors, kings, princes, and lords of Christendom, and say: Without me you would not be what you are. The Popes have saved antiquity and civilization, and Rome is worthy of remaining as a sanctuary in which to shelter all the precious treasures of the past."

But it is now time to devote a few words to the enemies of the temporal sovereignty of the Holy See, and their fate. The first great enemy was the Court of Constantinople. Though unable to defend its own territories, yet it ceased not for centuries by secret intrigues and open assault, like Piedmont of the present day, to disturb the peace of Italy. One instance will suffice to show the enmity which the eastern heretics bore to the Sovereign Pontiffs. Pope Martin had renewed the anathemas of his predecessors, and combated with zeal against the Monotholite heresy, of which the Greek emperor was the avowed patron. One day a hired band of assassins seized him at the very threshold of the Vatican, and hurried him away to the sea-coast. For fifteen months he was dragged in chains from island to island, and at length was exposed, as an enemy of the emperor, to the fury and insults of the mob in Constantinople. The aged Pontiff, barefooted, with tattered stole and tunic, and covered with filth and blood, yet praying aloud for his persecutors, was dragged through the streets and subjected to every insult. Soon after he expired in exile in the Chersonesus; but the miracles which were wrought at his tomb attested to the world how different was the judgment of God from that of man.

Had it not been for this false pride and hatred against Rome, ever inherent in heresy, the statues of Mahomet and Soliman and Amuret would not now wear their laurel wreaths in the eastern capital. The aegis of the Popes, as it sheltered Europe, so also would it have guarded the East from the Saracen sword, and instead of the half-moon, symbol of barbarism, the banner of the Cross would to-day be unfurled on the battlements of St. Sophia.

The names of Arnold of Brescia and Cola di Rienzi have of late years become familiar in the Protestant literature of England, which extols them as champions of liberty against the tyrannical government of papal Rome. Their history, indeed, has much in common with the revolutionists of modern times, but it is far different from what our novelists and socialists pretend.

St. Bernard wrote to Pope Innocent regarding Arnold of Brescia: "Beware of that youth from Brescia. His words are honey, but his tenets are poison: it is the scorpion with a dove's head. Already Brescia has cast him forth; France banishes him; Germany rejects him; it remains for Rome to anathematize him." A little later, in 1139, anathema was, indeed, pronounced against his tenets in the General Council of Lateran, yet Arnold would not submit. Many adventurers were attracted to his standard by his illusive cry of "Rome, the capital of the Italian republic." At the same time he solicited aid from the emperor of Germany, and, heedless of consistency, wrote to him: "Down with all who resist Cæsar: behold our cry! we are resolved to make thy dominion universal and unrivalled." Many, indeed, were the tumults which the followers of Arnold excited in Rome; in one of them even a Sovereign Pontiff, Pope Lucius II., was killed. Still the Romans refused to be led away by the deceptive visions of revolution. One day whilst the Pope was absent, the citizens assembled, and full of rage and disgust, caused Arnold to be summoned before them. A popular tribunal was extemporized: Arnold was declared to be a disturber of the public peace and an enemy to his country. In the popular frenzy he was beheaded; his body was burned, and its ashes were cast into the waters of the Tiber.

Cola di Rienzi, the last of the tribunes of Rome, walked

in the steps of Arnold, and met with a similar fate. He was one of those who, during the papal residence in Avignon, proceeded thither with Petrarch and other deputies of the Roman people to pray Pope Clement VI. to return to Rome. The Pontiff, knowing his energy and the popularity which he enjoyed, conferred on him the dignity and name of Tribune, with full power for the suppression of crime and brigandage in the territory of Rome. Led away by ambition, Cola di Rienzi soon indulged in every excess. Fully equipped, he proceeded to the porch of the Lateran Basilica, and there striking with his sword towards the points of the compass, he proclaimed that the whole world should thenceforward obey his rule. Rome was amazed at his folly, and, the citizens seizing on him, sent him in chains to the then reigning Pope Innocent. The clemency of the Pontiff after a while restored him to his liberty and his former dignity, taking care at the same time to appoint a cardinal legate to guide and control him in the government of Rome. The rage of the citizens was, however, soon again kindled against him: the popular voice accused him of heinous crimes, and at length he was murdered by an angry mob on the 8th of October, 1354.

The period of the residence of the Popes in Avignon has been well styled the seventy years' captivity of the people of Rome. Many times the Pontiffs were asked by their subjects to return amongst them. On one occasion Petrarch thus addressed the Pontiff: "Do you choose to arise on the last day with the Avignonese, or with the holy Apostles SS. Peter and Paul, with the martyrs Laurence and Stephen, with the confessors Gregory and Sylvester? And what can you answer, O holy Father, when, on the last day, St. Peter shall say to you, What reverence did you show my tomb? what love did you show my people?" The Popes, indeed, were more than desirous of returning to the holy city. Of one of them (Pope Benedict XII.) it is told that night after night he would mount the watch-tower of his palace in Avignon, and there sighing and praying, would stretch forth his arms towards his widowed Church. The intrigues of princes, however, and the tumultuous scenes in Italy, prevented the Popes from realizing their desire. It seemed as if Providence had decreed to make known to the world the necessity for the free exercise of the pontifical rule in Rome. Long had holy Church to weep for the schisms and other evils that sprung from this period of captivity. Rome itself well-nigh became a desert: its population was 150,000 when the Popes set out for Avignon; it numbered only 17,000 when they returned to the Vatican. At length an humble virgin, renowned for her sanctity, set out on foot across the Alps, and presented herself before Gregory XI. She spoke to him in the name of God: "It is the wish of Heaven that you fulfil your secret vow to return to Rome." The Pontiff stood amazed; he had, indeed, in the secret of his heart, vowed to return to Rome; but he had feared to make it known to anyone, so many were the difficulties that seemed every day to render its realization more and more impossible. It was St. Catherine of Sienna that thus spoke to the Pontiff in the name of God. He obeyed, and on the 17th of January, 1377, Rome rejoiced once more in the presence of its chief pastor and its sovereign.

I will not speak of the many attacks which, in succeeding times, were made against the Papal rule in Rome. The sack of the city, by the Lutheran army of De Bourbon, for a while menaced it with utter destruction. The frescoes of Michael Angelo, in the Pauline, still present traces of their fires; the sacred ceremonies of religion were travestied in the public streets by a drunken soldiery, and outrages to humanity and religion were perpetrated which awakened an outcry of indignation throughout all Europe.

At the close of the last century these scenes were again renewed in Rome, in the name of the Directory of France.

The venerable Pontiff, Pius VI., who for twenty-three years had ruled the Church of God, was commanded to leave the Holy City for a distant prison. To a priest, whom he had asked to accompany him, his words were: "Have you courage enough to accompany us to Calvary?" As he hastened to prison, he exclaimed: "How vividly do the early ages of the Church now recur to my mind—the ages of her triumphs." And well, indeed; for in his sufferings and his sorrows were once more sown the seeds of the Church's victory. His successor, Pius VII., was also destined to taste the bitter cup of persecution. Napoleon, at the zenith of his power, said to his ministers: "Can the sentence of the old man cause the muskets to drop from my soldiers' hands?" Yet so it was: the snows of Russia caused that very calamity to befall his hitherto victorious troops. Under the blighting sentence of excommunication, the faded laurels fell from Napoleon's brow; and, whilst the pinioned eagle was sent to pine away its days of misery on a dreary rock, the Holy Father returned to his capital, amidst the joyous acclaims of a grateful people.

"The Arabs have a fable that the great pyramid was built by the antediluvian kings, and alone, of the works of men, bore the weight of the flood. Such as this was the fate of the Popedom. It had been buried under the great inundation; but its foundations had remained unshaken, and, when the waters abated, it appeared alone amid the ruins of a world which had passed away." (Macaulay's *Essays.*)

And now we should turn our thoughts to the immortal Pontiff who so happily reigns. But his sorrows and his triumphs are household words in every home of Christendom, and hence they require no more than a passing reference. When, in 1848, revolution held out its promises, its friendships, and its richest boons, Pius IX., by his golden words, *Non devo, non voglio, non posso*, laid down the basis of Christian freedom, and drew the line of eternal separation between true liberty and communism. From that day all the storms of infidelity and socialism have raged around the throne of Pius IX.; but, thanks to Providence, they have raged in vain. Castelfidardo presented a glorious spectacle to the world. It was, indeed, the combat of the two standards; on one side, revolution, brute force, and injustice, personified in Victor Emmanuel and Cialdini, and exulting in a momentary triumph; on the other, religion, honour, and justice, with Pius IX. and Lamoriciere. Never, in the verdict of Europe, had the temporal power of the Popes so great a triumph—never did Christian chivalry present more glorious champions. The martyrs of Castelfidardo, combating for Pio Nono's throne, became sponsors for all that is good, and honourable, and just in society; they died in its defence, and by their death they secured its triumph.

Before concluding, I would wish to tell you who are the present enemies of the temporal sovereignty of the Popes. They are the socialists of Italy, combined with adventurers from every part—from Hungary and Poland, from France and Russia, and, I must add, from England, too—men fanatical in their hatred of the Catholic Church, or revolutionist in their principles, who rush with frenzy against the Popedom, which they instinctively recognize to be the mainstay of morality and social order. They are aided by all who wish to undermine society, or who, under the name of liberty, seek loose reins for libertinism and brigandage throughout Europe. They are aided by the anti-Catholic press of England: they are aided still more by England's funds. Even in Ireland, collections have been made in Protestant churches, which I could name, in aid of the attacks on Rome; and these collections have been enforced by some Orange landlords on their tenantry. St. Bernard, describing the Italian revolutionists of his day, says: "Odious to earth and Heaven, they have assailed both the one and the other; impious towards God, reckless towards things sacred, factious among themselves, envious of their neighbours, inhuman towards foreigners, . . . they love none, and by none are loved. Too impatient for submission, too helpless for rule; . . . importunate to gain an end, restless till they gain it, ungrateful when they have gained it. They have taught their tongue to speak big words, while their performances are scanty indeed." (*De Considerat.*, iv. 2.)

Who would not say that these words described the revolutionists of our own day? The oppression of the poor, the bankruptcy of the State, the plunder of monasteries, the insecurity of life and property throughout the whole Peninsula, public insults to religion, war against the helpless virgins of Christ, these be thy triumphs, O Italian revolutionists! So dreadful are the abuses, so horrible the crimes of these enemies of God and man, that the present meek Pontiff was forced thus to describe them in his Encyclical of 17th of October, 1867: "Cast your eyes around you, Venerable Brethren, and you will see and deeply deplore, with Us, the detestable abominations which now chiefly desolate unhappy Italy. . . . The venerable commandments of God, and the laws of Holy Church, are utterly despised, and impiety uplifts its head unpunished, and triumphs. Hence all the iniquities, all the evils and injuries We behold with the utmost grief of Our soul. Hence these numerous arrays of men who walk in iniquity, serving under the banner of Satan, upon whose forehead is written 'Falsehood,' and who, called by the name of rebels, and turning their mouths against Heaven, blaspheme God, sully and contemn everything sacred, and, treading under foot all rights, divine and human, breathe only carnage like rapacious wolves. These are they who shed blood, lose their souls by most serious scandals, and seek most unjustly to profit by their own malice, carrying off by violence other men's goods, afflicting the weak and the poor, increasing the number of widows and orphans, showing favour for reward to the impious; while they refuse justice to the poor, plundering and, in the corruption of their hearts, shamefully glutting themselves with all evil passions, to the very ruin of civil society itself."

Were we to listen to the infidel press of Europe, the Roman people should also have joined in the revolutionary war against the temporal sovereignty of the Holy See. But it is not so: the Romans have learned too well the fate of the usurped provinces and the sad tale of the adjoining kingdom, to seek to substitute a military despotism for their present mild rule. No; the Roman people have loved to prove on every occasion their devoted loyalty to the Sovereign Pontiffs. They proved it when with universal acclaim they welcomed Pio Nono returning from his exile. They proved it year after year, refusing to afford a plea to Piedmontese intervention, which was ever ready at the frontiers. They proved it when the French army was withdrawn, and when they formed special troops for the defence of the patrimony of St. Peter, and swelled the Zouave battalions to repel the Garibaldian bands. They proved it in the towns of the Sabina, which were entered by surprise by the invading revolutionists; but the inhabitants soon chased the freebooters from their walls with the rallying cry of *Viva Pio Nono*. They proved it, in fine, when unsolicited they formed volunteer corps of guards to maintain order in the city of Rome, whilst the gallant army of the Pope went forth in the name and with the blessing of the whole Christian world, to humble to the dust the Garibaldian pride on the plains of Mentana.

Yes, the Romans know too well the privileges they enjoy under the mildest and most beneficent rule of Christendom to associate themselves with the revolutionists of other kingdoms. No deaths from starvation are heard of in Rome; no emigration is forced upon its people to secure the means of subsistence; ruin is not brought upon its families by a sudden monetary crisis; for centuries the small holders are protected by an admirable tenant-right; its capital, the great centre of attraction for the *élite* of Europe, is enriched by an ever-increasing train of wealthy visitors: there is no form of human misery but has the noblest institutions for its relief: everything is done by the government to alleviate the condition of the poor: the whole revenue of the Pope is devoted to public works for the good of the country; the schools and universities present a gratuitous education, even in its highest branches, to all; there is no monopoly in its offices, and the highest post is open alike to the sons of the humblest artisan as to the scions of its noblest houses. Such are but a few of the special features of that rule which the Roman people refuse to exchange for the disgrace and misery and oppression and bankruptcy of their neighbours.

But let us suppose that the Roman people were at length to be seduced from their allegiance to the Sovereign Pontiffs. Should this suffice to justify the powers of Europe in acquiescing in such a revolutionary course? I unhesitatingly reply that it should not. It is not for itself alone that the patrimony of St. Peter enjoys the Papal government, but it is moreover for the common good of all Christendom. An American statesman has well illustrated this point. The district of Columbia, as the seat of government, enjoys a special independence. Now, were this State, he says, to proclaim itself desirous of being annexed to an adjoining State, surely no man of common sense in Congress would by his vote sanction their desire, for the plain reason that its exceptional government is given to it, not for itself alone, but for the benefit of all the United States. Even so, no change can be justified in the form of government of Rome without the approval and sanction of all Christendom. That sanction Christendom shall never grant, and never shall the powers of Europe permit the Holy See to be deprived of its principality, which is necessary for the du exercise of its sacred mission, and which is the sur guarantee of its freedom in its spiritual sovereignty. Th Christian pilgrims from afar shall not cease to fondly tur to that kingdom of the heart as to their home, and a Christendom, in the outpouring of its affections, shall fror age to age greet the Pontiff-city as we to-night salute her *Esto perpetua.*

II.

On the Feast of the Exaltation of the Holy Cross, in th year 1586, Pope Sixtus V., wresting a noble obelisk fron Augustus and Tiberius, erected it in front of that matchles sanctuary which, "of temples old or altars new stand alone with nothing like to it," and inscribed on it the word —"*Christ conquers, Christ triumphs, Christ reigns.*" Thi simple motto tells us the destiny of Christian Rome Divinely chosen to be the centre of God's Church, it mus show forth the power of God, and perpetuate, till time sha be no more, the victories and triumphs of the Cross. So, too till the fulness of time was come, did God choose, in th Jewish dispensation, one spot of this world which He wishe to be called His own—Jerusalem, "the city of perfec beauty, the joy of all the earth;" and there He placed th temple of His Majesty, the one well-spring of all joy, an hope, and peace, the one beacon-light which could guid man to heaven.

The Church of God was not to be confined merely to on city or people: it was to embrace all nations and tribes an tongues; and yet it was to be *one* kingdom, and its unit was to be the very proof of the divine power which sus- tained it. In the ways of Providence, Rome, chosen as th centre of that unity, was to reverse Rome's destiny. Hitherto the throne of Satan, and the citadel of the superstitions o paganism, it trampled the world under foot: now th capital of religion, and the city of Christ, it was to sanctify the world, and lift it up to breathe the pure air of the mountains of God.

During two centuries and a-half the foundations of this spiritual city were cemented with the blood of countless martyrs. Every age and condition of life, every clime and nation under the sun sent its chosen champions of faith to the triumph of martyrdom in Rome. The circus of the Emperor Nero was the first great theatre of these triumphs; and it was meet that on that hallowed spot should arise the noblest shrine of earth to the glory of God in honour of the Prince of the Apostles. Then the Colosseum was so steeped in Christian blood, that St. Gregory the Great could send a little of its dust, as a priceless relic, to Queen Theodolinda. Forty thousand Christians, from every province of the empire, were assembled to work as slaves in the erection of the great baths of Diocletian; how would they have rejoiced, and how would they have blessed their toil, did they know that the walls at which they laboured would one day be a glorious shrine under the invocation of her who is the Queen of Angels and Martyrs. Thus, year by year, Rome was purified, ennobled, and sanctified.

Around the new city of Christ, but concealed from pagan gaze, were silently raised up those mighty bulwarks of Rome's spiritual glory, the Catacombs. With their corridors and chapels they encompassed Rome on every side, and realizing the vision of the Apocalypse, the remains of the martyrs of Christ reposing beneath the altars, cried out by day and by night before the Redeemer's throne, "How long, O Lord, how long?"

Thus, in the ways of God, was mysteriously prepared that city of the Church which He wished to call His own. And now the heart of Constantine is subdued to Christian truth. There was but little, indeed, in the early career of that imperial ruler to give hope or promise to the Church of Christ. It was nothing but the power of God, miraculously shown forth in the heavens, and the glorious victory which the standard of the Cross achieved on the banks of the Tiber, that led him captive to truth. How altered was now the scene. St. Peter, Prince of the Apostles, on foot, clothed in poverty, and bearing a pilgrim's staff, had entered Rome by the *Via Triumphalis;* now, along that same route, the standard of the Cross is encompassed by all the splendour of the Imperial Court, and is unfurled in triumph by the victorious troops. The senate was convened in the Ulpian Basilica, where now the column of Trajan so majestically stands. It was feared, indeed, that a tumult would ensue; but when the imperial decree was proclaimed, that Christianity was emancipated and free, a shout of joy arose from the assembled multitude, "Great is the triumph of Christ." On that day religion came forth from her hiding-places; and thenceforth all that was richest and choicest and most beautiful, all the riches and splendour that the world could give, its gold and silver and precious stones, became the handmaids of faith, and were lavished with unsparing hand on the sanctuaries and shrines of Rome.

We would deceive ourselves, however, were we to suppose that, at the conversion of Constantine, the rulers of the Roman Empire, from being the chiefs and deities of paganism, became, by a sudden transition, the promoters and champions of the Christian faith. No; the ruling powers that guided the destinies of the empire continued as devoted to the cause of paganism, and as hostile to Christianity, as in the days of Nero and Diocletian. When the senate assembled, on the death of Constantine, they passed a decree enrolling him among the gods, and public sacrifices were offered in his honour. Four hundred pagan temples still crowded the city, and were frequented by the Imperial Court. The altar of victory, which stood in the senate house, was only finally removed fifty years after the emanpation of the Christians, by Gratian. The words of ılian the Apostate were received with applause, when, ›fore the assembled senators, he denounced Constantine as disturber of the ancient laws, and an impious transgressor : the sacred traditions of Rome. Even as late as Theodosius, ıe question was formerly proposed in the senate: "Should hrist or Jupiter be adored as sovereign Deity?"

But whilst the powers of this world continued to uphold ıe fabric of paganism, Christianity, resting on the power of od, was casting deeper and deeper its roots in the very eart of Rome. "In this period of the world," writes chlegel, "in this decisive crisis, between ancient and ıodern times, in this great central point of history, stood vo powers opposed to each other: on one hand, we behold ıe Roman rulers, the earthly gods, and absolute masters f the world, in all the pomp and splendour of ancient aganism, standing as it were on the very summit and verge f the old world, now tottering to its ruin; and, on the ther hand, we trace the obscure rise of an almost imper- eptible point of light, from which the whole modern world 'as to spring, and whose further progress and full develop- ıent, through all succeeding ages, constitute the true urport of modern history." (Schlegel, *Philosophy of Iistory*, i. 358.)

The government of Imperial Rome had clung to paganism: ıe day of avenging chastisement was now at hand. From he depths of the German forests mighty armies of barbarians ıshed in on the distant provinces of the empire; but this id not suffice to disturb the joyous festive routine of the even Hills. In her pride of heart the mistress of the vorld cried out: "I sit a queen, and sorrow I shall not ee;" and it appeared little more than a day-dream when he rumour first reached her that the bands of Alaric were ıarching onwards from the Alps towards Rome. "The rst emotions of the nobles and people," says Gibbon, "were those of surprise and indignation, that a vile barbarian should dare to insult the capital of the world. But their arrogance was soon humbled by misfortune." Famine compelled the senate to send ambassadors to the tent of Alaric; but when they menaced, that unless honourable conditions were granted, they would lead forth an innumerable host of armed citizens to battle against him, the barbarian chief haughtily replied: "the thicker the grass the easier it is mowed."

The storm was for the moment averted by liberating 40,000 slaves, and paying all the silver and gold demanded by Alaric. The pagans within the city now attributed all their calamities to the Christians. Tertullus, the consul, renewed the worst Gentile superstitions on the Capitol; and, addressing the senate, declared that these first steps were but a prelude to the speedy triumph of paganism over the hated religion of Christ. So execrable were the impious rites of pagan impiety at this time practised in Rome, that, as Sozomen relates, the most reflecting of the citizens looked upon the subsequent calamities of the city as a just judgment on its blind attachment to idolatry.

The wages of such impiety were not long delayed. The 40,000 slaves ceaselessly clamoured for revenge on their past masters. In the plains of Rimini, Alaric again marshalled his countless host. As he passed the Apennines, a holy hermit threw himself in his path, seeking to mitigate his wrath. "Servant of God," cried Alaric, "seek not to turn me from my mission: it is not from choice I lead my army against that devoted place; but some invisible power, which will not suffer me to halt a single day, urges me on by violence, continually crying out to me without ceasing, 'Forward! march upon that city, upon Rome, and make it desolate.'" (Socrat., *Hist. Eccl.*, vii. 10.)

At the hour of midnight, the Gothic army having advanced along the Salarian way, rushed into the city. And now all the evils that had been perpetrated by Rome during the sieges, and massacres, and plunderings of a thousand years, were mercilessly retaliated on herself. "One cannot relate without tears," says the Italian annalist, "the cruelties exercised on this occasion." The city was in flames: the forum, the temples, the streets were filled with the slain. The trophies and monuments of past triumphs were a chief object of the Gothic rage; and it is related by Orosius that some of the temples and public edifices which seemed to defy the brands of the barbarians, were struck with thunderbolts from heaven. (Oros., lib. 3, cap. 19.)

In the midst of all these terrors, Alaric caused it to be proclaimed that he warred not against St. Peter. The Churches of St. Peter's and St. Paul's were declared inviolable sanctuaries; and so strictly was this observed, that the barbarians not only halted in their career of slaughter, on arriving at these hallowed precincts, but many of them were seen conducting thither such as had moved them to pity, that, under the protection of the Apostles, they might be saved from the rage of others. (St. Augustine, *De Civit. Dei*, lib. 2.) One fact, commemorated by Orosius, suffices to make us realize how important was this source of safety to the remnant of the population of Rome. Whilst the barbarians were rushing through the city in quest of plunder, it happened that a sacred virgin, who had grown old in the service of the sanctuary, was discovered in her convent, on the Cœlian Hill, by a Gothic chief, who demanded all the gold and silver she possessed. To his surprise, she mildly told him that the treasures entrusted to her keeping were immense; but that they were the sacred vessels used in the divine mysteries at the altar of St. Peter, the Apostle. The chief sent intelligence to Alaric of the discovery he had made. An instant order was returned to have all the sacred vessels promptly conveyed, just as they were, to the Basilica of the Apostle, and to protect the nun and all the Christians who should accompany her on the way. Then, indeed, an astounding spectacle was beheld. Through the greatest thoroughfares of the city a solemn train advances, with the same order and measured step as if it moved not through scenes of slaughter, but along some hallowed aisles on a joyous festival. The barbarian troops, brandishing their battle-axes and swords, serve as a guard of honour; whilst the hymns of Christian praise, chanted by those who bore the sacred vessels, re-echo, like the trumpet of salvation, throughout the dread scene of havoc and destruction. The Christians, at these well-known voices, started from their hiding-places, and joined the gladsome procession. Many pagans, too, took up the hymn of Christ, thus to escape under the shadow of that sacred name. None were molested in that procession, and the barbarians vied with each other for the honour of marching as its guards.

Thus Heaven displayed its mysterious power, and prepared a harbour of safety for the objects of its solicitude; but, when the Christians had been separated, as if by angelic hands, from the doomed inhabitants, the city was devoted to utter ruin. The world was filled with consternation at the news that Rome was trampled on and burned to the ground. Even in the deserts of Judea, St. Jerome cries out: "Who would have believed it, that a city, I may say, constructed of trophies, that all-conquering Rome, the empress of the world, should lie crushed: that the cradle and home of so many nations should be changed, on a sudden, into one vast charnel-house?"

Nevertheless, the pride of Rome was not destroyed. When the barbarians had retired, the pagan fugitives, like a returning tide, hastened back to the ruined city; but they showed no signs of conversion or repentance. The Queen of the Seven Hills still refused the Cross: she chose rather once more to deck her brow with the laurel wreath; and again she had recourse to pagan oracles, seeking for some delusive promise of revenge and victory. Rome was the last citadel of idolatry; and so mighty was it, even in its humiliation, that it required the constant repeated blows of the most ruthless barbarians, during another century and a-half, to beat down its last bulwarks, and annihilate for ever, in its ruin, the last hopes of paganism.

About the middle of the fifth century, the Huns poured in a new tide of destruction on the decaying empire. They were led on by Attila, who styled himself "the scourge of God," and boasted that the grass should not grow where his horse would tread. After ravaging Thrace and Illyricum, we find him, in the year 447, invading Gaul, at the head of 700,000 warriors. Checked by the brave Aetius, on the plains of Chalons, his rage was turned against Rome. Deprived of all human aid, the citizens and senators looked to the great St. Leo as their only hope, and prayed him to avert the impending calamity. Robed in his sacred vestments, and accompanied by his deacons, the Pontiff went forth unarmed to meet the ruthless barbarian king. What words he used we know not; but Attila subsequently avowed, to his discontented chiefs, that, whilst St. Leo spoke, another venerable man appeared to him in the heavens, menacing death if he refused to abandon his enterprise against Rome.

The Vandals were more savage than the Goths, and the name of their leader, Genseric, was more terrible in Rome than that of Alaric himself. His armed nation of barbarians, as an ocean which had burst its boundaries, rushed in upon Italy, ravaging its fields, reducing its towns to solitude, and massacring or carrying away captive whole populations. When about to sail from Carthage, the pilot asked him to what coast should he steer. "Leave the direction to the winds," replied Genseric, "they shall guide us to that one with which God is in wrath." (Procopius,

De Bel. Vand., i. 8.) For a whole fortnight the blindest barbarian passions again wrought their terrible will on helpless Rome, and once more the only refuge was in religion. "Instead of a sally of the Roman youth," writes Gibbon, "there issued from the gates an unarmed and venerable procession of the Bishop at the head of his clergy. The fearless spirit of Leo, his authority and eloquence, again mitigated the fierceness of a barbarian conqueror; the King of the Vandals promised to spare the unresisting multitude, to protect the buildings from fire, and to exempt the captives from torture." Among the spoils borne away were the holy vessels, the table of gold, and the seven-branched candlestick which had been carried off by Titus from Jerusalem. They were now taken from the Temple of Peace, and shipped in triumph for Carthage.

Twice more, within twenty years, the city was forced to endure all the terrors of invasion. Italy was one vast wilderness. In Emilia and Tuscany it is recorded that not even one of the inhabitants survived. But though the Queen of Empires thus "saw her glories, star by star expire," she renounced not the service of paganism. Even on the anniversary of the delivery from Attila, St. Leo was forced to address to the citizens the words of the prophet: "In vain have I struck your children; they have not received correction." He warns them lest, imitating the perverseness of the Jews, they should incur their chastisement; and he adds: "It covers me with confusion to have to make this statement; but it must not be dissembled here, that more is said to be due in this matter to the demons of paganism than to the Apostles of our Lord, and that, while the insane exhibitions of the circus attract to-day overflowing multitudes, but few have gathered round these tombs of the martyrs, to thank Heaven for having preserved us through their intervention."

For Totila, a barbarian king, but famed for his temperance

and chastity, was reserved the task of demolishing the last vestiges of Pagan Rome, and setting aside for ever the institutions of Romulus. As he advanced towards the city, the deacon, Pelagius, who had spent his vast paternal wealth among the poor, was sent by the Romans to ask for a truce, even for a few days. The Goth received Pelagius with honour, and embraced him; but, at the same time, declared his unalterable resolve to level Rome with the dust. The city was given up to the fury of the barbarians, but Totila himself hastened to St. Peter's, and, at the prayers of the clergy, granted permission to any of the inhabitants that wished to fly from the doomed city. When the Goths retired from the Seven Hills, Rome was indeed a desert; even the city gates were torn down by the barbarians, and borne away as trophies of their triumph.

Whilst the power of paganism was thus broken in its very capital, Providence was gradually unfolding its mysterious designs for the salvation of the barbarian nations. For the first time brought in contact with Christian missionaries by these incursions, the barbarians soon became docile children of the Cross; and, before a century had passed from the invasion of Totila, Rome had avenged her sufferings by the spiritual triumph of faith in the very depths of the forests of Germany.

In the age of St. Gregory the Great, new enemies present themselves at the gates of Rome. Once more it is the angel of religion that wards off destruction, and the inhabitants find a refuge beneath the mantle of the Vicar of Christ. Alboino and his Lombard hordes, as an avalanche from the Alps, descended upon Italy: desolation everywhere marked their course. "Scenes of misery meet our eyes," writes St. Gregory, "and our ears are assailed with the cries of lamentation and suffering; no matter to what side we turn, the country is reduced to a wilderness, strewed with the ruins of towns and cities – there is no husbandman in the fields, no dweller in the villages; and it is our doom to see the trifling residue of the population that is still left, incessantly subjected to the horrors of the sword, or dragged into captivity. As for this city, once the queen of the world, judge ye who are spectators, of the immensity and variety of her disasters; how she is crushed and humbled to the earth by incessant shocks of invasion, by the carnage of her citizens, and the dread of dangers incessantly impending over her. All her mighty ones are taken away. What has become of the senate and the Roman people? Of the majestic order of the past not one trace is left; and after her people have perished, her walls and trophies fall of their own accord, and crumble into dust." (S. Gregory, *Com. in Ezechielem.*)

It was in vain that St. Gregory represented to the Court in Constantinople the sad misery of the Roman people. The Emperors, helpless against their enemies nearer home, could afford no protection to their subjects in Italy; nay, more, to cloak their own weakness, they never ceased to heap reproach and invective on the Pontiff, and to seek to frustrate his plans for the public safety. Yet, the untiring exertions of St. Gregory did save Rome, and he merited to be hailed by the citizens as "the father of his country." Even Gibbon admits his claim to their gratitude:—"The merits of Gregory," he writes, "were treated by the Byzantine Court with reproach and insult, but in the attachment of a grateful people he found the purest reward of a citizen, and the best right of a sovereign."

Succeeding Popes pursued the same course, shielding the shrines of the Apostles by the mantle of religion. A signal triumph awaited the exertions of Pope Gregory II. In the year 729 the Lombards, urged on by the Exarch, and paid by imperial gold, laid siege to the city. Gregory II. had no army to defend the walls; but, accompanied by an august retinue of the Roman clergy and nobles, he went forth to the

Vatican fields, where, close by St. Peter's, the enemy had pitched his tents. There the Pontiff made a moving appeal to Luitprand, reminding him of the sacredness of Rome, and of the mysterious Providence which had hitherto guarded its sanctuaries. He concluded with the words: "The city cannot be consumed without giving to the flames those churches and tombs which have been ever regarded by all nations far and near—and even by those little removed from barbarism—not only with veneration, but with the most thrilling religious awe: and is it to be credited that Attila, overawed by the mere apparition of the Apostles, retired from Rome, while the sight of their sepulchres, close to which he is standing, has no power to move a Christian king to mercy?" Luitprand could not conceal his emotion; he prostrated himself for the Pontiff's blessing, and then proceeding to the Basilica of St. Peter's, divested himself of his mantle, diadem, silver cross, and military belt, and offered these royal ornaments on the tomb of the Apostles, as a pledge that thenceforward his army should only fight in defence of Rome.

When, in after years, the Lombard chieftains again harrassed the cities of Italy, need I mention the devotion of Charles Martel, the piety and heroism of Pepin, the triumphs of Charlemagne? On Christmas Day, in the year 800, Charlemagne entered St. Peter's, arrayed in patrician purple, and, as he knelt before the shrine of the Apostles, Pope Leo poured on his forehead the sacred chrism, and placed the imperial crown upon his head, whilst the church resounded with acclamations of "Life and victory to Charles Augustus, most pious and pacific emperor, raised up by God."

This coronation of Charlemagne marks a new era in the history of the world. Thenceforth his title was "Carolus, by the grace of God, King of the Franks, devout defender of Holy Church, and, in all things, the helper and champion of the Apostolic See." All that was noble in the institutions of the ancient empire was now revived. The various tribes of barbarians became united with the Romance nations in the common bonds of imperial rule as of religion. Rome, the citadel of faith, was honoured by all as the centre of peace, and the source, not only of Christian piety, but also of every social blessing for the world. "A glorious empire," writes Florus of Lyons, in the year 850, "a glorious empire flourished under the lustre of a brilliant diadem: it knew but one prince and one people: all the cities had judges, and were secure under the shadow of the laws. The zeal of the priesthood was kept glowing by frequent councils: the sacred records were incessantly in the hands of youth enthusiastically devoted to study: there were everywhere schools in which those of a tender age were disciplined and prepared for the higher study of letters. In those bright days there came frequent embassies from realms the most remote. Rome herself, the mother of kingdoms, reposed under the protectorate of this nation: there it was, that its chief, sustained by the help of Christ, had received the diadem by Apostolic gift. Oh, thrice happy, had it but known its good fortune; this empire which had Rome for its citadel, and the key-bearer of heaven for its founder." (Florus apud Mabillon, *Analecta*, i. 388.) The Chronicler of Vulturnum adds: "At that time few were the fortress-castles in those regions; but scattered in all directions over the face of the land, were to be seen innumerable villas and churches. Nor was there any fear or apprehension of war; for peace the most profound, and security reigned everywhere, to the great felicity of Italy, until the time of the Saracens."

The Saracens, when assailing the western nations, had for their chief object the destruction of the Christian faith. The Roman Pontiffs were untiring in their efforts to arouse the princes of Europe to oppose them. The words of Pope John VIII. should have sufficed to awaken the ardour of the most slothful. To Charles the Bold he writes: "How many and how great are the things we have suffered, and are hourly suffering, at the hands of the Saracens. Why should I attempt to describe, when all the leaves of the forest, were they turned into tongues, would not suffice to narrate them? The blood of Christians is poured out like water; the people devoted to God are slaughtered. Captivity the most cruel, in perpetual exile, is the lot of such as escape destruction by the sword or by fire. Behold the cities, the walled towns, and the country villages bereft of inhabitants, have sunk into ruin; and their bishops, dispersed in flight, are sure of refuge nowhere but around these tombs of the Apostles. Wild beasts usurp the sanctuaries where stood their chair of doctrine. Behold, most beloved son, the sword has pierced to the soul: days have come in which we exclaim, 'Blessed are the wombs that have not brought forth.' The mistress of the nations, the queen of cities, the mother of churches, the consolation of the afflicted, the harbour of refuge for all who are in distress or danger, the seat of the Apostles, Rome, sits desolate and overwhelmed with distress." And, in another letter: "Within the walls the remnant of the people who have survived so many disasters, are reduced to the most trying distress: all beyond the walls is a solitude; the basilicas of the saints and their altars they have destroyed; of the priests and holy nuns, some they have dragged into captivity, others they have put to every species of most cruel death; and all the people redeemed with the blood of Christ, through a vast circuit, they have slain."

In the year 903, ambassadors from Southern Italy presented themselves at the camp of the Saracen Emir, now master of Sicily. He did not even vouchsafe an audience to them; but, after some days, he sent the message: "Let them begone from hence, and tell the wretches who sent them, that to take care of all Italy is my concern; and that as for those that dwell there, it is for me to dispose of their destinies at my pleasure. Do they dare to hope that my arms can for a moment be resisted by the despicable Greeks or Franks? Would that I could catch them some place where they could not escape by flight. But why waste my breath with these Christian dogs? Let them begone; and tell them that it is not their doom alone which is sealed: the city of that old dotard, Peter, also, I have doomed to destruction." There was, indeed, no prospect of human aid; but there was a higher Power to guard the Shrine of the Apostles. A few weeks passed on; and, whilst the emir matured his plans of conquest, naught but prayer and penance was seen on the Seven Hills. One night, as he set out to continue his devastating career, he slept in a chapel of St. Michael the Archangel; on a sudden, the camp was aroused by the intelligence that their emir was no more. Summoning the leaders of the army to his bedside, he told them, as he expired, that that night St. Peter, in the form of a venerable bishop, clothed in sacred robes, stood before him, and with the pastoral staff transfixed his breast.

Throughout seven centuries, with rare intervals of peace, that war, under the varying names of Saracen, Mussulman, and Turk, was waged against the Cross by the disciples of Mahomet. For St. Pius V. was reserved the glory of achieving the final discomfiture of the restless enemy. On the morning of the 7th October, 1571, the allied fleets of Venice, Spain, and Rome, sailed out from the port of Lepanto, and, under the standard of St. Peter, shattered for ever the Mussulman power. Rome decreed to Colonna, the victorious commander, all the honours of a triumph. In the pageant which welcomed him within the walls were set forth all the joyous memories of the past—all the cheering prospects for the future of Christian civilization. The sainted Pontiff, with the assembled cardinals, advanced to the threshold of St. Peter's Basilica, and there embraced the triumphant soldier of the Cross; and a thrill of joy reverberated through every Catholic heart whilst the kiss of peace was thus given to Christian heroism by the Vicar of Christ.

Three hundred years have passed since that glorious day. The Dominican novices still linger at Santa Sabina. The orange-tree planted there by St. Dominick has not decayed. The room where that great saint lived of old, and where St. Pius V. prayed at the moment when the battle raged at Lepanto, still breathes the fragrance of their piety. But when the Christian pilgrim now visits that hallowed spot, and looks down on the present sad condition of Rome, how must he sigh for the day when the present heir of the virtues, as of the name of Pius, may once again, at the threshold of the Shrines of the Apostles, give the kiss of peace to the triumphant chivalry of Catholic Europe.

Modern writers of history for the British public (and permit me to name two of the most recent works that I have seen: *Rome, from the Fall of the Western Empire*, by the Rev. George Trevor, Canon of York; and the *Historical Essays* of Mr. Freeman) heap obloquy on the name of Alexander III., whilst they extol the Emperor Frederick Barbarossa as the man of his age, a model of princely wisdom, the beneficent ruler of a grateful people. With such writers, envenomed hatred of the Holy See takes the place of history, and facts are represented, not as they really were, but as these writers would wish them to have been.

Barbarossa was, indeed, a man of genius, and his empire possessed such military resources that, had he been inspired by religion, and guided by the dictates of conscience, a golden era might have smiled on the Western Church. It was, however, the one object of his reign to crush every germ of civil liberty, and to establish an imperial despotism both in Church and State.

On the day when the cardinals elected Alexander III. to the chair of St. Peter, the agents of Barbarossa rushed into the Conclave, tore off the sacred vestments from the newly-elected Pope, and hurried him and the cardinals to prison: "Great," says an eye-witness of these scenes, "was the grief of the clergy; the judges and seniors of Rome were weighed down with sorrow, and a helpless stupor seized the people, until, at length, when the august victims of persecution had been three days in the dungeons of Trastevere, the spirit of Frangipani, and the other nobles, could brook the outrage no longer: they marched at the head of the Roman people, seized the fortress, and restored the prisoners to liberty." Three anti-Popes, in succession, were intruded by Barbarossa into the See of Peter, seeking, by unrelenting tyranny, to oppress the whole Church of God.

And here let me remark, that it was precisely one of these anti-popes who, to flatter the Emperor, solemnized, in 1161, the canonization of Charlemagne; for, Barbarossa wished to appear heir of the virtues and heroism of that great prince. Nevertheless, this canonization is precisely one of the matters of reproach adduced by the Canon of York against the memory of the Popes. (*Rome from the Fall of the Western Empire*, page 134.) How true is the proverb, *mendacem oportet esse memorem.*

When Barbarossa captured Milan for the first time, he convened a synod of Jurisconsults at Roncaglia, and there it was published with acclamation that the Imperial will was the supreme principle of law: *quod principi placuit legis habet vigorem.* His cruelty, on the second capture of Milan, excited the indignation of all Europe. He himself describes in a letter to the Count of Soissons the destruction which fell upon this fair capital of North Italy; "the walls and their fosses we make level with the ground: we destroy the towers; of the entire city we make a ruin and a solitude." (D'Achery, *Spicilegium*, iii. 536.) On the 30th of May, 1167, he renewed the same scenes of havoc and plunder in Rome. "The Germans, on this occasion," writes the historian Höfler, "wreaked their vengeance on the environs of Rome and on the city itself in a dreadful way: even the nephew of the Emperor, Frederick of Rottenburg, set fire to the Basilica of St. Peter's—that most august sanctuary of the Catholic world, which the Saracens themselves had, so to say, respected."

But he, whom the power of man could not control, was now humbled by the hand of God. Half the Imperial army was carried off by pestilence before it could fly from Rome. Three months from the pillage of the city saw the deputies of the towns of North Italy hastening to the convent of Pontita, where, under the guidance of Pope Alexander III., the famous Lombard League was formed, which soon restored liberty to the Italian Communes, and led on their hitherto dispirited troops to the decisive victory of Legnano. The united cities had, in the meantime, built a new fortress, to which, in honour of their great leader, they gave the name of Alessandria. When Barbarossa sued for peace, one condition, above all, he insisted on, viz., that the fortress should no longer bear the hated name of Alexander III., but be rather styled in his own honour, *Cesarea*. The representatives of the League easily assented to this empty condition, but popular feeling, more consistent in gratitude and honour than the diplomatists of that age, refused to sanction their decree; and that fortress to the present day bears its historic name of Alessandria. New disasters fell in quick succession on the devoted head of Barbarossa. Even his great crusade, in which 100,000 men, marching under the banner of the Cross, threatened to subjugate the entire East, brought him no honour; and Barbarossa miserably ended his days, drowned in the river Cydnus. The German poet and historian, Schiller, commenting on the course pursued by Pope Alexander in regard to Barbarossa, makes the following just remarks: "From traits like this may the spirit be recognised which animated the Roman Court, and the inflexible firmness of the principles which every Pope, setting all personal considerations aside, saw himself following. Emperors and kings, illustrious statesmen and stern warriors, were seen to sacrifice their rights under the pressure of circumstances, to prove false to their principles, and to yield to necessity. This seldom or never happened to a Pope. Even when he wandered about in misery, possessed not of a foot of land in Italy, not a soul that was gracious to him, and lived on the compassion of strangers, he still held firmly to the prerogatives of his See and the Church. If every other political community at certain times has suffered, and suffers still, from the personal qualities of those to whom their government is confided, this has hardly ever been the case with the Church and her Head. How unlike soever to one another the Popes might be in temperament, mind, and capacity, their policy was ever firm, uniform, immutable. Their capacity, their temperament, their mind, seemed not to be infused into their office at all. Their personality might be said to melt away in their dignity; and passion, in their case, was extinguished under the triple crown. Although on the decease of every Pope, the personal chain of succession to the throne was broken, and with every new Pope was pieced afresh; although no throne in the world changed its master so often, and was so tempestuously assailed: yet was this the only throne in Christendom which never seemed to change its possessor; because only the Popes died, but the spirit that animated them was immortal."

Whilst the Pontiffs laboured to guard the city of Rome from foreign assailants, the spirit of revolution within the walls more than once attempted to revive the rule of Romulus at the shrine of the Apostles. The first great leader of revolt was Arnold of Brescia. Expelled from the religious order to which he belonged, "he," as Otho of Frisinga writes, "endeavoured, by an unheard-of temerity, to rehearse the pagan tragedies of old, and re-establish the reign of murder and tyranny on the Seven Hills." Even Barbarossa turned away in disgust from his arrogant and unmeaning words. His tragic fate is described by Otho of Frisinga, who tells us that he received its details from the lips of Barbarossa himself. For some time Arnold was defended by the Visconti, who, however, soon surrendered their *protégé* into the hands of the Imperial Prefect of Rome. By order of the emperor he was brought to the stake, and the Imperial Prefect caused the ashes of the pyre, on which the wretched man was burned, to be swept into the Tiber. (Baronius, ad. an. 1155, page 41.)

The next great revolutionary leader was Nicola di Lorenzo, better known by his popular abbreviated name, Cola di Rienzo. He was a fanatical worshipper of the Rome of the Gracchi and Cæsar. "His letters," writes Sismondi, "are full of mystical fanaticism: his references to the ancient heroes of Rome are always mingled with invocations to her Christian saints." He was treated mercifully by the Popes, and eceived pardon at their hands, but the people could not olerate his crimes. His last discourse on the Capitol was nterrupted by the cries of the assembled populace. Seeking safety in disguise and flight, he was discovered, and dragged by the people to the platform of the palace, on the Campidoglio, and there an assassin plunged a dagger into is breast. Gibbon adds: "He fell senseless at the first stroke; the impotent revenge of his enemies inflicted a thousand wounds; and his body was abandoned to the dogs, he Jews, and to the flames."

Need I remind you of the sad desolation brought by the Ghibelline factions on the fairest districts of Italy? Their ury reached its summit when the Imperial agent, an Albiensian heretic, abetted by Sciarra Colonna, dared, in nagni, to lay hands on the Vicar of Christ. And yet never as Boniface VIII. more noble than at that moment. Assuming his pontifical robes, he courageously confronted his aptors: when threatened with deposition, he fearlessly plied, "I am ready to suffer everything, sooner than betray the freedom of the Catholic Church; and, as Vicar of Christ, I can well endure the sentence of deposition at the hands of heretics." Even Dante, though deeply imbued with Ghibelline prejudices, can find no words sufficient to reprobate this crime of Anagni:

"Veggo in Alagna entrar lo fiordaliso,
E nel Vicario suo Cristo esser catto:
Veggolo un' altra volta esser deriso;
Veggo rinnovellar l'aceto e il fiele,
E tra vivi ladroni essere anciso."

From that day dates the ruin of Anagni. A traveller, in 1526, thus describes its sad condition:—"The town is deserted and in ruin: tottering walls are seen on every side, especially where once stood the palace of Pope Boniface. I asked an aged inhabitant, whence came this ruin? He said to me, it dates from the insult offered to Pope Boniface; from that day decay set in, and pestilence, war, and domestic strife have completed its destruction." (Raccolta di Viaggi, *Viaggio di Alessandro Bolognese*, A.D. 1526.)

I have mentioned the name of Dante. He was an ardent friend of the Ghibelline party, and strenuously supported their cause. Yet we would, perhaps, seek in vain for a more elegant or faithful description of the destiny of Christian Rome than that presented to us by this prince of poets:

"Figlia e madre d'eroi, che in pace e in guerra
Sempre sul l'Universo avrai l'impero,
Roma, che sei de' Numi emula in terra
Con lo splendor de' Cesari e di Piero.

"Innanzi a te, *quando in follie non erra*,
Sorge a vertù l'attonito pensiero:
Innanzi a te l'ossequio mio s'atterra,
Chè in te sol veggio il grande, il bello, il vero.

"Il tempo, che *qualunque* umana altezza
Transforma, strugge e alfin copre d'obblio,
Ti guarda sì ma il tuo poter non spezza.

"Sull' Aventin, dove a seder si pose,
Dante un giorno così gridar s'udìo:
E: Sia così! l'Eternità rispose."

Petrarch was heir of the piety as well as of the genius of Dante. The laurel crown was awarded to him in the Capitol amid popular applause, but Petrarch hastened in solemn procession from the Capitol to St. Peter's and suspended his crown as a votive offering at the shrine of the Apostles. Rome was, at this time, deprived of the presence of the Popes, who had taken up their residence in Avignon. Petrarch addresses them in the name of Christendom: "Rome stretches out towards you her emaciated and withered arms; the bosom of Italy is agitated with sobs of grief, imploring your return." And, again, he writes to Pope Urban V.: "Remember that the Church of Rome is your spouse. You will say that the Universal Church is the spouse of the Roman Pontiff: it is true. Far be it from me to wish to restrict your jurisdiction: I would rather assign to it no limits but those of the world; for all true worshippers of Christ must obey your rule. But, Holy Father, this does not prevent Rome from having special claims on you: other Churches have their own bishops; Rome has no bishop but you. . . . And when you are summoned to the tribunal of Christ, do you choose to arise in Avignon, or not rather with Peter and Paul, Apostles; with Laurence and Stephen, martyrs; with Gregory and Sylvester, confessors; with Cicily and Agnes, virgins?" At length, Martin V. returned to Rome, and the widowed city was once more comforted by the presence of the Vicar of Christ. We shall hear from Platina the condition of the city, and the joy of the Romans welcoming him on his return: "He was hailed as the propitious star, and last hope of their country, by what still was left of the Roman people and princes. They marked that day as one of the brightest in their annals. Rome he found in a condition so dilapidated and forlorn, that it no longer presented the appearance of a city. The houses you might see tottering and nodding to their fall; the churches prostrate, the streets deserted: everything wore the appearance of decay, of neglect, long-continued and beyond redress. Want and misery were stamped on the visages of the inhabitants. Of the festive crowds, the concourse, the polished air and brilliancy of city life, there was no vestige to be discovered; but it looked as if the offscouring of the whole country had been swept together in that dingy, forlorn place." (Platina, *Vit. Pont. in Vit. Martini V.*)

I need no more than mention the memorable sack of Rome in 1527, which renewed all the horrors of the invasions of the Goths and Huns. Two armies, the one of German Lutherans, under the command of Fraunsberg, the other of Spanish troops, led on by the Constable de Bourbon, made a joint attack on the city, on the morning of the 6th of May. Fraunsberg, pointing to Rome, said to his soldiers: "Behold your plunder. Luther has promised it to you; if you hold back, famine and death await you." Their subsequent excesses baffle all description. Ranke writes: "Restrained by no leader, the blood-thirsty soldiery, hardened by long privations, and rendered savage by their warfare, burst over the devoted city. Never fell richer booty into more violent hands; never was plunder more continuous or destructive." Fraunsberg, as he marched to Rome, wore on his neck a chain of massive gold; and it was his boast that with it he would strangle the old dotard of the Vatican. On the morning of the assault, as he joyfully advanced towards the apparently defenceless city, he was seized with apoplexy, and fell lifeless to the ground. The other leader, the Constable de Bourbon, as he mounted the walls in triumph, was struck down by a bullet, and, being borne along by his soldiers, expired at the threshold of St. Peter's.

This sack of Rome was destined, in the ways of God, to purify it from the corruption with which an immoral literature had begun to flood the entire Peninsula. During the first years of the revival of Grecian art, the restoration of letters, and the Lutheran heresy, men's minds, moreover, seemed infatuated with a new Capitoline mania, and began to idolize the ideas and the passions of the pagan age. Thenceforward, these profane fires were extinguished in Rome. The arts, indeed, hallowed by religion, attained their highest perfection under the benign patronage of the Vicar of Christ. They were no longer, however, the slaves of impiety, but the handmaids of faith; and the whole city, with its countless monuments, became one vast trophy of religion, symbolizing the triumph of Christ, of His Apostles and martyrs, over the pride, and passions, and superstitions of paganism.

Towards the close of the last century, the statesmen of Europe, led away by Voltarian ideas, sought to make the Church of Christ subservient to their political schemes. The great Pontiff, Pius VI., saw the See of Peter at one and the same time assailed by Ferdinand of Naples, Joseph of Austria, Charles of Spain, Leopold of Tuscany, the Bourbon of Parma, and even Louis of France—all nominally Catholic sovereigns, but all combined to enslave the Church of God. Again were the Psalmist's words repeated: *Quare fremuerunt gentes, et reges convenerunt in unum.* The Reign of Terror, and the principles of 1789, overturned these thrones, and scarce the memory remained of all their plotting against the Vicar of Christ.

In 1799, the storm fell upon Rome. The aged Pius VI., venerable for his fourscore years, his virtues, and his great deeds, was treated with brutal violence by the Calvinist Haller and his associates, who, in the name of the French Republic, dragged the saintly Pontiff from the Vatican, and hurried him off to the prison of Valence. The infidels of that day gloated over the downfall of the Papacy, and boasted that the last of the Popes was in their hands. Even an official decree was promulgated in Rome, that the cardinals would not be allowed to elect a successor in the place of the dying Pope. Yet the august prisoner, when yielding his spirit to Heaven, the 29th of August, 1799, took from his finger a precious ring, presented to him by the good Queen Clotilda of Sardinia, sister of Louis XVI., and commanded one of his attendants to consign it to his successor in the See of Peter. That same autumn, the armies of France, ignominiously flying from Italy, left Venice free for the Conclave. A change, too, had come over the rulers of France; and, whilst the newly-elected Pope Pius VII. enters his capital, amidst the acclamations of his people, Napoleon, on the field of Marengo, proclaims his determination to uphold the rights of the Sovereign Pontiffs, and to build up the ruined altars of his country. He sent an ambassador to Rome, and gave him the instruction: "Comport yourself towards the Pope as if he had an army at his back of 200,000 men."

A few years rolled on, and Napoleon, blinded by his unprecedented success, renounces the protectorate of the Sovereign Pontiffs: the Papal States become an imperial province, and his son is styled the King of Rome. To the threat of excommunication he replied: "They say I am to be denounced to Christendom. Nothing but ignorance, the most profound of the age in which we live, could have suggested such a notion; the date involves an error of a thousand years. Does Pius VII. imagine that the arms will fall from the hands of my soldiers?" Need I tell you the result? He whose breath scatters the mightiest hosts, and causes the earth to tremble, looked down in His wrath on that imperial pride. The arms did fall from the hands of Napoleon's soldiers; and he himself was led away a captive, to end his years on the rocks of St. Helena.

Little more than twelve months have passed since another Napoleon abandoned another saintly Pontiff of the name of Pius. And, again, need I mention the result? Step by step, as the French troops recede from the walls of Rome, the German armies penetrate into the heart of France. The capital of Christendom surrenders to the Piedmontese troops, and Napoleon appears as a suppliant at the tent of Bismarck. Victor Emmanuel enters the city of the Popes, and France has the humiliation of witnessing the Prussian triumphant entry into her capital.

Thus, is the unmistakable characters of unchanging truth, history traces for us the divine decree, that Rome is the city of the Vicar of Christ, the heavenly-guarded centre of the Church of God. Every arm raised against it shall surely perish. God may permit His enemies to triumph for a while, but all their efforts must be subservient to His wise designs. The fire of the Chaldeans was allowed of old to purify the temple and cleanse away the iniquities of Judah ; yet did not Sion cease to be God's own city till the plenitude of ages had come. Even so, the enemies of religion may revel for a time amid the sacred glories of Rome, but the lessons of history, as well as the teaching of faith, are our guarantee that present sufferings are the harbingers of a glorious future for the Church of God.

Thus, gentlemen, I have essayed to illustrate, by the facts of history, the destiny of Christian Rome. If I have dwelt particularly on the calamities which in past times have pressed upon this new Jerusalem, this line of reasoning was suggested by the afflictions which at the present moment overwhelm the Vicar of Christ. In the long line of Pontiffs, none has been more glorious, none has guided with more steady hand the barque of St. Peter; yet none has been more fiercely assailed by the storms of infidelity, indifferentism, and revolution, and none had surpassed him in his sorrows. When Pius VI. was in captivity, an humble Camoldolese, who subsequently wore the tiara as Gregory XVI., published his work, entitled *The Triumph of the Holy See;* and in its first lines he writes: "It will occasion surprise to many that I should, at the present moment, speak and write of the triumph of the Holy See, whilst the Pope is a prisoner, and the princes of the Church are dispersed, and all sacred things are overthrown in every part of Italy, and throughout the greater portion of Europe; yet I pursue this course because all these things only serve to prove of how little avail are the utmost efforts of the enemies of God, and how true are the words of St. Chrysostom, that it would be easier to extinguish the sun in the heavens than to extinguish the Church of Christ." In God's own time the present storm shall also cease. I am not a prophet; yet I do not hesitate to foretell that some of you whom I now address, will, at no distant day from the present trials of Pius IX., and the victory of his sacred cause, as well as from the punishment of the assailants of the Holy City, derive a new argument to set forth the true, unchanging destiny of Eternal Rome.

IV.

THE CIVILIZATION OF IRELAND BEFORE THE ANGLO-NORMAN INVASION.

(*Lecture delivered in Sydney, for the benefit of the St. Vincent de Paul's Society, 27th of April,* 1885.)

At the request of the gentlemen of the St. Vincent de Paul's Society, who labour with unwearying devotedness to alleviate the distress of the poor of every denomination among our citizens, I will address you this evening on the Civilization of Ireland before the Anglo-Norman Invasion. There are but few, indeed, who will venture at the present day to question the fair fame of Ireland for culture and science and religion during the centuries that immediately followed the Apostolate of her Apostle St. Patrick. For four centuries, at least, all Christendom resounded with her praises, and the nations of Europe, rejoicing in the gifts and graces lavishly bestowed on her by Heaven, reverently saluted her as the bright star of learning for the western world, the sanctuary of Religion, the Island of Saints. The chronicler Marianus—whose great work is of itself a standing proof of Ireland's civilization, for he led the way among all the chroniclers of the middle ages—treating of the sixth century, attests that "Ireland, the Island of Saints, was to a sublime degree full of holy men and of innumerable wonders." The Anglo-Saxon, St. Aldhelm of Malmesbury, writing in the eighth century, is not less emphatic in his praise, and describes Erin as a country "rich in the wealth of science," and "as thickly set with learned men as the firmament is with stars." What wonder, then, that the illustrious German writer, Goerres, should cry out, "When we look into the ecclesiastical life of the Irish people, we are almost tempted to believe that some potent spirit had transported over the sea the cells of the Thebaid, with all their hermits—its monasteries with all their inmates, and settled them down in this western island; an island which in three centuries gave eight hundred and eighty saints to the Church, won over to Christianity the North of Britain and a large part of Germany, and, while it devoted the utmost attention to the sciences, cultivated with especial care the mystical contemplation in her communities, as well as in the saints whom they produced." Surely a people such as this must not be stigmatized as barbarous, but rather is it justified in claiming for itself a foremost place among the most civilized nations of the middle ages.

Without entering into minute details in this matter, which presents such a wide field for historical inquiry, a few general remarks may suffice to bring before you in its true light the civilization of Ireland at this period.

From the fifth to the ninth century schools and monasteries were everywhere multiplied throughout the length and breadth of the land, and became so many centres for learning and higher studies, fountains of sacred wisdom, homes of discipline, sanctuaries of religion. There was Clonard, with its bright array of saints, following the rule of St. Finnian the Wise. The ancient writer of St. Finnian's life declares that from that monastery "like the sun in the firmament, he enlightened the world by the rays of his virtues, of salutary doctrine and miracles: for the fame of his good works invited many illustrious men from divers parts of the world to his school, as to a holy repository of all wisdom, partly to study the Sacred Scriptures, and partly to be instructed in the rule of the religious life." In the school of Beannchuir, in the "Valley of Angels," four thousand disciples used to assemble under the guidance of St. Comgall. St. Bernard styles it "a very noble monastery, and head of several others: a place truly sanctified, abounding in saints, abundantly fruitful to God: so much so that one of the religious of this holy congregation, named Luanus, was said to be the founder of an hundred monasteries:" and he adds, that "its disciples not only filled Ireland and Scotland, but swarms of its saints spread themselves over foreign countries; one of whom, St. Columbanus, coming to our shores of Gaul, founded the monastery of Luxeuil." The other countless monasteries had each its distinctive grace. Thus, Derry was famed for the angelic life of its religious; Saigher, for its almsgiving; Iniskeltra and Glasnevin, for meditation on the Sacred Scriptures; Lismore, for the study of the classics; Aghabhoe, for geometry; Clonmacnoise, for history; Clonfert, for missionary enterprise. The Aran islands, off the western coasts, were at first popularly known as Aran of the Flowers, but so many were the holy men who flocked thither to lead a heavenly life under the Abbot St. Enda, that thenceforward they became known only as Aran of the Saints. For centuries all these great monasteries have been little more than shapeless ruins, yet the spirit of God seems to linger around each hallowed spot ennobled by such heroism of piety and sanctified by so many virtues. Not many years ago a few devout pilgrims knelt together within the ruined enclosure on Aran-more, where St. Enda was interred, and where likewise repose the relics of a countless army of white-robed saints. One of those pilgrims subsequently wrote: "We can never forget the scene of that morning: the pure, bright sand, covering the graves of unknown and unnumbered saints as with a robe of silver tissue, that glistened in the sunshine; the delicate green foliage of the wild plants that rose here and there, as if wrought in embroidery upon the white expanse; on one side the swelling hill crowned with the church of Benignus, and on the other the blue sea, that almost bathed the foundations of the venerable sanctuary itself: the soft, balmy air that hardly stirred the ferns on the old walls; and the fresh, happy, solemn calm that reigned over all."

In those early centuries, travellers had not the railways and steamers which facilitate communication in modern times. Nevertheless, countless strangers, from all the European nations, flocked to Ireland, that, at the pure fountains of her schools and monasteries, they might satiate their thirst for science and religion. Dr. Johnson does not hesitate to say that, throughout all this period, "Ireland was the school of the West—the quiet habitation of sanctity and literature." Bishop Nicholson also writes: "Within a century after the death of St. Patrick, the Irish seminaries had so increased, that most parts of Europe sent their children to be educated there, and drew thence their bishops and teachers." Montalembert attests that "Ireland was then regarded by all Christian Europe as the principal centre of knowledge and piety. In the shelter of her numberless monasteries a crowd of missionaries, doctors, and preachers were educated for the service of the Church, and the propagation of the faith in all Christian countries. A vast and continuous development of literary and religious effort is there apparent, superior to anything that could be seen in any other country in Europe. The monasteries, which gradually covered the soil of Ireland, were the hostelries of a foreign emigration. They were open to all: the poor and the rich, the slave as well as the free man, the child and the old man, had free access, and paid nothing. Nor did the Irish monasteries confine the benefit of their literary and religious instruction to the natives of Ireland. They opened their doors, with admirable generosity, to strangers of every country and every condition. Above all, to those 'ho came from the neighbouring island, England; some to nd their lives in an Irish cloister; some to go from house) house in search of books, and masters capable of explain-ıg those books. The Irish monks received with kindness uests so greedy of instruction, and gave them both books nd masters, the food of the body and the food of the soul, 'ithout demanding any recompense. From the seventh to ıe eleventh century, Anglo-Saxon students flocked into :eland: and for four hundred years the schools of the land maintained the great reputation which brought so ıany successive generations to dip deeply there into the ving waters of knowledge and faith."

This influx of devoted men from the sister island, in the ursuit of science and piety, is further attested by Camden, ho writes: "No men came up to the Irish monks for ınctity and learning; and they sent forth swarms of holy ıen all over Europe, to whom the monasteries of Luxeuil ı Burgundy, Pavia in Italy, Würzburg in Franconia, t. Gall in Switzerland, and so many others, owe their :igin. The Saxons, at that time, flocked to Ireland from l quarters, as to a mart of literature. Wherefore it is ıat we frequently meet, in our writers of the lives of the ıints: 'He was sent over to Ireland for education.'" But, we go back eight hundred years before Camden wrote, e will find the same fact attested by Venerable Bede, who,)eaking of the seventh century, says: "Many nobles and hers of the English nations were living in Ireland, whither ıey had repaired either to cultivate the sacred studies, or lead a life of stricter discipline. Some of them became onks; others chose rather to apply to reading and study,)ing about from school to school through the cells of the asters; and all of them were most cheerfully received by ıe Irish, who supplied them gratuitously with good books ıd instruction."

The brightest name on England's calendar of missionary

saints is St. Willibrord. He spent twenty years in th schools of Ireland, preparing himself to do God's work, an laying up a rich store of those spiritual treasures of whic he was to be the bearer to distant lands. The Litany c St. Ængus, composed in the eighth century, commemorate several Britons, Picts, and Saxons, and also Gauls, Germans Romans, and Egyptians—holy men who went to Ireland i the pursuit of the science of salvation, and chose it for thei resting-place. As late as the eleventh century, we fin Bishop Sulgen, from Wales, setting out for the Irish shores as we read in his metrical life :—

"Exemplo patrum commotus, amore legendi
Ivit ad Hibernos sophia mirabile claros."

"By his ancestors' bright example moved,
He sought in Erin the science which he loved,
And in her schools those skilful masters found,
Whose wisdom is throughout the world renowned."

But not only was Ireland thus rich in the blessings o Christian civilization at home, she was, moreover, chosen in the ways of Providence, to be the dispenser of thos blessings to almost every nation of Europe. So numerou were the Irish missionaries who laboured in the cause o religion and civilization throughout France, that the con temporary Eric of Auxerre cries out: "It would seem as i a whole nation of Christian sages had landed on our shores." Other ancient writers compare those missionaries to swarms of bees that, quitting their parent hives, hastened to less favoured regions to enrich them with their honied store and St. Bernard declares that "from Ireland, as from ar overflowing stream, crowds of holy men descended on foreigr nations."

The testimony of a few historians not prejudiced in favour of any of Ireland's claims may serve to place this important fact in its true light. Mosheim writes: "That the Irish were lovers of learning, and distinguished themselves in hose times of ignorance beyond all other European nations, ravelling through the most distant lands with a view to mprove and communicate their knowledge, is a fact well-nown; for we see them, in the most authentic records of ntiquity, discharging with the highest reputation and pplause the functions of teachers in France, Germany, and taly." Thierry, in his *History of the Norman Conquest*, hus speaks of Ireland: "It possessed a multitude of saints nd learned men, venerated alike in England and in Gaul; or no country had furnished a greater number of Christian nissionaries, animated by no other motive than pure zeal nd an ardent desire of communicating to foreign nations he learning and the faith of their native country. The rish were great travellers, and everywhere they gained the earts of those whom they visited." So, too, the German ntiquary, Wattenbach: "Above all others, the Irish went orth into every part of the world. They filled England and he neighbouring islands. In France they were every-vhere to be met with, and they made their way even into he heart of Germany." Montalembert also writes: "A haracteristic still more distinctive of the Irish monks, as of ll their nation, was the imperious necessity of spreading hemselves without, of seeking or carrying knowledge and aith afar, and of penetrating into the most distant regions o watch or combat paganism. This monastic nation be-ame the missionary nation *par excellence*. While some ame to Ireland to procure religious instruction, the Irish nissionaries launched forth from their island. They covered he land and seas of the West. Unwearied navigators, they anded on the most desert islands; they inundated the ontinent with their successive immigrations."

It is at least a thousand years since the sons of Ireland hus laboured in building up the bulwarks of religion and civi-zation throughout the continent of Europe. Nevertheless heir memory is still held in benediction, and their names are enrolled among the patron saints of the chief nations of Christendom. One hundred and thirty Irish saints have found a place in the calendars of Germany; forty-five are honoured as patrons in France; thirty in Belgium, and several others in Italy, Switzerland, and even in remote Iceland. What is most remarkable, we meet with those Irish pilgrims and missionary saints in the most out-of-the-way places—in the depths of the Black Forest in Germany, in the remotest and most sequestered hamlets in France, on the highest peaks of the hills of Switzerland. Let me take one instance. On the face of a precipice above the Lake of Thun in Switzerland, there is the cave in which an Irish patron of the district, St. Beoadh—Latinized *Beatus*—dwelt. It would be difficult to find a more romantic spot. The path that leads to it threads along the edge of precipices overhanging the green lake. Tufts of wild flowers cling to the rock and dangle their glorious harmonies of colour at dizzy heights over the tranquil water. About thirty feet below the mouth of the cave a large stream rushes out of the rock, and forming a silvery cascade of eight hundred feet, plunges into the still mirror of the lake. The cave of the saint is itself screened by a fir wood clinging to the rock ledges. Its wide entrance was once walled up, so as to leave only a door and a window, but the stones have fallen. The rude altar, too, is now overthrown. For a time after the triumph of Zwinglianism in Berne the faithful pilgrims continued to visit the sanctuary of St. Beatus, till at length the civil authorities drove them away at the point of the spear. At present a little chapel bears the name of the saint at Lungern, on the nearest point of the adjoining Canton of Obwalden, where the ancient faith still maintains its ground, and thither flock crowds of pilgrims every year to honour the memory of their Apostle on his feast, the 9th of May.

But to return to the subject before us. We may conclude

·om these few remarks, that so far from Ireland being sunk ı ignorance and barbarism in those days, it was enabled, :om the overflowing abundance of its literary and religious fe, to yield rich streams of true Christian civilization to ıe most favoured countries of Europe.

We might desire, perhaps, no better proof of the develop- ıent of studies in the Irish schools than the high perfection ttained in the cultivation of the native tongue. The ınguages which now hold the foremost place in civilized ations were as yet only in their first rudiments, whilst the ·ish tongue was being perfected in all the branches of terature in poetry and prose. It is no small tribute to the oility with which the Irish scholars of those days culti- ıted their native language that we find the most learned :ofessors of comparative philology in modern times in the niversities of Paris, Leipzic, and Berlin, as well as in New ork, Edinburgh, and Oxford, devoting their time and lents to illustrate the Celtic fragments that have been ·eserved to us from those golden ages of Irish literature.

The Ollamhs, or Masters of the Sciences, were every- here treated with marked honour, and in all the assemblies e highest place—after that of the monarch himself—was ssigned to them. Nor was it so easy a matter for them to tain that rank. Their course of instruction occupied relve years; eight of these were devoted to the study of ıilosophy and grammar, and the cultivation of the Irish nguage, and the four remaining years were spent in the mposition of treatises in poetry and prose in their native ngue, to prove themselves qualified for the degree to which ey aspired.

It is from those ages that the Brehon laws have come own to us. They lead us back long before the Justinian ws, and they present the minutest details of a system of gislation sanctioned by religion, which of itself would ffice to prove the high civilization of Ireland a thousand years ago. The publication of those ancient Celtic laws ha been carried on for twenty years under a Royal Commissio and the four volumes already published are most valuab as illustrating the character and institutions of the Iris people in those days. Lord O'Hagan—who has been s lately snatched from a wide circle of friends who loved hi and from the country which he loved so well—in an essa on the Study of Jurisprudence, writes, that "To the stud of those Brehon laws which for so many ages held sway i Ireland, some of us, children of the soil, will be attracte as by ancestral voices from the buried past. And for a the learned of Europe, who have interest in the history Jurisprudence and the Archæology of Law, they must l the subject of intelligent curiosity and careful investiga tion."

It appears to me that I have said enough to justify th statement which I made, that during the centuries whic immediately followed the death of St. Patrick, Ireland d servedly held a foremost place among the civilized nation of Christendom.

But there are some writers who would fain persuade that this bright era of civilization closed with the nin century; that before the Norman invasion Ireland ha become degenerate and had relapsed into barbarism. He how a brilliant English writer, who but a few weeks a paid a hurried visit to the Australian shores, describes t Ireland of those days:—"The Irish, when the Norma took charge of them"—thus writes Mr. Froude—"were, wi the exception of the clergy, scarcely better than a m of armed savages. They had no settled industry, and settled habitations, and scarcely a conception of propert . . . The only occupation considered honourable w fighting and plunder. . . . The religion of the Iri Celts, which three centuries earlier had burned like a st in Western Europe, had degenerated into a superstitio and no longer served as a check upon the most ferocious passions. . . . Their chief characteristics were treachery, thirst for blood, unbridled licentiousness, and inveterate detestation of order and rule. As a nation," he adds, "they have done nothing which posterity will not be anxious to forget;" they "have little architecture of their own, and the forms introduced from England have been robbed of their grace;" in fact, they are "unable to boast of one single national work of art." (Froude, *The English in Ireland*, i. 14, 22.) Of this semi-barbarous people the Normans came to take charge, thus "fulfilling the work for which they were specially qualified and gifted. . . . The true justification of the conquest lay in the character of the conquerors. They were born rulers of men, and were forced, by the same necessity which has brought the decrepit kingdoms of Asia under the authority of England and Russia, to take the management, eight centuries ago, of the anarchic nations of Western Europe." Thus, with the Norman victors, everything was fair and bright; whilst the island which they invaded was plunged in the depths of ignorance and barbarism.

Such are the views which many who have made a mere superficial study of Irish history, are only too eager to adopt. Now, there are several ways in which we may test the accuracy of those statements, but there is one which commends itself particularly to me; and, as it not unfrequently happened in days of chivalry, that whilst hostile armies were marshalled face to face in battle array, some chosen combatant from either side would enter the lists to decide by personal combat to whom should be awarded the palm of victory, so, too, I will lead into the arena before you two illustrious champions, each a fitting representative of the race to which he belonged—the Irish monarch, Brian, and William, the Norman conqueror. They present to us, indeed, many features in common. Each of them successfully usurped an imperial power; they were wise and prudent in council, brave and valorous in the field; victory smiled upon their arms in countless battles, and on the day of their greatest triumphs, at Clontarf and at Hastings, they were alike engaged under the banner of religion; so, too, they have both received from posterity the title of "the Great," and by their respective races they have been honoured with an uninterrupted chorus of unrivalled applause; and hence, it seems to me that the distinctive merits of their imperial rule may, without the risk of partiality, be fairly accepted as a test of the civilization which they represent.

Brian entered on his career, pledged to free Ireland from the oppressive yoke of the Danes. Wave after wave of these northern barbarians had, for a hundred and fifty years, swept over the fairest territories of Erin, and long and painful was the bondage which they imposed upon her people. The richest shrines and sanctuaries were plundered, and the whole country was laid waste. The leaders of these pagan bands even assumed the title of kings of Ireland; and, indeed, more than once they seemed to have secured for themselves a complete mastery over a great part of the island. The chieftains of the subjugated districts were led away to work as slaves for the Danish lords; a Danish soldier was billeted not as a guest, but as a master in every household; each church and monastery had a pagan chieftain appointed to it, and a heavy tax was imposed as well on those who administered, as on those who received the sacred rites of religion. Wherever the invaders went the schools were closed and the teachers slain, and it was an imperative command that all books which were met with in their devastations should be burned or carried away. In sadness the annalists add: "No Irish chief was able to give deliverance from the foreigner because of the excellence of their armour, the greatness of their prowess, their strength and valour, and the excess of their thirst for the fruitful, grassy lands of Erin." Together with material conquest they sought to insure the triumph of paganism. Their leader, Thorgils (who is better known by his Latinized name, Turgesius), caused himself to be proclaimed in Armagh the head of the religion in Ireland, whilst his wife, Otta, was enthroned as high priestess on the high altar of the great church of Clonmacnoise, and proceeded to deliver thence her pagan oracles.

The Dalcassians of Munster were among the foremost and bravest in resisting the tide of invasion. They had vowed that their battle-axes would know no repose so long as Ireland was not entirely free from the Danish thraldom; and they were faithful to their vow. With the chieftaincy of the Dalcassians, Brian had inherited that pledge; its fulfilment was the one great purport of his life; and he lived long enough to see it crowned by a glorious triumph. But let us examine somewhat in detail the chief features that marked this monarch's career.

The first great feature of Brian's rule that presents itself is his disinterestedness. Though victory after victory attended his arms, we nowhere find that riches or plunder or personal aggrandizement were his aim. When a decisive battle forced the Danes of Munster to submit to his authority, the one condition of peace imposed was that every Irishman held by them in bondage should be set at liberty; and the annalists add that thousands of captives were at once seen joyfully returning to their homes. So, too, when as monarch of Ireland he again broke the Danish power, his decree went forth that every Irishman held in bondage throughout Erin should be free, and once more thousands of noble captives were restored to their homes and to freedom.

Though Brian had vanquished the Danes, he took no steps to exterminate them or to banish them from the kingdom. On the contrary, he recognized the element of strength which, as faithful subjects, they would add to his power, and he permitted them to remain in the chief seaports, thus to promote commerce and to develop the resources of the country. He made use of them too to carry the war into the enemy's camp. He gathered together a mighty fleet from all the Danish harbours, and, accompanying it with a chosen band of his own Dalcassian heroes, sent them to pursue the marauding Vikings and to ravage the islands off the Scottish coast and the more northern islands which they had made their resting-place. The fleet returned laden with an immense booty; the Vikings were forced to acknowledge the superior sway of the victor, and Brian was now able to assume the proud title of chief monarch of Ireland and of all the Danish isles.

Brian was also renowned for his hospitality. The Danes of Dublin were compelled to supply to his palace at Kinkora 360 butts of wine every year, and a proportionate quantity was exacted from the Limerick Danes. Each Irish chieftain paid so many head of cattle as his tribute, and whatever was thus received was devoted to enhance the hospitable fame of the royal residence. Its halls were open to all, and rich and poor, chieftains and pilgrims, were welcome to the hospitality of the Irish monarch.

He applied himself in a special manner to repair the material ruin that had resulted from the Danish invasions. The bridges were everywhere repaired, the causeways were restored, new roads were made, the residences of the Irish chieftains were rebuilt, and his own palace at Kinkora was adorned with a magnificence befitting the abode of Ireland's monarch.

In his reverence for the Church and her clergy, the Irish king proved himself to have at heart the true interests of his people. There is no surer test of a monarch's merits in the work of Christian civilization than his dealings with the Church. All the nations of the civilized world are indebted to her in this, that by her they have been lifted up from the mire of pagan barbarism, and have received at her hands the crown of religious and social blessings that adorns them. The truths of heaven are upon her lips; her mission is divine. She does not seek to intrude her authority into the secular domain; but, nevertheless, her beneficent influence permeates the whole body of the State. Whosoever seeks to fetter the Church whilst she guides her children in their heavenward course, is an enemy of civilization, and it matters but little that these fetters be of iron or of gold. True civilization gives freedom to the Church of God, and aids and sustains her in that wondrous mission of beneficence which has been confided to her by her Divine Founder. Such was the freedom given by the monarch Brian to the Irish Church; such the generous aid with which he strengthened her and encouraged her to achieve her glorious work. At his visit to Armagh he offered twenty ounces of gold at the altar of our Apostle; and when a few years later he again visited the same shrine, he repeated the same rich gift. Guarded by his protecting hand, religion went forth arrayed in heavenly comeliness, and her blessings were multiplied throughout the land. Her schools and institutes of piety were revived, the poor were protected, councils were held, strict discipline was enforced, and distant nations began once more, as of old, to look with delight towards our tranquil shores, and to repeat, rejoicing, the Prophet's words: "Blessed is the people whose God is the Lord." And this hallowed influence of the Church continued throughout the whole of this period down to the Anglo-Norman invasion; the monasteries of Ireland flourished, her cloisters were adorned with the maturest fruits of virtue, and peace poured out its richest blessings upon her people. We find a St. Celsus in Armagh, a St. Gillibert in Limerick, a Malchus in Lismore. There was St. Laurence O'Toole, the fearless champion of the liberty of the Church—aye, and of the liberty of his nation, too; and, together with these, there were a thousand other saints and learned men, forming a galaxy of bright and glorious names of which the greatest nations of Christendom would be justly proud.

The contemporary writer of Brian's life attests that, besides restoring the religious houses which the Danes had plundered, he founded seven new monasteries. Everywhere the churches were clothed with a new splendour, the desecrated shrines were adorned, and the deserted chancels resounded once more to the praises of God. He erected no fewer than thirty-two round towers;[1] those characteristic monuments of Irish architecture which, whilst as beacon-lights they served to guide the weary pilgrim to the sanctuary wherein he would find repose, offered, at the same time, in case of any sudden irruption of the barbarians, a safe retreat and a secure defence for the inmates of the monasteries and the relics and the shrines of their holy founders, and the other sacred treasures which have been at all times so dear to the piety of our faithful people. So, too, the schools of Ireland, in a particular manner, engaged the attention and the solicitude of the Irish monarch. And allow me to add that, after the Church, there is no more powerful factor in the work of civilization than the school, for religious education enlightens the mind and strengthens the will; it teaches man his duties, and disciplines him to be faithful to them; it makes known to him his rights, and enables him to assert and defend them. The schools of Ireland flourished during Brian's reign; and throughout this period of our country's history, the Universities of Armagh, and Bangor, and Lismore, won for themselves a world-wide renown. It is recorded that no fewer than 7,000 students' names were inscribed on the roll of Armagh. There is one special feature of Brian's patronage of science

[1] Mac Liag, in the Irish MS. *Life of Brian:* "By him were founded cells and churches. . . . It was Brian that gave out seven monasteries, both furniture, and cattle, and land, and thirty-two cloicteach."

to which I may particularly refer; for it teaches a great lesson which many of the rulers of the world at the present day, notwithstanding all our boasted civilization, have not wisdom enough to learn. Wherever throughout Ireland a youth was found whose talent gave promise of being suited for the higher branches of learning, it was the monarch's wish that he should be trained to science, and his education was provided for from the royal revenues. But, better than any words of mine, the ancient chronicler will set before you the boundless munificence which thus distinguished the reign of the Irish monarch. In the old English translation of the *Annals of Clonmacnoise*, under the year 1002, we read: "The whole realme was overrunn and overspread by the foreigners. The churches, abbeys, and other religious places were by them quite razed and debased, or otherwise turned to vile, base, servile, and abominable uses. . . . . But King Brian was a meet salve to cure such festered sores; in a small time he banished the Danes, made up the churches and religious houses, restored the nobility to their antient patrimony and possessions, and, in fine, brought all to a notable reformation."

Again, *The Wars of the Gaedhil* records that: "By him were erected in Erin noble churches and their sanctuaries. He sent professors and masters to teach wisdom and knowledge, and to buy books beyond the sea and the great ocean, because the writings and books in every church and sanctuary had been destroyed by the plunderers, and Brian himself gave the price of learning and the price of books to everyone separately who went on this service. Many churches were built and repaired by him; bridges and roads were made; the fortresses of Munster were strengthened. . . . He continued in this very prosperous, peaceful, hospitable, just-judging, venerated—with law and rule among the clergy; with honour and renown among the laity—powerful, secure, for fifteen years in the chief sovereignty of Erinn." (Page 139.)

We cannot be surprised that under such munificent patronage the arts and sciences would once more have flourished; they even attained a high perfection, and added new lustre to Ireland's ancient fame. The art of illuminating was cultivated with particular care. So perfect were the Irish copyists in this beautiful branch of art, and so wonderful was their skill, that the first Norman invaders could find no words sufficient to express their admiration; and Giraldus Cambrensis, contemplating one of their masterpieces, cried out, in astonishment, that it was the work not of men, but of angels. "Among all the miraculous things of Kildare," he writes, "nothing surprised me so much as that wonderful book said to have been written from the dictation of an angel. This book contains the Four Gospels according to Jerome's version, and is adorned with almost as many richly illuminated figures as it has pages. Here you see the majesty of the Divine countenance, there the mystical figures of the Evangelists, together with other designs without number, which, if carelessly surveyed, seemed rather blots than intertwined ornaments, and appeared to be plain work, where there was, in truth, nothing but intricacy. But, on close examination, the secrets of the art were evident; and so delicate and subtle, so laboured and minute, so intertwined and knotted, so intricately and brilliantly coloured did you perceive them, that you were ready to say they were the work of an angel and not of man. The more intently I examined them, the more was I filled with fresh wonder and amazement. Neither could Appelles do the like; indeed mortal hand seemed incapable of forming or painting them." Mr. Westwood, in his classical work, *Palæographia Sacra*, after examining the *Book of Kells* and other works still treasured in the home libraries, adds, "Ireland may justly be proud of the *Book of Kells*. This copy of the Gospels is unquestionably the most elaborately executed manuscript of early art now in existence. At a period when the fine arts may be said to have been almost extinct in Italy and other parts of the continent, the art of ornamenting manuscripts had a perfection almost miraculous in Ireland. The invention and skill displayed, the neatness, the precision and delicacy far surpass all that is to be found in ancient manuscripts executed by continental artists." Several Irish illuminated manuscripts, dating from the period of which we treat, are still preserved in the continental libraries, and not long ago a distinguished German writer pronounced the following judgment on them:—"The ornamental pages, borders, and initial letters exhibit so correct an architectural feeling in the distribution of the parts, such a rich variety of beautiful and peculiar designs, so admirable a taste in the arrangement of the colours, and such an uncommon perfection of finish, that one feels absolutely struck with amazement." (Waagen, in *German Art Journal*, No. 11.)

It is a constant tradition that the monarch Brian cultivated the study of music, and was himself skilled in the harp. Certain it is, at least, that music was at this period highly prized among our people. Polydore Virgil and other chroniclers attest that the Irish people were *musicæ peritissimi*. Wherever the Irish missionaries found a home they were sure to introduce a passion for poetry and the music of the harp, as at the monastery of St. Gall, where the use of that instrument continued long to be taught by Irish masters. The Normans were enraptured with the strains of the Irish harp, and Geraldus Cambrensis, to whom we have already referred, did not hesitate to write that "Irish musical skill was incomparably superior to that of any other nation. For their modulations are not slow and morose, as in the instruments of Britain, to which we are habituated; but the sounds are rapid and precipitate, yet sweet and pleasing. It is wonderful that the musical proportion is preserved amidst such precipitate velocity of the fingers, and that the melody is rendered full and perfec by an undeviating art, amidst such trembling modulations such organic tones so infinitely intricate, possessed of suc pleasing swiftness, such unequal parity, such discordan concord. . . . They commence and close their modula tions with so much subtilty, and the tinklings of the slende strings sport so freely with the deep tones of the bass cords so delicately pleasing, so softly soothing, that the perfectio of their art lies in concealing art."

In gold and silver work the Irish schools attained a higl perfection, as may still be seen in the cross of Cong, the shrine of St. Manchan, and other precious fragments tha happily escaped the ravages of later times. The work o art known as the Tara Brooch, now preserved in the Roya Irish Academy, Dublin, is described as "formed of white bronze as a base which is covered with a variety of orna- ments in gold, silver, niello, variously coloured glass and enamel. No language can convey an idea of the wonderful delicacy of the workmanship of this brooch." It was exhibited at the South Kensington Museum in 1863, and a writer in *The Times* referred to it as "more like the work of fairies than of men." A most practised jeweller who examined this and other works of the Irish artists of those days, attested, that "so wonderful is their workmanship, that they cannot be imitated exactly at the present day. They have been executed in a peculiar manner, unknown to modern times." But in this matter I may be permitted to cite the words of Dr. Stokes, who in our own day has proved himself second to none in labouring to restore the study of ancient Irish art. In his *Life of Petrie* he thus writes:—"It is in the variety of form and the exquisite tracery in metal work that the skill and taste of the old artificers is mainly shown. The jewelled shrines of the consecrated bells, as well as many of the earlier and even of the later croziers down to the fifteenth century, exhibit great power both in design and execution. To him whose sense of beauty and of excellence is not narrowed or tied down by formulæ, it has in all the qualities of proportion, variety, and gracefulness a singular and unapproachable beauty. If it be true that the characteristic of a savage art is its want of progression, the rule does not apply to that of Ireland. Incontestable evidences of the rise, progress, and final decay of art in this country were long ago pointed out by Petrie, and it seems to have culminated in the latter part of the twelfth century. From this time, the period of the Anglo-Norman invasion, it gradually declined, until, after more than three centuries of anarchy and war, it died away, leaving its old monuments, its beautiful shrines, its sculptured crosses, decorated churches, and illuminated MSS. to tell of its former lustre." (Page 271.)

To the munificent patronage of Brian—to the impulse given by him to restore the religious monuments of Ireland—we are indebted that Church architecture was developed to a wonderful degree. Suffice it to name St. Cormac's chapel at Cashel, the chancel arch at Tuam, the churches of Clonfert, Roscrea, Inishmain, and Kilmacduagh—all of which date from this period, and which—so beautiful even in their ruins—are admitted to be some of the noblest monuments that the twelfth century presents to us. The twelfth century was, indeed, a period of great architectural revival in England and throughout the Continent; yet the ablest writers on the subject are now agreed that in richness of ornament, and perfection of minute detail, the architectural remains, which Ireland still preserves, belonging to this period, are unsurpassed and unrivalled by any contemporary monuments. And here I wish to recall to your mind two of those groups of monuments—Clonmacnoise and Glendalough—which, though they belong in part to a much earlier age, yet received, at the period of which I treat, that crown of loveliness which, even in their desolation and decay, they have never ceased to wear. It it not very long ago that an illustrious statesman of England, who for years had been familiar with all the great monuments of England, visited Glendalough, and declared that, as a group, he had seen nothing in Great Britain to surpass it. It would seem as if nature had chosen this singularly interesting valley to be a tranquil retreat for religious seclusion and for prayer. High mountains arise to the north, and west, and south, which serve as impenetrable barriers to repel the intrusion of the world on its solitude. Towards the east alone the valley expands to welcome the first rays of the rising sun. The still waters of the lake mirror the glory of the Creator, and the varied beauty of nature, and the grandeur of the surrounding scenery, raise up the mind to the contemplation of heavenly things. No wonder that, as far back as the sixth century, St. Kevin and countless other saints should have loved to dwell there. No wonder that it should be known to the Fathers of the Irish Church as the Valley of God—the Rome of the Isles of the West. And what shall I say of Clonmacnoise, standing, as it does, on the banks of the lordly Shannon—its majestic stone crosses, its lofty towers, its causeways, its churches and sanctuaries—all leading back our thoughts to those days when its monastery was the chief retreat of learning and piety, when the bells of those towers gave joy to the distant traveller, and those churches resounded to the praises of the Most High? And here I may adopt the learned Petrie's words: "There is not, perhaps, in Europe a spot where the feeling heart would find more matter for melancholy reflection than among the ancient churches of Clonmacnoise. Its ruined buildings call forth national associations and ideas. They remind us of the arts and literature, the piety and humanity, which distinguished their time, and are the work of a people who, in a dark age, marched among the foremost on the road of life and civilization, but who were, unfortunately, checked and barbarized by those who were journeying in the same course, and ought to have cheered them on."

Such were the schools of Ireland—such the wonderful development of every branch of art which bespeaks the refinement and civilization of its people. By the invasion of the Anglo-Normans all this was undone, and from the period of their arrival precisely dates the nation's decline. But, on this growth of art in the eleventh and twelfth centuries, and its rapid extinction subsequent to the landing of the Anglo-Normans on our shores, you will permit me to cite two authorities whose testimony cannot be gainsaid:—

"It is a remarkable fact," writes Dr. Stokes, "that as Ireland was in the vanguard of progress in religion and art in Western Europe, from the seventh to the twelfth centuries, so, also, does it seem to have been foremost in decline; and though in other countries mediæval art touched its finest point in the thirteenth century, Celtic art had reached its full perfection a hundred or two hundred years before. This art sprang from the heart and instinct of the native population, and drew its indescribably minute perfection of execution from the intense devotion of the holy men who carried it to its highest point; and so, for the secret of its premature decay, the student of her history will not long search in vain. Ireland became the scene of intestine war; her monasteries were rifled, her libraries burned, her precious reliquaries robbed or destroyed; . . . her native energies were paralyzed, and her aspirations chilled, by the long years of suffering thus entailed."

Not less explicit is Petrie's testimony: "The progressive decline of the fine arts in Ireland, from the end of the twelfth century, is as yet an unwritten chapter in the history of our country. Nevertheless, there are few circumstances in our annals that more strongly depict the debasement which it was the unhappy fate of Ireland to have suffered in those troubled times, or that more strikingly indicate the indissoluble connexion which ever exists between the cultivation of the fine arts, and the civilization, greatness, and happiness of a people. If, in such a state of barbarism as Ireland was then reduced to, genius had arisen, it would have died like a flower of the desert, unnoticed and unknown; for it was not the warrior's rude and bloody hand that could preserve and cherish it, nor his yet ruder mind that could appreciate its excellence and beauty: the seed should be wafted to some more genial clime before it could be nurtured into vigour."

There was another feature in the Irish monarch's rule which must not be omitted; this was his firm repression of crime and the even-handed justice which he meted out to all. Order and contentment and social happiness followed in the train of this just rule, and the annalists relate, not as a matter of poetic imagery, but as a stern fact, that in those times of peace a fair maiden decked out with precious jewels, and bearing rich treasures in her hands, could traverse the whole island from shore to shore, without injury or insult being offered to her.

And now we come to the closing scene. If, during his reign, Brian displayed the wisdom of a Christian monarch, the close of his career was one which merited for him the aureola of a Christian hero. The Danes had resolved to make a last effort for the conquest of Ireland, determined that one spot at least should remain in Europe where triumphant paganism would enjoy an undisturbed control. From the Isle of Man, and the Scottish coasts, and the northern islands, the Vikings gathered together their bravest troops, and left nothing undone to ensure their success. The chief figure in the confederation was the apostate Viking, known in the Irish annals by the name of Brodir. He is thus described in one of the northern sagas:—"He had been a Christian man, and was a deacon by ordination but he had thrown off his faith, and became God's dastard, and now he worshipped ıeathen fiends, and was, of all men, the most skilled in ›orcery. He had on him that coat of mail which no steel ould bite. He was both tall and strong, and had such ɔng black locks that he tucked them under his belt." This postate leader, fired with hatred of the Christian faith, allied all the Northmen's strength to secure the triumph of aganism. So manifest and so terrible were his dealings vith the evil one, that his brother, Ospak, at length declared the Christian faith must be true which the demon thus ssails," and, quitting Brodir, he hastened to receive the 'aters of baptism, and bore to Brian the first intelligence of ıe imminent danger that now threatened him. The Irish ıonarch, on his part, lost no time to summon his forces round him, and all that was best and bravest in the land astened to his standard to ensure the victory of the Cross. 'n Good Friday, the 23rd April, in 1014, at morning's awn, the pagan troops and their allies stood marshalled in attle-array on the plain of Clontarf. Their mighty fleet ɔde tranquilly beneath the shelter of the Hill of Howth, ıd, besides furnishing them with supplies, offered them a ıfe retreat should disaster attend their arms. The city of 'ublin did not then extend beyond the district around hrist Church: all that now is Abbey-street, and Sackville-reet, and thence down to Ballybough-bridge, was covered y the sea-shore. Along the valley of Clonliffe the Danish :mies extended their lines towards Dublin, and, as the ıy advanced, the battle seems to have grown warmest ıere, for the Danes left nothing undone to maintain, whilst ıe Irish troops spared no effort to cut off, their communica-ons with the city. Foremost among the Danish con-derates was a picked band of 2,000 men, encased from ɔad to foot "in polished, strong, triple-plated armour." The ›ven banner, their enchanted standard, was borne before ıem, and Brodir took their command. But neither the ıven banner nor the coats of armour could save them from the Dalcassian battle-axe, and at sunset on that eventf day almost all of that chosen band lay lifeless on the plai The whole number of the invading army is supposed to ha been about 80,000, and so sure were they of success th they had brought with them their families, resolved to mal Ireland their adopted home. "The Northmen," writ Adhemar, "came at that time to Ireland with an ir mense fleet, conveying even their wives and children, wi a view of extirpating the Irish, and occupying in their stea that very wealthy country." (Apud Labbe, *Nova Bibliot. MSS.*, tom. ii., page 177.)

The Irish monarch formed his troops into line of batt along the rising ground where All Hallows College no stands. He addressed only a few words to them, tellir them to hold in mind that it was on Good Friday they we called upon to fight for their religion and their countr The Cross was their banner, and Brian's son their leade The aged monarch himself, now in his eighty-seventh yea retired to his tent, and there, like Moses of old, with ey and hands uplifted towards heaven (*Marianus* in Chronic "manibus et mente ad Deum intentus") remained i prayer while the battle raged around him. As evenir came on it became apparent that the Irish troops wer victorious along the whole line, whilst the high tide th had set in rendered the escape of the invaders to their ship impossible. Thousands of them were driven into the sea and found there a watery grave. The contemporary annalis gives the total Danish loss in this battle at no less tha 60,000. But whilst the power of Danish paganism wa thus broken for ever, Brodir, with a few companions, ha cut his way through the Irish lines, and, passing by th royal tent, espied the aged monarch wrapt in prayer. Fu of Satanic rage he rushed in, and dealt him his death-blow

Thus closed the heroic career of Brian, laying down hi life, in the moment of victory, for his country and for th

Christian faith. The day after the battle the Abbot of Swords, with his religious brethren, conveyed the monarch's body with religious pomp to that monastery of St. Columba, and hither the Archbishop of Armagh and the clergy from all parts of Ireland came, and they paid him all honour as a true Christian hero, and conveyed his remains, in triumphant procession, to the Cathedral of Armagh. There, after seven days' vigils, his body was laid in the tomb close to that sanctuary of Ireland's Apostle, which, during life, he had loved so well.

I have thus endeavoured to sketch for you the distinctive features of the rule of the Irish king. They do not bear with them the impress of a semi-barbarous condition of things; on the contrary, it seems to me that if we lay aside preconceived prejudices, and take the witness of history as our sure guide, we must consider the monarch Brian as a sovereign of whom any nation in Christendom might be justly proud.

And now we may turn our attention to the champion of Norman civilization, and see what were the distinctive features of his rule. I need not dwell on the valour shown by William the Conqueror in the field of battle, of his prowess in arms, or of the vast resources of the kingdom which he won by the sword; for such material strength and such success are not the true tests of civilization that history presents to us. Like the Irish monarch, he had usurped a crown which was not his of right, and his chief battle was won under the banner of religion. Yet, even here, there is a great disparity between both princes. Brian grasped the sovereignty of Ireland for his country's good, to combine its strength against its Danish oppressors; but William seized the English crown as a matter of selfish aggrandizement and personal ambition. Brian, at Clontarf, was, in truth, the champion of religion, and his victory was the triumph of the Faith; but William had procured from the Pontiff by intrigue and by false representations the religious banner under which he fought; and thus from the outset he made a mere pretext of religion the better to further his political aims.

But to enter more particularly on our inquiry into the distinctive traits of the Norman monarch's rule, the first reat feature that presents itself is the cruelty with which he exercised his irresistible power in extirpating those who had shown themselves bravest in defending their country and their homes against him. The Northumbrians were reckoned among the most valiant of the English race, and more than once they had made the armies of William dread their assault. On the approach of Christmas, in the year 1069, William entered York, the Northumbrian capital, in triumph. The North was at length hushed before him, the Northumbrians had returned to their own firesides, and there was no longer an army to oppose his progress. How did he use his victory? I will not detail to you in any words of mine his dealings with the unhappy men who had now accepted him as sovereign. I will rather read for you the words of Mr. Freeman, who, by his historical researches on this period of English history, has won for himself immortal renown. He thus writes:—"The king took the work of destruction as his personal share of the conquest of Northumberland. He left others to build his castles in York, but he himself went through the length and breadth of the land, through its wildest and most difficult regions. That all who resisted were slain with the sword, was a matter of course: Harold had done as much as that in his great campaign against Gruffydd. But now William went to and fro over points a hundred miles from one another, destroying, as far as in him lay, the life of the earth. It was not mere plunder, which may, at least, enrich the plunderer: the work of William at this time was simple unmitigated havoc. Houses were everywhere burned with all that was in them; stores of corn, goods, and property of every kind were brought together and destroyed in the like sort; even living animals seem to have been driven to perish in the universal burning. . . . The long-abiding traces of the destruction which was now wrought were its most fearful feature. The accounts of the immediate ravaging are graphic and terrible enough, but they are, perhaps, outdone in significance by the passionless witness of the great Survey, the entries of 'waste,' 'waste,' 'waste,' attached through page after page to the Yorkshire lordships, which seventeen years after had not recovered from the blow. Indeed, we may be inclined to ask whether northern England ever fully recovered from the blow till that great development of modern times which had reversed the respective importance of the north and the south. For nine years, at least, no attempt was made at tilling the ground. Between York and Durham every town stood uninhabited; their streets became lurking-places for robbers and wild beasts. Even a generation later the passing traveller beheld with sorrow the ruins of famous towns, with their lofty towers rising above the forsaken dwellings, the fields lying untilled and tenantless, the rivers flowing idly through the wilderness. Men, women, and children died of hunger; they laid them down and died in the roads and in the fields, and there was no man to bury them. There were those who did not shrink from keeping themselves alive on the flesh of their own kind. Before the end of the year Yorkshire was a wilderness. The bodies of its inhabitants were rotting in the streets, in the highways, or on their own hearth-stones; and those who had escaped from sword, fire, and hunger, had fled out of the land."

Such was the devastation of Northumbria; and yet, amid such harrowing scenes, William did not hesitate to keep the Christmas feast with special pomp and rejoicings at York.

Another feature of William's reign was his selfishness; that is to say, his readiness to sacrifice the country's weal in order to gratify his own thirst for amusement and pleasure. There was no lack of hunting-grounds in England: hunting had been a favourite pastime of its royal princes for centuries before William's conquest. All these, however, did not suffice for William's amusement. He wished for some new theatre of pleasure, reserved entirely to himself and his favourite courtiers; and he marked out Hampshire for such a hunting-ground. Hampshire was, at this period, "the most civilized and best cultivated part of the kingdom. To find room, therefore, for William's sport a fertile district, thirty miles in extent, was deliberately laid waste. In the days of Edward, and the kings before him, it had been a flourishing land, full of the habitations of men, and thick-set with churches, where the worship of God was duly paid. At William's bidding, men were driven from their homes, their houses were pulled down, their churches were rooted up, and the fruitful land became a wilderness. The historians of both races raise their indignant wail over the homes of men which were changed into the lairs of wild beasts. The great Survey calmly gives us the names of the Englishmen who were driven forth from their wasted homes, and shows how a few of them were allowed to retain small scraps of land beyond the limits of the sacred precincts of William's sport. There, we are told, amid the desolation which he had wrought, the Conqueror would gladly have spent his life, rejoicing in the slaughter of the lower animals during the short intervals of the slaughter of mankind. But we are told also that the scene of William's greatest crime was the scene of the heaviest blows which were dealt upon his house. A curse seemed to brood over the region from which man had been driven to make room for the wild beasts. The wilderness which William had made was fatal to his sons, and to his sons'

sons." (Freeman, *Norman Conquest*, vol. iv., p. 613.) I may add the testimony of a contemporary chronicler, otherwise an eulogist of the king, but who thus complains of the selfishness of the monarch :—

"He took great sums, both by right and also with much unright, from his people, and for little need: he was fallen on coveteousness, and greediness he loved altogether. He made great deer chases, and therewith laid down laws that whoso slew hart or hind he should be blinded. . . . . His great men complained of it, and the poor men murmured; but he reckoned naught of them all, and they must altogether—

"'Follow the king's will
If they would live or have land—
Land or goods, or even a quiet life.
Woe, woe! that any man should be so proud;
Should so lift himself up, and reckon himself above all men.'"

The dealings of a sovereign with the Church are, as I have already remarked, one of the best tests of true civilization. William showed but little reverence towards the Church, except when it was the purpose of his policy to make her an instrument in accomplishing his designs. Abbots and bishops, not subservient to his interests, were set aside: if some of them received rich gifts, it was done to bind them the better with golden fetters to his throne. The churches and monasteries had hitherto been regarded as inviolable sanctuaries, and several of the nobility had deposited their family treasures in them. "But the thresholds of the English saints proved no safeguard against the Norman king. Early in the year 1070, in the course of Lent, William caused all the monasteries of England to be searched, and all deposits of this kind to be carried to the royal treasury." (*Ibid.*, iv. 328.) The historian compendiates, in one short sentence, the systematic policy of William towards the Church: "The prelacy of England was to be used as a means for riveting the fetters of England."

(*Ibid.*, iv. 131.) It is true that Lanfranc and St. Anselm shone as brilliant stars in the English Church during this period; but they were foreigners. Lanfranc was a Lombard from Pavia; and when he entered the Norman monastery of Bec, which was to become so famous under his guidance, he found that the brethren were "neither well-lettered nor much trained in religion." Anselm, too, was an Italian, a native of "wild Aosta, lulled by Alpine rills." The name of St. Thomas of Canterbury alone remains—a name which, indeed, must not be forgotten. It was not, however, as an apostle or as confessor that he adorned the Church. His aureola is that of martyr; and it is no proof of Norman civilization that the chief agents in his martyrdom were the English monarch and his Norman courtiers.

It is set forth in eulogy of William's reign that every crime against property was inexorably punished; so that a theft or robbery was a thing unheard of throughout England. The law of justice, however, is not one-sided: it teaches that property has its duties as well as its rights; and it is particularly by the fulfilment of those duties that true civilization is made known. William had distributed to his Norman knights almost the whole property of the kingdom, and they had made themselves secure in their strong castles against every attack. From time to time William extorted large sums of money from the knights whom he had thus enriched, and they, in their turn, extorted still larger sums from the unfortunate natives subject to them. Thus the significant word *unlaw* was, for the first time, introduced into the annals of England: it implied, as the historian of the conquest writes, "a state of things where law was on the mouth of men in power, but where law itself became the instrument of wrong." (*Ibid.*, iv. 621.) The contemporary chronicler records that all classes shared in the general corruption, and that "little righteousness was in this land amid any men: and as man spake more of right law, so man did more of *unlaw*.

All that was abominable to God and oppressive to man was common in William's time." (*Chronicle of Peterborough*, written in 1087.) The system of feudal extortion thus introduced by William, long continued to bear its bitter fruits. I will read for you one passage from the Saxon chronicle, under the year 1137:—"Every powerful man made his castles, and held them against the king, and they filled the land full of castles. They cruelly oppressed the wretched men of the land with castle-works. When the castles were made, they filled them with devils and evil men. Then took they those men that they imagined had any property, both by night and by day, peasant men and women, and put them in prison for their gold and silver, and tortured them with unutterable torture; for never were martyrs so tortured as they were. . . Wretched men died of hunger; some went seeking alms who at one while were rich men; some fled out of the land. Never yet had more wretchedness been in the land, nor did heathen men ever do worse than they did; for everywhere at times they forebore neither church nor churchyard, but took all the property that was therein, and then burned the church and all together." (*Anglo-Saxon Chronicle*, ii. 231, published under the direction of the Master of the Rolls, by Benjamin Thorpe.)

This was the feudal system which the Normans a few years later introduced into Ireland; and can we be surprised that it should have produced the same sad fruits of iniquity and oppression? The brave chieftain, O'Melaghlin, fully appreciated this feature of Norman rule when he sent the remarkable message to Henry II.: "Notwithstanding his promise of supporting me in the possession of my wealth and dignities, he has sent robbers to invade my patrimony. Avaricious and sparing of his own possessions, he is lavish of those of others, and he thus seeks, at our expense, to enrich libertines and profligates who have consumed the patrimony of their fathers in debauchery."

We now come to the closing scenes of William's reign. To none more truly than to princes can the motto *Qualis vita, finis ita*, be applied: their end is too often the picture of their career. We have seen how the death of the monarch, Brian, was in every way worthy of the Christian hero. He died in the moment of triumph over the enemies of the Cross, adding the martyr's crown to the many laurels of a glorious reign. Strange, indeed, is the contrast that the death of William presents.

In the beginning of August, 1087, he sailed for the coast of France to avenge some words of insult that had been uttered by the French king. "When the corn was in the fields, and the grapes in the vineyards, and the apples in the orchards, he led forth his troops to gather in the rich spoil of the fruitful season. All was laid waste; the thought of mercy passed utterly away from William's mind." (Freeman, *Norman Conquest*, vol. iv. 701.) At last he reached the city of Mantes, and he resolved to make that city an example of utter ruin. On the 15th August the gates were opened to him, and he issued the order that the city should be burned to the ground. "On that day all was destroyed; the houses and goods of the citizens perished; the churches were burned, and holy recluses, who deemed it a crime to leave their cells even at such a moment, were burned with them. William's heart was gladdened at the sight: he rode, and bade his men heap on fuel to make the flames burn yet more bravely." Whilst thus engaged, his horse stumbled on the burning embers, and the king, unwieldy in his weight, received his death-wound.

The dying king was carried to Rouen, and there on his death-bed he acknowledged aloud the many faults of his iniquitous career: he had won England by no right, by no claim of birth; he had treated the sons of the English soil with harshness; he had cruelly wronged nobles and commons alike; he had despoiled many wrongfully of their inheritance; he had slain countless multitudes by hunger or by the sword. The harrying of Northumberland rose up before his eyes in all its blackness. He told how cruelly he had burned and plundered the land; what thousands of every age and sex among the noble nation which he had conquered had been done to death at his bidding.

On the 9th September, 1087, King William died. The knights and nobles who had hitherto attended him, without delay mounted their horses and hastened homeward with all speed, not knowing what deeds of lawlessness might now be witnessed. Not one knight remained to show honour to his deceased sovereign. The servants and other followers set to work at once to make spoil of the royal chamber: "they stripped the deserted house, and the very corpse of the dead, of all that they could lay hands upon, and made off with their prey: weapons, clothes, vessels, the royal bed and its furniture, were carried off, and for a whole day the body of the Conqueror lay well-nigh bare on the floor of the room in which he died." (*Ibid.*, iv. 713.)

Well, indeed, might the contemporary, Ordericus Vitalis, cry out: "O magnificence of the world, how worthless thou art, and how vain and frail: like the rain bubbles of the shower, swollen one moment, burst into nothing the next. Here was a most mighty lord, whom more than a hundred thousand warriors just now eagerly served, and before whom many nations feared and trembled; and now by his own servants, in a house not his own, he lies foully stripped, and from the first to the third hour of morning is left deserted on the bare floor."

None but a plain Norman gentleman, named Herlwin, was found to convey the king's remains to Caen, where William had expressed a wish to be interred. At Caen a numerous body of clergy and nobility awaited the remains and formed a solemn funeral procession. As the procession was on its way, flames were seen to issue from a house, and in a little time a great part of the town was on fire. Clergy and laity alike hastened to check the flames, and a few religious men alone kept on their way bearing the body to St. Stephen's minster. Everything seemed to conspire that he who had received during life such court and homage, should be treated with dishonour and contempt in death. The horrors however, of that funeral are not yet complete.

On the interment day, all the great knights and nobles of Normandy, with the bishops and abbots and clergy, had assembled in St. Stephen's minster. The Bishop of Evreux delivered the funeral harangue, and at its close called on all who were present to forgive the deceased monarch anything he might have sinned against them. At once a knight named Ascelin arose amid the vast assembly, and declared that he forgave him not. "This ground where ye stand," he said, "was the site of my father's house, which the man for whom ye pray, while he was yet but Count of Normandy, took away by force from my father, and, in spite of law and justice, built this church upon it by his might. I therefore claim the land: I forbid that the body of the robber be covered by my mould, or that he be buried within the bounds of mine inheritance." (*Ibid.*, iv. 719.) Terrible, indeed, were these words; and yet the justice of this bold claim was admitted by the assembled nobles and clergy; and before the ceremony was proceeded with, the ground had to be purchased from Ascelin.

One misfortune more was still in store for William's remains. The corpse was removed with royal state from the bier in the centre of the minster to the stone coffin, which was to be its last resting-place. But by the unskilfulness of the workmen the stone coffin was too small for the unwieldy corpse of William. "In the efforts which were made to force it into its narrow room, the body burst; a fearful stench filled the church, which the burning of incense and of all sweet savours could not overcome." Such is

:r. Freeman's narrative. (*Ibid.*, iv. 720). Sir F. Palgrave still ore vividly describes this last terrific scene: "The debt as paid, the price of that narrow plot of earth, the last d of the Conqueror. Ascelin withdrew his ban: but as e swollen corpse sank into the ground it burst, filling the cred edifice with corruption. The obsequies were hurried rough; and thus was William the Conqueror gathered to s fathers, with loathing disgust and horror."

Such was the inglorious end of William's eventful reign. lfishness and personal aggrandizement and the oppression his subjects were the most prominent features of his rule. u will probably conclude with me, that they merited the shonour and ignominy which accompanied its close.

I have endeavoured thus briefly to set before you the ief events that in a distinctive way marked the reigns of e monarchs, to each of whom posterity has awarded the le of "the Great." One of these rulers presents to us ltic life as it was before the Normans set foot upon the sh shores; the other exemplifies the Norman customs, d the habits of those whose mission, forsooth, it was to ng the blessings of civilization to Ireland. It seems to most clear—and, unless I have entirely misconceived the timony of the documents to which I have referred, it will your judgment also—that the verdict of authentic history l pronounce William, notwithstanding his mighty power, have been little better than a semi-barbarous prince, ilst it will award to Brian the palm and the crown of a e Christian monarch. And looking back upon the argu- nts which I have endeavoured to compendiate in this ef address, I will ask you to draw from them the conclu- n that, during the period that preceded the Anglo-Norman asion, Ireland was not immersed in ignorance and bar- ism; but, on the contrary, was justly ranked among the st civilized nations of Christendom.

V.

JOAN OF ARC.

What is to be said of Joan of Arc? Are we to adm her claim to our admiration and respectful homage, shall we brand her as an impostor whose very achiev ments are little better than a blot upon the fair escu cheon of her native land? For more than two centuri after her death this latter opinion was popular amo the countrymen of those who fled before her on the battl fields of France. Shakespeare, for instance, who may just be said to represent the public opinion of England in h day, can find no better names for Joan than "ugly witch "enchantress," a "fell banning hag," a "foul accurs minister of hell," and he introduces her as communing wi the evil spirits, and guilty of the foulest crimes. In lat times this prejudice has died away, and able writers ha done justice to her memory, and perhaps no brighter pag of eulogy of the Maid of Orleans are to be found than tho embalmed in modern English literature. In France, t fellow-citizens of Joan have very generally cherished h memory. We must except Voltaire and his school, wh left nothing undone to asperse her character, that thus th might cast reproach upon the Holy Church of which t Maid of Orleans was at all times a devoted child. Son twenty-five years ago the original documents connected wi her marvellous career were at length discovered and pu lished in Paris, and since then all the writers of any nan in England, France and Germany have united in a chor

eulogy, presenting Joan to the world in her true character
a heroine of patriotism and a heroine of religion.

The beginning of the fifteenth century was one of those
ark and dreary periods when men instinctively looked to
eaven for help. France, hitherto the foremost nation of
hristendom, was sunk in the lowest depths of humiliation
nd misery. The Christian world, paralyzed by years of
hism, appeared to have lost its vigour and innate energy.
he Hussite heresy had occupied Bohemia and lower
ermany, and the Moslem enemy, whilst knocking at the
ates of Constantinople, had pushed on the triumphant
rescent into the heart of Europe. It was when the hour
as darkest that Heaven intervened. Within a few years
e victory of the Christian arms at Belgrade gave a breath-
g time to Europe; the Hussite heresy melted away so
hat scarce a trace of it remained. The great schism was
ealed by the Council of Constance; and, thanks to the
umble Maid of Orleans, France was lifted up from her
egradation to rank once more among the foremost of
hristian nations, a post which she has ever since retained.

The village of Domremi, where Joan was born, on the
east of the Epiphany, in 1411, is picturesquely situated on
e banks of the Meuse in French territory, but on the im-
ediate borders of Lorraine. It takes its name from St.
emi, the great patron of France, and at present, to distin-
uish it from other places of similar name, is known as
omremi-la-Pucelle. The humble house in which Joan was
orn is still standing. In a niche over the doorway there
a bronze statue of the heroine, who is represented as clad
armour, but in a kneeling posture, her hands clasped in
rayer.

From her childhood Joan was remarkable for her gentle-
ess and docility, and as she grew in years was unwearying
industry. She took the lead in all the village pastimes,
nd being singularly fair, was idolized by her fond parents,

who regarded her as their child of promise. Like S[illegible] Genevieve and Cousin, she tended her father's small flock [illegible] sheep, and she never was more happy than when summone[illegible] to assist in knitting or weaving or the other humblest duti[illegible] of the household. Through the disturbed condition of t[illegible] country she was deprived of the blessings of education, a[illegible] she never learned to read or write. Her parents, howeve[illegible] instructed her in the "Our Father," the "Hail Mary," and t[illegible] Apostles' Creed; and a marvellous simplicity of heart, wit[illegible] a burning love of God abundantly supplied what was wanti[illegible] in her instruction. She rose before break of day, that s[illegible] might assist at Holy Mass, and again after the day's to[illegible] she hastened to the church, where she knelt in prayer, h[illegible] eyes and her heart fixed upon the crucifix, or upon t[illegible] statue of our Lady of Dolours. Every Sunday she made [illegible] pilgrimage to the hermitage of Notre Dâme de Vermon[illegible] which was not far distant, and she brought with her wreat[illegible] of wild flowers as her offering at that venerable shrine.

From her fourteenth year her patrons, SS. Catherine an[illegible] Margaret, in mysterious voices announced to her th[illegible] she was marked out for a special mission by Heaven. "T[illegible] weak things of this world," they said, "are chosen to ove[illegible] come the strong: it would be her mission to save Franc[illegible] and she was unceasingly to form her heart to piety that s[illegible] might be faithful to those designs of Heaven." So famili[illegible] did this communing with her patrons become, that she r[illegible] garded them as her daily companions, and in every dang[illegible] and difficulty invoked their aid. When humiliations an[illegible] sorrows crowded around France, the voices of those patro[illegible] more distinctly assigned to Joan her divinely-appointe[illegible] mission; and when at length Orleans was besieged, and, i[illegible] human judgment, its fate was inevitably sealed, they co[illegible] veyed to her the express command to hesitate no longer, b[illegible] to take her place in the front of the battle-field. She wa[illegible] chosen, they told her, to give victory to the French arm[illegible] o relieve Orleans, to lead the king in triumph to Rheims, nd to see him crowned there: but after that her lot would e betrayal and death.

To understand the purport of this mission we must cast hurried glance on what men now regarded as the hopeless ondition of prostrate France. The question that presentec self to men's minds was simply this: Is France, so long ie bulwark of Europe—the France of Clovis, of Charlemagne, St. Louis—to be blotted out from the roll of nations? The ormans, who four centuries before had conquered England, ad grown in prestige and power, and now, restless in their nbition, steadily pursued the design of adding their mother untry, France, to their dominions.

The battle of Agincourt, fought on the 25th of Octor, 1415, had revived the humiliations of Crecy and oictiers, and brought the fortunes of France to the lowest b. An army of 15,000 men, commanded by Henry V. of ngland, had defeated the French army of more than 60,000 en. The chivalry of France was laid low upon that bloody ld, and the few of the nobility who escaped death were l off to the dungeons of England. The whole of the ngdom north of the Loire was quickly overrun and declared nexed to the Crown of England. At the same time men's nds were confused, and the nation paralyzed by party tions and civil war. The Duke of Burgundy, the most werful of the French nobility, had flung aside his loyalty d allied himself to the invaders. The words of Shakespeare thfully depict the ruin that this treason brought upon ance. In his *Henry VI.*, part the first, he introduces an of Arc thus addressing the Duke:—

> "Look on thy country, look on fertile France,
> And see the cities and the towns defaced
> By wasting ruin of the cruel foe!
> As looks the mother on her lowly babe,
> When death doth close his tender dying eyes,
> See, see the pining malady of France;

> Behold the wounds, the most unnatural wounds,
> Which thou thyself hast given her woeful breast!
> O, turn thy edged sword another way;
> Strike those that hurt, and hurt not those that help!
> One drop of blood drawn from thy country's bosom
> Should grieve thee more than streams of foreign gore;
> Return thee, therefore, with a flood of tears,
> And wash away thy country's stained spots."

To such a degree did party factions prevail that fou bishops were slain in the streets of Paris. The King France, Charles VI., smitten with imbecility, had become tool in the hands of the English faction. The Queen open espoused the cause of England, and the parliament a sembled in Paris declared the King of England Regent France and heir of the French crown. Perhaps no scene humiliating was ever before or since witnessed in th history of France. The King, the Queen, the Duke Burgundy, the Parliament—all united in excluding th Dauphin from the throne, and in handing over the kingdo to triumphant England. This added strength to the Englis cause, and Henry V. was enabled to pursue his career conquest with all the prestige of legitimate authority. Th deaths of the two kings within a few months, in 1422, i stead of leading to peace, only served to add to the gener confusion. Henry VI. of England, though as yet a mino received with solemn pomp the crown of France. Ho strange that this young prince, the only king of Englan who from the time of the Norman invasion has been remar able for piety, should before his death see himself depriv of both crowns, whilst nevertheless he continued strenuous to win for himself the eternal crown! The Dauphin w saluted by his adherents under the title of Charles VI but could not approach Rheims, where alone he could crowned in conformity with the traditions of France, f Rheims was in the hands of the enemy. In the meantin the English commanders, the ablest military leaders of tho days, knowing their opportunity, pressed forward and redoubled the ardour of their troops to complete the national triumph. The Dauphin was contemptuously styled the King of Bourges, the city where his Parliament assembled, and in all human calculations the day could not be far distant when even this mockery of a title would be wrested from him.

Orleans, situated on the Loire, was the last hope of the French monarchy. Even of this strong fortress the defence had become almost hopeless. The Earl of Salisbury, in 1428, had ravaged all the country around, and occupied the adjoining fortresses. When he was slain by a cannon-ball, the Earl of Suffolk, who succeeded in the command, pressed the siege with an army of 20,000 men. He built a triple line of redoubts in order to cut off supplies, and the intrenchments being gradually completed between these redoubts, it appeared certain alike to friend and to foe that in the approaching springtime the city would be forced by famine to surrender. The battle known as the Herrings' battle added to the despondency of the friends of France. At the approach of Lent, in 1429, a body of 2,500 men set out from Paris to convey a large convoy of herrings and other Lenten provisions to the besieging army. The French could only muster a force of 4,000 men to intercept them; but those being badly equipped were defeated with slaughter. The fort called Tournelles, which guarded the approach to Orleans by the bridge over the Loire, also fell into the hands of the besiegers, and was at once transformed into the foremost bastion for the assault of the city. Thus defeat followed upon defeat, and Orleans, which hitherto had more than once proved the bulwark of France, was marked out for inevitable ruin. Hume writes that "the eyes of all Europe were turned towards this scene, where it was reasonably supposed the French were to make their last stand for maintaining the independence of their monarchy and the rights of their sovereign."

There was no longer a French army in the field, and the was hardly a general to command an army. It was at th moment that Joan of Arc appeared upon the scene. Sh was in her eighteenth year when she quitted her father house for the theatre of war. She is represented by th contemporary writers as of medium height, of fair propo tions, and capable of enduring great fatigue. Her feature were expressive of rustic honesty and innocence. Her voic was strong, yet of great sweetness, and her manner was s full of dignity and grace as to soften and subdue the rudes of the soldiery. She rode at the head of the army, clothe in a coat of mail, and armed with an ancient sword, whic had long been suspended at the sanctuary of St. Catherin de Fierbois. She carried in her hand a white standard c her own design, embroidered with golden *fleur-de-lys*, an having on one side the representation of our Saviour en throned in majesty, and on the other the image of th Blessed Virgin Mary.

When Joan made known to the civic authorities of th district of Domremi her mission, and her intention to visi the king, she was laughed at as a maniac. Repeated solici tations, however, and the every-day increasing wants o France, wrung a reluctant consent that she might procee to the Court. It was on the 13th February, 1429, that accompanied by a few friends, she set out for Chinon, wher the Court was then held, to declare her mission to the king Three hundred courtiers of every rank were assembled there and the king in disguise mingled with the throng. Never theless, Joan walked straight through the crowd, and heedless of all the rest, knelt before the Dauphin. H reproved her, saying he was not the king. She replied "Yea, sire, thou art my sovereign, and I am commissioned by God to lead thee in victory to Rheims to wear the crown of France." She then made known to him, as proof of her mission, some details regarding his contemplated fligh rom France, and his prayers to Heaven for succour, which e declared were known to Heaven alone. It was not, however, till the 21st of April that all difficulties were overcome, nd that Joan, accompanied by a chosen band of knights, vas permitted to set out for Orleans. She crossed the nglish lines unobserved, and entered Orleans after sunset n the 29th of April. Within three months she fulfilled her nission, freeing Orleans, driving the enemy before her in very battle-field, and leading the king in triumph into Rheims.

On entering Orleans, Joan assembled the citizens in the athedral, and told them to prepare for combat on the next lay. The fort of Tournelles, which had become the key of he enemy's position, was the first place which she assailed. As she advanced at the head of the troops she was struck by an arrow in the shoulder; but she plucked it out and lung it aside. Three times she led the citizens to the ssault, and three times they were driven back. Their ast hope seemed lost when, whilst mounting a ladder, Joan was stunned by a blow of a stone and fell to the ground. She was, however, on her feet again in an instant, and waving her sacred banner, called on the fugitives to make a ast effort. The enemy could no longer resist their ardour. The defenders of the bastion were all slain or made prisoners, and Joan re-entered Orleans in triumph. In eight days the siege was raised, and on Sunday, the 8th of May, Joan, holding in her hand her victorious banner, amid the acclamations of the citizens, proceeded to the cathedral to assist at solemn thanksgiving. With the rapidity of lightning Targeau and other fortresses were stormed, and at length, on the 29th of June, the decisive victory of Patay wiped away the disgrace of Agincourt.

The English commanders had chosen their own ground, and had gathered all available forces to check the advance of the French troops. On the eve of the battle Joan sent orders to the cavalry to look well to their spurs. Whe one of the officers remonstrated with her, saying that suc orders implied cowardice, as if they meant to fly from th battle-field, she replied: "It is not so; but the English wi so quickly take to their heels that we shall require all ou speed to overtake them." With a far inferior force, Joan, th next day, fell upon the English army, and her words wer literally verified. The field was covered with the slai of the enemy, whilst most of their leaders fell into th hands of the victorious French. On the 9th of July, Joa took by assault the important city of Troyes, which wa supposed to be impregnable, and a few days later the city c Rheims opened its gates to its sovereign. On Sunday, th 17th of July, the mission of Joan was in a great measur fulfilled, when she knelt beside the altar in the Cathedral c Rheims, her sacred banner floating over the throne, whils Charles was with solemn rite crowned King of France. I must not be forgotten that in all these victories Joan re ceived but little aid from the French commanders. The looked upon her plans as visionary and impracticable; the thwarted her in her designs, and even when she wa victorious grudgingly awarded her the meed of praise.

In all her battles, Joan manifested the sincerest pity for th vanquished enemy. More than once she wrote to th English commanders, asking them to desist from the inva sion of France, and to unite in a crusade against the Turks She always claimed it as her special duty to protect th prisoners and the wounded. Once when she saw an Englis soldier dangerously wounded, she threw herself off her hors to kneel beside him, and to give him every physical an spiritual comfort that she could impart. She never use her sword to strike an enemy. Her standard was her usua weapon, even of defence, and she could not restrain he tears when she saw brave enemies stretched lifeless on th battle-field. On the eve of battle she insisted on the soldier preparing for the conflict by approaching the Sacrament of Penance. She herself assisted at Holy Mass every morning. Wherever she stayed in a town or village, it was her delight to see the children assembled in the church, to join them in their hymns to the Blessed Virgin, and to receive the Holy Communion with them.

We have seen how the first part of Joan's mission was fulfilled. She had led the king in triumph to Rheims, and she had encircled his brow with the crown of St. Louis. Now betrayal and death awaited her. There appeared, indeed, to be some contradiction in the messages which the mysterious voices had conveyed to her; for whilst at times they spoke to her of betrayal into the enemy's hands, they at other times referred to a glorious victory that would be her lot. There was, however, no contradiction in all this, for her heroic death was to be the crowning victory of her wonderful career. On the 24th of May, 1430, the vigil of the Ascension, Joan combatting before the walls of Compiegne, fell into the hands of the Burgundian troops. She had thrown herself into that beleaguered fortress, and headed the garrison in a sortie on the side of the bridge across the Oise. But she was encountered by an enemy vastly superior in numbers. Twice she drove the Burgundians from their entrenchments; but being compelled to retreat, the survivors of her heroic band were admitted within the walls. Unaided she still continued the combat, and the gates being shamefully closed, she was struck down, and became a prisoner in the enemy's hands.

Tidings of decisive victory could not bring greater joy to the English army than the capture of the Maid of Orleans. Amid public rejoicings the *Te Deum* was solemnly sung in Paris, and the English Regent purchased the prisoner from her Burgundian captors for a sum of 10,000 francs. One who visited the old town of Compiegne in our day relates that the battlements of that fortress of Picardy have long since mouldered away; the fosse choked by the fallen fragments is once more on a level with the plain; even the old bridge has been replaced by another higher up the stream; yet amidst all these manifold changes the precise spot where Joan was made prisoner is still pointed out by popular tradition to the passing stranger.

Nothing could exceed the cruelty of the treatment meted out to Joan during the twelve months of imprisonment that preceded her execution. The English regarded her as the one cause of all their misfortunes. She had checked them in their hitherto uninterrupted career of victories. She had plucked the laurels from their triumphant standard and encircled with them the brow of the French monarch. But beyond all this, she had evoked in her countrymen throughout all France an unconquerable spirit of devotion to their country, and had inspired them with a confidence of victory which foreboded evil to the designs of the invaders. How were they to undo the work of Joan? Her victories and achievements could not be gainsaid. They could nevertheless vitiate them in their source. Joan had announced that her mission was from Heaven: they would brand her as a sorceress, and they would impute to diabolical agency all her success. Her work should therefore be abhorred by all well-disposed men, as having for its object to promote a wicked cause and to thwart the designs of God. This was what the English agents now sought to effect by her trial, for so long as the French people were persuaded that her mission was from Heaven, the invaders felt that their sword was broken, and that the wished-for conquest of France would be a hopeless and forlorn task.

Her trial was a mere parody of a court of justice. Every vilest accusation was advanced without proof, and wholesale statements, which on the face of them were untrue, were accepted as unanswerable proof of her guilt. For instance, one accusation was to the effect that she had never in her life assisted at Holy Mass; had never received the Holy Communion; had never been to Confession. Her very victories and marvellous success were accepted as proof of diabolical agency; whilst her listening to the heavenly voices was interpreted as taking counsel from the fairies and giving adoration to false gods. So intense was the enmity against Joan, that no one dared to appear in her favour. A Breton woman having presumed to say in the hearing of others that Joan was in truth commissioned by God, she was herself sentenced to death and burned at the stake on Sunday, 3rd September, 1430.

Joan was led by the English to Rouen, and imprisoned in the great tower of the castle, where she was kept in an iron cage, her feet being secured by a heavy chain. She was treated by the guards with the grossest contumely. Her judges were bought with English gold. She underwent fifteen examinations before them, and was led to the tribunal clad in military attire, but loaded with chains. Yet her courage did not fail.

When the Earl of Stafford visited her in prison, pretending that he was about to ransom her, she replied: "Ah! *mon Dieu*, you are mocking me. You have neither the will nor the power to ransom me. I know well that the English have resolved upon my death, thinking that after my death they will win the kingdom of France; but I tell them that, even were they a hundred thousand soldiers more than they are, they shall never have this kingdom."

The most insidious questions were put to her; but her unaffected simplicity so baffled her opponents that one of the English leaders who were present could not forbear exclaiming, "She is truly a worthy woman—if only she were English." One of the questions put to her was whether she knew herself to be in the grace of God? Had she answered in the negative, she would have been held as guilty on her own confession; did she answer in the affirmative, she would have been found guilty of arrogance and presumption. She replied, "If I am not in the grace of God, I pray God that it might be vouchsafed to me; if I am, I pray God that I may be preserved in it." She was asked whether it was to the standard or to herself that so many victories were to be ascribed? She replied, "Whether the victory came from the standard or from me, all was due to our Lord. The victory was His, and my hope of victory was founded on Him alone." One of the most insidious questions was: "Do your patrons, SS. Catherine and Margaret, love the French and hate the English?" She replied without a pause: "They love what our Lord loves, and hate what He hates." But the question was urged: "Does God hate the English?" She fearlessly replied: "Whether God loves or hates the English, I know not; but I know that they will every one flee out of France, except those who die in it, and that God will make the French victorious over the English." She knew that a cruel death awaited her, and though at times she wept and shuddered at the thought of it, yet she ever renewed her courage and resignation. "I only ask of God," she said, "the deliverance of France, the salvation of my soul, and to be received into Paradise. After my death I ask nothing of the king, but to have Mass said for those who have given their lives for him."

On the 29th of May, 1431, sentence of death at the stake was pronounced against her, and the next morning she was led out to execution. In the old market-place of Rouen, a pile of wood was prepared of prodigious height, traversed in every direction with hollow spaces for the creation of air-currents, the better to ensure that the whole mass would be consumed. On the summit of this pile Joan was fastened to a stake with iron chains. A huge cap was set upon her head with the inscription, *Heretic, Sorceress, Idolater.* She asked for a cross. An English soldier, breaking a piece of wood, formed with it a rude cross which she affixed to her breast. Her confessor alone stood by her. He caused a crucifix to be brought from a neighbouring church. She again and again pressed it to her lips, and asked that it would be held aloft, that her last look on earth might fall on the blessed sign of Redemption, and throughout her sufferings she kept her eyes immovably fixed upon it. Before the fire was kindled, one of those who had been instrumental in urging on her execution rushed to the scaffold and implored her pardon, which joyfully she accorded him.

She knelt for a considerable time in prayer; and she called on all present, whether they were her enemies or not, to unite with her in imploring the divine mercy. She pardoned all who had betrayed her, or done her an injury; and, with a loud voice, she declared that if she had been guilty of any fault, it was to be imputed to herself alone, and that the king, her sovereign, was not to blame. As the flames began to ascend, she warned the confessor, who stood entranced at her side, to beware of his danger. He gave her the last absolution, and retired. By a last effort, she thrice pronounced aloud the Sacred Name, and her martyrdom was complete. An English soldier, who was animated with special hatred, had sworn that morning that he would have a share in her death. At the last moment, he hurried to cast a bundle of faggots upon the burning pile. Whilst doing so, he heard her last cry; and, looking up, saw a white dove taking its flight from the ashes towards heaven. He swooned away, crying aloud: "We have put to death a saint." An English officer, who was also present, seeing her demeanour in death, exclaimed: "Woe to us! woe to us! she is a saint."

Not to dwell upon the other details of her execution, there is one tribute to her heroism which must not be omitted. As she was led to the stake, there were 10,000 enemies assembled in the public square of Rouen, who clamoured for her blood. It may be said that they hated her with a national hatred, and with a personal hatred; and their hatred was more and more inflamed by the tales industriously circulated regarding her sorcery and other manifold wickedness. There was not one of those 10,000 but was moved to tears at witnessing the piety and heroism with which she endured her martyrdom. They all instinctively felt assured that she was a true Christian heroine; and they went away from that scene of suffering overwhelmed with shame, and proclaiming aloud, what has since become the clear verdict of history—that Joan was a heroine of patriotism and a heroine of religion.

We have said that the voices of her patrons had announced to her the close of her career with a glorious victory. Was not the prediction fulfilled? What nobler victory could Joan have achieved than that by which she vanquished all her enemies in her heroic martyrdom? The result of her death was quite the reverse of what the English aimed at. The French soldiers and people became more and more convinced that her mission was divine. They were fired with a national and religious enthusiasm which nothing could withstand; and the English invaders, who for years had marched from conquest to conquest, and from victory to victory, saw city after city, and territory after territory, snatched from their hands. Paris welcomed back its sovereign. The Duke of Burgundy returned to his allegiance. The Duke of Bedford, Regent of France for the English king, expired in the very house where Joan had been imprisoned—his laurels faded, and himself worn away by sorrow and anguish. Within a few years, the English were driven from every foothold in France, and the prediction of the Maid of Orleans was literally fulfilled. But, besides these immediate results, an undying spirit of patriotism was evoked, which revived the energy of the nation, and imparted to its people an unparalleled vigour and strength; so that France has ever since held a foremost rank among the civilized powers.

Joan may be said to have blended into one, French piety and French patriotism; and M. Guizot writes, that it is precisely from this period that we are to date the downfall of feudalism, and the awakening of the national spirit in France. "Joan of Arc," he says, "sprang from the people. It was by the sentiments, creed, and passions of the people that she was inspired and sustained. She was looked upon with distrust, scorn, and even enmity, by the people of the Court and the chiefs of the army; but she had the soldiers and the people ever at her side. It was the peasants of Lorraine who sent her to the succour of the burghers of Orleans. Thus began the formation of the French nationality. Up to the reign of the Valois, it was the feudal character which dominated in France—the French nation, the French mind, French patriotism did not yet exist. With the Valois commenced France properly so called." The position of Joan of Arc is unique in history. Neither profane nor sacred history presents to us a heroine cast in the same mould. Her memory and fame have triumphed over every enmity. After years of culpable lethargy, the king and court of France awoke to their duty, held an official inquiry into her cause, and proclaimed to the world her incomparable merit. A statue, to perpetuate her fame, has long since been erected in Orleans, the first theatre of her victories; but the proudest monument to her honour is the undying affection by which her memory ever lives in the hearts of her countrymen.

And now I have only to add that, in historical pursuits, we should have three angels for our guides. The first shall explore the monuments of the past, and gather together the dusty rolls and decaying parchments which we call the records of history. The second, who is the Angel of Truth, shall blot out the falsehoods that defile so many pages of those records. The third, the Angel of Resurrection, shall breathe upon the gathered dust of past ages, and quicken it into life; so that we may see the facts of history in their true light, and may realize their purpose in the designs of Providence. These three angels have faithfully guarded the honour of the Maid of Orleans. They have placed her upon an exalted pedestal of fame. They proclaim to the world that a providential mission was assigned to her—a mission which she faithfully fulfilled; and they teach us that, by the fulfilment of this mission, she has merited to hold a high post of honour among Christian heroines, for her love of religion and her love of her native land.

VI.

THE ST. BARTHOLOMEW MASSACRE IN FRANCE.

(*Paper presented to the Historical Society of St. Kieran's College, March,* 1875.)

The 24th of August, 1572, marks a rubric festival in the annals of France; for it recalls a terrible deed of vengeance executed by the Court and by an outraged nation against the Huguenots. It is also a rubric feast in the calendar of those who assail the Catholic Church in this kingdom, whilst it affords a popular theme for disclaiming against her persecuting spirit; for all the crimes and horrors of that bloody day are laid at the door of the Sovereign Pontiff and of the Catholics of France. That no link might be wanting in the terrible accusation, the French infidels of the last century supplied an abundance of imaginary details, all of which were accepted without hesitation by the agents and abettors of the Protestant tradition of England. The words of Chenier were repeated in English pulpits: that the Cardinal de Lorraine had blessed the poignards of the assassins at the Louvre, and had given the signal for the massacre. It mattered but little that that illustrious cardinal was at the time far away from France, not having as yet returned from Rome, whither he had gone to take part in the Conclave for the election of Pope Gregory XIII. The words of Voltaire were also accepted as historic truth: that the clergy were the active agents of this butchery, and that the assassins immolated their unhappy victims, wielding a dagger in one hand, and holding a crucifix in the other; and yet it was well known that this wicked picture rested solely on the fancy of that prince of infidels, and proceeded from his diabolical hatred against the Catholic priesthood, and against the cross, the symbol of redemption.

Three years ago the second centenary of this massacre was not forgotten amongst us; and then these stories were once more eagerly repeated in the pulpit and in the press, with all the earnestness that Protestant fanaticism could inspire, and with such variety as each one's imagination could supply. The Westminster Abbey celebration merits to be specially referred to; though many would, perhaps, expect that at least the Dean of Westminster would be raised high above such prejudices. Nevertheless, he availed himself of his sermon on that occasion to inform the British public that the massacre was perpetrated "with the express approbation" of the Sovereign Pontiff. A few years earlier, Froude, in his *History of England* (Vol. x.), had pictured in minute detail all the particulars that could be imagined connected with that St. Bartholomew's feast, repeating the most childish tales regarding it. Since then the very same tales have once more found a place in his pages; whilst he accused the Catholics of Ireland of a premeditated massacre of their Protestant neighbours in the memorable year of 1641. By such imaginative writers, the Catholics of France, accused of every crime, are painted in the darkest colours, and, at the same time, the harmless Huguenots are set before us in the light of peaceable citizens, only desirous of permission to practise the religion which they professed—innocent victims, involved in sudden ruin by the fell, persecuting spirit and treacherous intolerance of Rome. And yet, why should we complain of Voltaire, or Froude, or Dean Stanley, or the many other apostles of the Protestant tradition of England, when we find Lord Acton, and writers of his school, who, though professing the Catholic faith, yet seek to give the stamp of history to such calumnies, and to fan the flame of popular fanaticism against the Holy See, by accusing it of guilty complicity in this dreadful massacre?

You will not expect, however, that in this short paper I would analyze, much less refute in detail, all the calumnies that have been uttered, and the mis-statements that have been made on the subject of this St. Bartholomew's bloody festival. The task which I assume is a much simpler one—to present a brief but truthful narrative of the leading facts connected with that terrible day; and in doing so I will endeavour to arrange my remarks under the three following heads:—

First. The principal events connected with the massacre;

Second. The causes of that widespread discontent which prompted so many persons throughout France to deeds of violence against the Huguenots;

Third. In fine, a few of the chief questions which have arisen regarding this festival of St. Bartholomew.

I.—During the first months of the year 1572, the policy of the French King and Court was wholly favourable to the Huguenots. The leaders of the party were summoned to the capital; many of the highest offices of state were intrusted to them; and every civil or religious privilege that they contended for was readily accorded them. In a most special manner, dignities and honours were conferred on the Admiral Coligny, who was their ablest champion as well in council as in the field; and, to crown all, the king, Charles IX., offered his sister in marriage to the young Prince Henry of Navarre, on whom the Huguenots had now centred all their hopes of securing for themselves, one day, the great prize of the diadem of France. This marriage, being contrary to the disciplinary laws of the Catholic Church, met with a stern and uncompromising opposition from the Holy See. Charles, however, persisted in his design, and, in defiance of the most solemn repeated prohibitions, the marriage was celebrated in Paris, with extraordinary pomp, on the 18th of August, 1752. (White, *Massacre of St. Bartholomew*, page 358.)

Walsingham was at this time English ambassador at the French Court. In his despatches he gives free expression to the feelings of delight with which he witnessed this happy course of events, so favourable to the Huguenots, who were the open friends and secret allies of England. He does not, however, merely record the favours and privileges accorded to his friends; he further attests that the king, being solely intent on enjoying the silly amusements of the Court, was wholly guided by the counsels of Coligny; and he even ventures to express a hope that ere long they would witness "the king's revolt from Papistry."[1]

Catherine de Medici, the Queen-mother, was not one who would acquiesce without a struggle in the paramount influence thus acquired by the Huguenot leaders. She had long been their friend and patron; but now that they would seek to undermine her power, and set aside her authority, she became at once their most determined and most unscrupulous enemy.[2] Charles IX., her son, being only in his tenth year on his accession to the throne of France, in 1560, Catherine, with the approval of the Council of State, assumed the authority, though without the title, of Regent; and

[1] See extracts from these despatches in Sir James Mackintosh's *History of England*, iii. 220.

[2] The policy pursued by Catherine, whilst Queen-Regent of France, during the minority of Charles, is thus faithfully described by Hume: "She had formed a plan of administration more subtle than judicious, and balancing the Catholics with the Huguenots—the Duke of Guise with the Prince of Condé—she endeavoured to render herself necessary to both, and to establish her own dominion on their constrained obedience." (*History of England*, chap. xxxviii.)

even after the king had attained his majority, she continued, with supreme and undisputed power, to rule the kingdom. The Guises were at first her only rivals, and, as they were the recognised leaders of the Catholic party, it became to her a matter of supreme political interest to foster the restless followers of the reformed tenets; and, though she publicly avowed her resolve to administer justice with even balance to all the contending parties, she never failed, when an opportunity presented itself, to throw her protecting mantle over the Huguenots, and to sustain them by all the influence which she could command. Catherine, from her childhood, had imbibed the notorious principles of Macchiavellian policy, which then held sway in the Court of Florence, and these were her only guide in the government of France. It will, therefore, not surprise us to learn that for a time the project was seriously entertained by her of adopting the reformed tenets as the national religion (Capefigue, *Histoire de France*, tom. iii., chaps. xxxviii. and xli.); for thus it was hoped that the Catholic party would be inexorably crushed, and that Protestant alliances would be secured for France against the growing power and encroachments of Spain.[1] Catherine, moreover, allowed sermons to be preached by the Huguenot ministers in the halls of the palace, and she took care that the young King would sometimes assist at these instructions.[2] Her daughter, Margaret of Valois, does not hesitate to write, in her *Memoirs*, that the whole Court was

[1] Charles IX. hated Spain. In his confidential correspondence with Noailles, 11th May, 1572, we read: "All my thoughts are bent on opposing the grandeur of Spain, and seeing how I can most dexterously do it."

[2] Letter of the Nunzio Santa-Croce, 15th November, 1561, inserted in *Actes Eccles. civiles et Synodales*, tom. i. The famous Calvinist, Duplessis-Mornay, says, of some of his brother-ministers, that "se fesoient faire la presche en la chambre de la royne mere du roy pendant son disner, estant aydès à ce faire par ces femmes de chambre, qui estoient secretement de la religion." (Cantù, *Storia Universale*, vol. viii., page 412.) "Elle leur donne à entendre qu'elle veut faire instruire le roi son fils en leur religion." (*Discours Merveilleux*, page 21.)

"infected with heresy," and that her brother, the Duke of Anjou, "had not escaped the unhappy influence; for he often used to throw her prayer-book into the fire, and give her Huguenot hymns instead." (*Memoires de Marguerite de Valois*, page 27, *seq.*) Many French writers are of opinion that Catherine herself "was affected with the venom of Calvinism" (*Laboureur*, vol. i., page 167); but Mr. White, after a profound investigation as to her character and government, concludes that she had but little of any religion, and that she believed "more in witchcraft and astrology than in GOD." (White, *Massacre*, page 167.)[1] The Spanish ambassador, writing to his court, in 1570, says that in Catherine's Royal Council of State "five, out of the eight members, were atheists or Huguenots." (Bouille, *Simanca's Archives*, ii., page 454.) The King himself was weak and vacillating, and wholly intent on the pursuits of pleasure. He was, moreover, impulsive in his anger; and a writer, whom none will accuse of partiality to the Catholic cause, does not hesitate to style him "a furious madman." (*History of the United Netherlands*, vol. i., page 43, by John Lothorp Motley: London, 1867.)

Now, however, that the growing influence of Coligny awakened suspicions and alarm in the mind of Catherine, and made her fear lest she would lose her hold of the royal power, she vowed the destruction of the Huguenot leaders. It was rumoured in Court circles that the administration of the government would soon pass into more vigorous hands, and that Coligny would rule supreme as President of the Council, and Captain-General of all the forces of the kingdom. "What do you learn in your long conversations with the Admiral Coligny?" said Catherine one day to the King. "I learn,"

[1] Ranke writes that Catherine "adopted the policy of the Huguenots because she had hopes that by their aid her youngest son, the Duke of Alençon, would mount the throne of England." (*Hist. de la Papauté*, iii. 83.)

he hastily replied, "that I have no greater enemy than my mother." (White, page 374.) These words sealed the doom of Coligny.

Most of the leading Huguenots had hastened to Paris to be present at the marriage festivities of the Prince of Navarre, and they availed themselves of this opportunity to complete their political organization, and to make an imposing display of their numbers and strength in the French capital. The public festivities had not as yet concluded, when Coligny, passing through the streets, received two gun-shot wounds at the hands of an assassin, on the evening of the 22nd of August. The wounds, though dangerous, were not judged mortal. The public voice instinctively traced the attempt to the Queen-mother, and authentic history has fully justified that verdict.[1] In arranging the details of the attempted assassination, Catherine had for her only assistants her son, the Duke of Anjou, and the Duchess of Nemours, whose first husband had been murdered by the Huguenots.

Had Coligny been slain on the 22nd of August, it is probable that no further massacre would have taken place, and Catherine, without opposition, would have at once resumed her place at the helm of the State. Now, however, that Coligny still lived, and that their party was strengthened by the universal sympathy which the attempted assassination had awakened, the Huguenots vowed immediate vengeance against the assassins. They brandished their swords marching past the Hotel des Guise (Lavallee, *Histoire des Français*, i., page 594; Dargaud, *Histoire de la liberté religieuse*, iii., page 255); menacing words were even uttered against the King, and it became their common boast, that the broken arm of Coligny would cost their enemies 40,000 heads. (Despatch of the Ambassador, Giovanni Michicli,

1 A number of contemporary authorities will be found in two valuable articles of the *Revue des Questions Historiques*, published by Victor Palmé, Paris, 1866, livr. i., page 11; and livr. ii., page 322; also in White, page 400, *seqq.*

in *La Diplomatic Venetienne*, page 548.) Above all, angry words were freely used in regard to Catherine. This artful woman, having failed in this attempt to rid herself of her defiant rival, saw that not a moment was to be lost to save herself from utter ruin.

On the morning of the 23rd she hastened to the King, and unfolded to him the details of a conspiracy,[1] which the Huguenots had planned against the State, as well as against himself and the members of the royal family: one course alone was open to him—to anticipate the traitorous designs of the conspirators, and to turn on themselves the ruin they meditated against France. "The Huguenots won over the King (thus writes the acute historian Ranke), and appeared to supplant Queen Catherine's influence over him. This personal danger put an end to all delay. With that resistless and magical power which she possessed over her children, she re-awakened all the slumbering fanaticism of her son. It cost her but one word to rouse the populace to arms; and that word she spoke. Every individual Huguenot of note was delivered over to the vengeance of his personal enemy." (Ranke, *Histoire de la Papauté pendant le* 16*me siècle*, iii. 83.)

Charles, at the request of his mother, signed, without hesitation, a royal mandate for the execution of the Huguenot leaders; and to a chosen band of their enemies was allotted the arduous task of carrying it with secrecy into effect. The evening of Saturday, the 23rd, rolled on with all the stillness of a summer vigil in the French capital, and not a murmur foretold the storm that was so soon to burst

[1] Froude thus describes the discourse of Catherine to the King: "She told him that, at the moment that she was speaking, the Huguenots were arming. Sixteen thousand of them intended to assemble in the morning, seize the palace, destroy herself, the Duke of Anjou, and the Catholic noblemen, and carry off Charles. The conspiracy, she said, extended through France. The chiefs of the congregations were waiting for a signal from Coligny to rise in every province and town." (*History of England*, x. 401.)

upon the heads of the unsuspecting Huguenots. But no sooner had the clock of Notre Dame struck three, on the morning of St. Bartholomew's feast, than the bell of St. Germain d'Auxerre tolled the signal for the massacre. The morning's sun of the 24th August saw completed the work of blood, so far as it had been planned by Catherine; but the passions of the populace being once let loose, it was not easy to withdraw them from deeds of violence, and two or three days passed by before order could be fully restored in the capital.[1]

On the evening of the 24th, the King addressed royal letters to the governors of the various cities of France, commanding them to maintain tranquillity, and to preserve the lives of the Huguenots. But the example of Paris proved too contagious for the excited populace, and as soon as the terrible news reached Orleans, Rouen, Lyons, and other towns, fresh scenes of rioting were witnessed, and new names were added to the roll of the murdered Huguenots.

Two days after the fatal festival of St. Bartholomew, the King, by a public order, assumed to himself the whole

[1] It is amazing to find with what carelessness the standard Protestant historians deal with the events which they profess to register. Thus, for instance, Hume, in his account of the St. Bartholomew massacre, writes that it began on the evening of the 24th of August. "On the evening of St. Bartholomew, a few days after the marriage, the signal was given for a general massacre of those religionists, and the king himself in person led the way to these assassinations." (*History of England*, vol. v., page 147.) For this statement regarding the king there is not even a shadow of authority; and all the contemporary writers are agreed that the massacre took place, not on the evening, but on the morning of the 24th of August. Beza writes that "c'etait au point du jour." (*Mem. de l'Etat de France*, i. 217.) M. Puygaillard, in a letter of the 26th August, 1572, says: "Dimanche matin, le Roi a faict faire une bien grande execution à l'encontre des Huguenotz." (See *Revue des Questions Hist.*, page 340.) To omit other equally explicit statements, the Duke of Anjou attests that the King and the Queen-mother, with himself and some trusty counsellors, met at the Louvre soon after midnight of the 23rd of August, and at early dawn of the 24th, "ainsi que le jour commençait à poindre," sent a messenger to withdraw the order which had been given for the massacre; but it was too late, the deed was already done. (White, *The Massacre*, page 416.)

responsibility of the dreadful massacre; and before the Foreign Ambassadors and Parliament, assembled in the Gilded Chamber of the Palace of Justice, he made the solemn announcement, that that execution on the leaders of an incorrigible faction which they had witnessed, had been done "by his express orders, not from any religious motive, or in contravention of his edict of pacification, which he still intended to observe, but to prevent the carrying out of a detestable conspiracy, got up by the Admiral and his followers, against the person of the King, the Queen-mother, her other sons, and the King of Navarre." (The "Official Declaration," in White, page 449.) Without a dissentient voice, the Parliament passed a vote of thanks commending the King's foresight and energy, and adding its official sanction to the royal sentence already executed against the traitors. To add greater solemnity to the occasion, the whole Parliament and Court, with Charles at their head, walked in procession to the Cathedral of Notre Dame, and there offered up solemn thanksgiving to God that so great and imminent danger had been averted from the kingdom. Medals were struck to commemorate[1] the event, and it was ordered that the public procession and thanksgiving of parliament should be annually repeated, to perpetuate the memory of their providential escape from the dreadful conspiracy. (Saint-Victor, *Tableau Historique de Paris*, xiii. 210.)

It is almost impossible to form an exact estimate of the numbers that were massacred in Paris, and throughout France, on this occasion. Each writer, as impelled by passion or blinded by prejudice, increases the number of the victims, and varies the details of the horrible massacre.

[1] A facsimile of one of these medals is given in vignette of title-page by White in *Massacre of St. Bartholomew*. It bears the motto, "*Virtus in rebellss*," and serves to confirm the opinion that the Huguenots were punished, not as heretics, but as rebels.

Thus, for instance, Perefixe calculates that 6,000 Huguenots were slain in Paris alone, and that the number of the sufferers throughout France was 100,000. Claude Haton writes that more than 7,000 were put to death in the city.[1] Davila and others increase the number to 10,000. Froude (*History of England*, x. 408) states that about 2,000 were murdered in Paris, and, "according to the belief of the times," 100,000 men, women, and children throughout France. He adds, however, the significant note, that in this case, as "with all large numbers, when unsupported by exact statistics," it is safe to divide the number "at least by ten." Sully reckons the whole number of victims throughout France as 70,000. Ranke, in his *History of the Papacy*, had registered them at about 50,000;[2] but, in his *History of the Wars in France*, he reduces the number to "about 30,000." Hume estimates the slain in Paris alone as "500 gentlemen and men of condition, and 10,000 of inferior sort." He does not assign the precise number of the myriads who were slaughtered elsewhere.

De Thou, writing for the express purpose of promoting infidel philosophism against the Church, calculates the total number of the slain in France at 20,000. La Popeliniere, who flourished at the time, and published his History (*Histoire de France, depuis l'an 1550 jusqu'en 1577*, edit. Paris, 1581, livre xxix., page 66) a few years after the event, numbers the Parisian victims at 1,000, and the sufferers throughout the whole kingdom at 20,000. Papyr Masson reduces the whole number in France to 10,000: Alzog, to less than 4,000. Caveirac writes that 1,100 were slain in Paris, and 2,000 throughout the rest of France. Barthelemy adopts the opinion of La Popeliniere as to the city of Paris,

1 "Plus de 7,000 personnes bien connues, sans autres jetées dans la riviere, qui ne furent connues." (White. page 470.)

2 "On a tué près de cinquante mille." (Ranke, *Hist. de Papauté*, etc., iii. 84.)

but reduces the total number of victims throughout the kingdom to 2,000.[1] Lingard, after a minute examination, concludes that the total number of the Huguenots slain in all France did not exceed 1,600. The *Huguenot Martyrology*[2] is, perhaps, the most important contemporary Huguenot record connected with the St. Bartholomew massacre. It was published in 1582, with the approval of the whole Huguenot body, who applauded it as an accurate and authentic register of their martyred brethren. Its authors had access to several public documents which have since perished, and every local return which they sought for was readily forwarded by the various Calvinistic congregations, that thus the work might be as full and complete as possible. This official *Martyrology*, when presenting to the reader a general statement regarding the massacre, calculates the total number of the victims at 30,000. Subsequently, however, when setting forth the details for the various districts, the number is reduced to little more than 15,000; and when, again, it proceeds to calendar the names of the sufferers—the special purpose for which it was composed—it can only discover 786 victims in the whole kingdom.

Amid so many conflicting opinions regarding the number of the Huguenots who thus fell victims to the perverse policy of the French Court, there is one thing, at least, which we may affirm with confidence: that there is great uncertainty as to the extent of the massacre, and that it is a manifest exaggeration to speak of the St. Bartholomew crime as a general slaughter of all the French Huguenots.

[1] The dissertation of M. Ch. Barthelemy, "La Saint-Barthelemy," is one of the best that has appeared on the subject; it is found in *Erreurs et Mensonges historiques*, Paris, 1863. The same dissertation is inserted in *Dictionnaire de controverses historiques*, par L. F. Jehan, Migne, 1866; but without the name of M. Barthelemy.

[2] The following is the full title of this work, to which we will have to recur more than once: *Histoire des Martyrs persecutés et mis a mort pour la verité de l'Evangile, depuis le temps des Apôtres jusqu'en* 1574, printed in 1582.

When, however, we take into account the perfect organization of the Huguenot congregations throughout France, and when we consider the official weight of the *Huguenot Martyrology*, and the precision with which it registers in its lists the names even of the humblest sufferers, we cannot be far from the truth when we assert that Lingard, in his computation, has allowed a very wide margin for all possible omissions, and that the total number of the murdered Huguenots cannot have exceeded 1,500.[1] Nothwithstanding this massacre of August, 1572, the Huguenots in the following year are found in the field with regularly-equipped armies, and fearlessly setting at defiance the whole power of the French monarch. For a while, victory even smiled upon them, and, when at length they were overpowered by superior strength, the most honourable terms were accorded to them.[2] Their independent organization remained unaltered; and, indeed, it was not till the time of Richelieu that they at length ceased to form a distinct military power in the kingdom. But it was not the St. Bartholomew massacre, nor their defeat in the field of battle, that effec-

[1] The popular songs of the period point to a very small number of victims. The following, written at the time by Cappler de Vallay, is published by Cantù:—

"L'Eternel Diel veritable,
Qui descouvre tous les secretz,
A permis de droit equitable,
Les perfides être massacrez;
Car la dimanche vingt-quatriesme,
Furent tués plus d'un centieme,
Fautueurs de la loi calvinienne,
Dupuis on a continué
De punir les plus vicieux," &c.

(*Historia Generale*, viii. 754.)

[2] White (page 179) estimates the number of Huguenots in France, in 1561, at about 1,500,000. After the massacre, in 1572, it was calculated that they numbered about 2,000,000. (Mackintosh, *History of England*, iii. 238.) When we take into account that in the intervening period they had been overcome in three civil wars, as we will see hereafter, but little room remains for an extensive massacre of their party on the feast of St. Bartholomew, 1572.

tually broke the power and lessened the numbers of th French Huguenots. For this result France was indebte far more to the spirit of religion that was awakened through out the nation by St. Francis de Sales, St. Vincent de Paul and the clergy formed in their school, whose piety and zea at length brought back these erring sons into the savin fold of the one true Church of Jesus Christ.

And now, before we quit this portion of our subject there are a few circumstances connected with the St Bartholomew massacre which merit our special attention although they are generally passed over in silence b modern historians.

In the first place, it is an important fact that no Bisho or Priest, or other representative of Catholic feelings an Catholic interests, was allowed any part in the Council o Catherine de Medici, and the massacre was planned an devised solely as a matter of State policy. Even the Papa Nunzio was left a stranger to the plot, and, as Sismond writes, "he only learned the death of Coligny and the rest when all had been accomplished."

Then, again, several Catholics fell victims to the rage o their enemies on that bloody festival. Sir James Mackintos expressly asserts, that "Catholics were involved in th slaughter: private interests and personal animosities bor-rowed the poniard and the mask of religious fury." (*History* iii. 225.) The *Huguenot Martyrology* (*Histoire*, &c., fol. 731) cites the following words of Mezeray, an eye-witness of th scenes of slaughter: "Whoever possessed wealth, or hel an enviable post, or had hungry expectant heirs, was put down as a Huguenot." When recording some individual instances of the massacre, the same *Martyrology* informs us that the Governor of Bourdeaux caused wealthy Catholics as well as Protestants to be thrown into prison: from Catholics and Protestants alike he demanded a ransom, and he deliberately put to death all for whom the ransom was not paid. Again, he states that at Bourges, a priest was thrown into prison and murdered; that at the town of La Charité, a Catholic matron received the assassin's dagger; and that at Vic, the Catholic Governor was himself murdered. It also states that in Paris two ecclesiastics of high dignity, Bertrand de Villemor and Jean Rouillard—the latter a Canon of Notre Dame—fell victims in the general massacre. And yet these are only a few cases incidentally mentioned in this record, otherwise so hostile to everything Catholic.

The Protestant historian, La Popeliniere, further assures us that the Catholics of France loudly protested against these deeds of blood being imputed to them, and they readily contributed as far as was in their power to secure the Huguenots from further attacks. "Many more would have been slain," he says, "were it not that some of the Catholic nobility, satisfied with the death of the leaders, used their efforts to appease the mob; several Italians, too, on horseback, and with swords drawn, drove back the rioters in the faubourgs and in the streets, and threw open their houses as a secure refuge for the sufferers." (La Popeliniere, *Histoire*, liv. 19.) He adds the names of several leading Catholics who thus distinguished themselves by sheltering the Huguenots from danger, as the Dukes D'Aumale, de Biron, de Bellievre, &c. The British Museum preserves a curious letter addressed from Paris, in the month of September, 1572, to the English Government, which accurately describes the feelings of the Catholics of Paris in regard to the massacre: "It is lamented (it says) to see the King's cruelty, even by the Papists: many be sorry that so monstrous a murder was invented, and at present they dread their own lives. The Duke of Guise himself is not so bloody, neither did he kill any man himself, but saved divers. He spoke openly that for the Admiral's death he was glad, but that the King had put such to death as, if it had pleased him, might have don good service."[1]

Nor must we suppose that this sympathy of the Catholi citizens for the Huguenots was confined to the capital. I every city of France similar instances were found of tha true charity which has ever characterised the Catholi Church, and which, on the present occasion, sought t stem the tide of massacre, and to shield the sufferers b the protecting mantle of religion. Thus, the *Hugueno Martyrology*, to which we have so often referred, attest (*Histoire*, &c., fol. 716) that very many of the sufferers wer sheltered in the monasteries from the fury of the populace and, as an instance, it states that "the monasteries serve as a safe shelter for the Huguenots in Toulouse." Again, i says that at Bourges "some peaceable Catholics saved th Huguenot sufferers from an infuriated mob." It adds that, in the town of Romans, "sixty Huguenots were seized by the mob, but the peaceable Catholics delivered forty of them out of their hands, and the governor delivered thirteen others. The remaining seven were murdered by private enemies, because they had been found with arms in their hands." (Page 718.) At Troyes, a priest was foremost among those who sought to rescue the unfortunate sufferers; whilst at Bourdeaux "several were saved by the clergy and others from whom no such favour could have been expected." (Fol. 730.) This triumph of charity over hatred and revenge was nowhere more manifest than at Nismes, notwithstanding

[1] MSS., Br. Mus.—"News from France," Sept., 1572: Froude, *History*, x. 410. There is also a Letter of Walsingham, on the 13th of September, in which he writes that "this manner of proceeding is, by the Catholics themselves, utterly condemned." The Venetian ambassador affirms the same in his "Relazione," published in *La Diplomatie Venitienne*: "Conciossiache dispiaccia oltremodo tanto ai Cattolici quanto agli ugonotti, non dicono tanto il fatto quanto il modo e la maniera del fare; parendo loro di strano che uno la sera si trovi vivo e la mattina morto; e chiamano questa via e modo di procedere con assoluta potestà, senza via di giudizio, via di tirannide; attribuendolo alla Regina," &c.

the memory of the bitter sufferings to which the Catholics of that city had been a short time before subjected by the triumphant Huguenots. The Catholic citizens, on the first rumours of a massacre, put forth all their strength, and invited the Huguenot leaders to unite with them in order to prevent the shedding of blood. All the city gates were closed except one, and there a body of armed Huguenots were stationed, together with the Catholic troops, to repress every attempt at massacre.

It would not be difficult to multiply proofs of the spirit of charity and forbearance thus shown by the French clergy. The city of Lyons is often cited as an instance of the activity of the priests in the work of slaughter,[1] but Montfalcon, the learned librarian of the public library of Lyons, though writing bitterly against the Catholics, has proved from official documents that the clergy had no part, direct or indirect, in the massacre or other disorders of that city. (Montfalcon, *Guerres de religion à Lyon*, page 420.) Fleury attests that the clergy, heedless of what they themselves had so often suffered, used every endeavour to protect the Huguenots:[2] he adds, that the Catholic body in Paris, and throughout all France openly avowed their disapproval of the massacre. At Lisieux, the governor, thinking it would please the Court, gave orders that the Hugnenots should be put to death; but the illustrious bishop, John Hennyer, preached with all his zeal against such cruelty, and he not only had the consolation of preserving his flock from the shedding of a single drop of blood; but, moreover, the Huguenots, moved by the charity thus shown them by this good pastor, became docile to his instructions, and very many of them were restored to

[1] As, for instance, by M. Dargaud, in his *Histoire de la liberté religieuse*, iii., page 362. Notwithstanding its many exaggerations, a prize was awarded to this work by the French Academy.

[2] "Le clergé, tout maltraité qu'il avait été par les heretiques, en sauva tant qu'il put en differents endroits." (Fleury, *Hist. Eccles.*, sixteenth century, sect. xii.)

the fold of Christ. (Becchetti, *Istorio degli ultin i quattro socoli della chiesa*, xii. 160.) Throughout Burgundy, as De Thou informs us, "little blood was shed, and nearly all the Protestants returned to the religion of their ancestors." (De Thou, tom. vi., page 432: so also La Virotte, in *Annales d'Arnay*, 1837.) When the Governor of Dauphiny, Bertrand de Gondes, a devoted Catholic, was told that it was the King's order that the Huguenots should be put to death, he replied that the King's power was abused by others, and that it was his duty to preserve the King's subjects for him." He, accordingly, issued an order that "any attempt upon the lives of the Huguenots would be punished with death." (Long, *Guerres de Religion dans la Dauphine*: Chorier, *Hist. Dauphine*, ii. page 647.) At Dieppe, the governor assembled the leading Huguenots in the great hall of the Palace of Justice, and having announced to them the fate which had fallen on the rebels in Paris and elsewhere, said he was sure that there were no rebellious or seditious citizens amongst them; "wherefore," he added, "children of the same Father, let us live together as brothers, and having for each other the charity of the Good Samaritan." No blood was shed in Dieppe, and, touched by the words of charity addressed to them, many of the Huguenots vowed to live and die in the Catholic faith. (White, *Massacre*, page 469.)

The question as to whether a royal order was addressed to the governors of the various cities and provinces commanding them to proceed with the punishment of the Huguenots, is one of but little importance in our present inquiry. There seems to be but little doubt that some such order was addressed to a few of the governors, if not by the King himself, at least by some of the courtiers, in his name. One thing, however, is now agreed on by friendly as well as by hostile historians: that no scheme of general massacre had been arranged by the Court, and communicated to the ocal governors before the festival of St. Bartholomew. ndeed it suffices to inspect the dates at which the massacres ccurred in the various districts, to be convinced that they ere not the result of any such preconcerted scheme. At [eaux the massacre was carried out on the 25th of August; ; La Charité on the 26th; at Orleans on the 27th; at amur and Angers on the 29th; at Lyons on the 30th; at royes on the 2nd September; at Bourges on the 11th; at ouen on the 17th; at Romans on the 20th; at Toulouse n the 25th: at Bourdeaux, not until the 3rd October. Had ie massacre been executed in accordance with any premedi-ted scheme, these deeds of blood would undoubtedly have een perpetrated on the same day throughout France, and ie mere recital of the respective dates must suffice to prove iat the thirst for blood proceeded from the contagious ex-nple of the capital rather than from any orders conveyed the whole kingdom. Nay, more, in some instances these cal massacres were in direct opposition to the express mmand of the King and Parliament, as at Toulouse, where, me days before the massacre began, "the parliament pub-hed a royal order, to the effect that no one should be lowed to molest those of the reformed tenets, but that, on e contrary, every favour should be extended to them."[1] *'he Huguenot Martyrology*, fol. 730.)

II.—The question will probably have ere this suggested self: Why were the passions of the Parisian populace so sily excited against the Huguenots, and why, in other wns, were so many people ready, when their hands were osened, to commit such deeds of bloodshed against these retched sectaries? Several reasons may be assigned for e bitter feeling thus displayed by the French nation. For it will suffice to refer to some few of them.

[1] It adds that, in like manner, "the king, by several letters, informed authorities in Bourdeaux that he did not intend the massacre to oceed further or to extend beyond Paris."

1. In the first place, there was a universal alarm throug out France, lest the Huguenots should seize the helm government, and enter on the administration of the kingdoı In a neighbouring state, from which they were separat only by the British Channel, they had an example of wh they might expect under Protestant rule. They heard the confiscations and imprisonments to which the Catholi of England and Ireland were subjected; the tortures eı ployed to extort confession of guilt from the confessors the faith; the savage cruelty exercised towards them on tl scaffold, and even after death: and they said to one anoth —Protestantism has triumphed in England, and this is tl result: the era of Nero and Diocletian has been revived, aı unheard-of cruelties have been exercised against the Catholi of that kingdom. Are we to permit the same intolera spirit of persecution to rule in our Catholic nation? was not that the Queen-mother or the Court of France fe aggrieved by the persecuting edicts of Queen Elizabeth. few days after the St. Bartholomew massacre, Catheri addressed a letter to the French ambassador in London, aı when setting forth the reasons of state why the death Coligny and the other factious leaders should not interru the friendly relations that existed between the two poweı she asks: "Did the Court of France manifest displeasu when the Queen of England ordered the death of those wl troubled her at home? No; and even were she to ord the execution of all the Catholics of England, we would n allow such a matter to interfere with our mutual frien ship."[1] Seldom, indeed, are such cynical and heartle words to be found even in the annals of diplomacy. (another occasion, however, Catherine displayed a little mo of the national spirit: for when Elizabeth instructed tl French ambassador to convey to the King the expression

[1] "Nous ne vous en empêcherions ni altérerions aucunement l'ami d'entre elle et nous." (*Correspondance Diplomatique*, tom. vii., page 347.

her hopes that he would be friendly to the Huguenots, the Queen-mother dictated, in reply, that her royal son could not follow a better guide than his good sister of England, and he would be careful to imitate the example which she would set in her dealings with her Catholic subjects.[1]

The French people felt none of that heartless indifference which ruled at Court. They were fired with indignation at the recital of the atrocities to which their fellow-Catholics were subjected in these countries, and it was openly declared that if the Huguenots were allowed to triumph, then the same scenes of butchery would be witnessed among themselves. The feeling in Paris was particularly intense. It is thus described by a modern historian, who, I may remark, is most repulsively prejudiced against everything Catholic: "Honest Catholics, they said, would fare no better in France than they did in England, where, as it was well known, they were every day subjected to fearful tortures. The shop-windows were filled with coloured engravings, representing, in exaggerated fashion, the sufferings of the English Catholics under bloody Elizabeth, or Jezabel, as she was called; and as the gaping burghers stopped to ponder over these works of art, there were ever present, as if by accident, some persons of superior information, who would condescendingly explain the various pictures, pointing out, with a long stick, the phenomena most worthy of notice. These caricatures proving highly successful, and being suppressed by order of the Government, they were

[1] Digges, page 246: Lingard, vi. 139. In 1567, several of the German princes, including the Palatine of the Rhine, and the Dukes of Saxony and Wurtemberg, despatched an embassy to the King of France, also interceding in favour of their co-religionists. Charles replied that he would be a friend of theirs only so long as they abstained from meddling in the affairs of his kingdom; and he added: "I might also pray them to permit the Catholics to worship freely in their own cities." (White, page 272.) How little changed is the attitude of these German governments towards their Catholic subjects, even after 300 years!

repeated upon canvas on a larger scale, in still more conspicuous situations, as if in contempt of the royal authority which sullied itself by compromise with Calvinism." (Motley, *History of the United Netherlands*, i. 42.)[1]

2. Another alarming example was at their own doors, in Switzerland, and this came the more closely home to them, because Calvin was in reality the prime-mover of all the Huguenot disorders, and, from his mountain retreat in Switzerland, was accustomed to boast that, before he died, his Reform would be triumphant in his own native France. Calvinism was, indeed, triumphant in Switzerland; but it was triumphant, as Erasmus attests, "by the slaughter of more than 100,000, young and old" of the brave Catholic Swiss peasantry. (Erasmus, *Opera*, tom. iii., part i., page 900.) And lest anyone should perchance entertain a doubt as to the tendency of their principles, the French Huguenots, in their Synod, held in Paris, in 1559, had openly adopted the tenets and discipline of the Swiss Calvinists, and, true to the spirit of their founder, they had further enacted the severe statute that "heretics should be punished with death," and that it was "the duty of the State to enforce such punishment."[2] Protestant writers, whilst accusing their Catholic brethren of intolerance, should not be unmindful of these decrees of their Continental co-religionists —decrees the more revolting and intolerable, because they were enacted in the name of liberty, and under the specious

[1] A few years later the same argument was made use of by the French agent who sought to engage Philip II. in a war against England: "I cannot refrain from placing before your eyes the terrible persecutions which the Catholics are suffering in England; the blood of the martyrs flowing under so many kinds of torments; the groans of the prisoners, of the widows and orphans; the general oppression and servitude, which is the greatest ever endured by a people of God under any tyrant whatever." ("Memorial of Mendoza," in Motley's *History*, i. 129.)

[2] See the excellent dissertation by Alzog, in Wetzer & Welte's *Dictionnaire Encyclopédique*, ii. 358.

pretence of asserting the outraged principles of religious equality.[1]

3. But there was yet another reason why the French populace were so easily roused to vengeance; and, as it is one of vital importance for understanding the relative position of parties in France at the period of which we treat you will pardon me if I dwell on it at some length.

The Huguenots had been labouring for many years, partly by intrigue and partly by force of arms, to overthrow the religion of the nation, and to establish the tenets of Calvin in its stead. To attain this great object of their ambition, all means seemed lawful to them. They sought by turns to oppress the Catholics, to revolutionize the State, and to dismember the kingdom. The result was faithfully sketched, a few years later, by the Duke of Burgundy: "I do not now speak," he said, "of the calamities produced by the new doctrines in Germany, England, Scotland, or Ireland—I speak only of France. Nor shall I enumerate one by one

[1] Beza writes: "Those who are unwilling to put heretics to death are more guilty than those who allow parricides to live with impunity: we desire to exterminate those who disturb the Church." (*Profession of Faith*, point fifth, page 119.) It was also a saying of Luther that "We live in such peculiar times that a prince may gain heaven more readily by shedding blood than at other times by prayer." When Condé consulted the Calvinist Synod assembled at Orleans about tolerating the Catholic worship, "that impracticable body, while claiming absolute liberty for themselves, would have denied it to those whom they called atheists, libertines, and anabaptists." (White, page 230.) We need not, however, go beyond Great Britain for this teaching of intolerance. John Knox, in his *Appellation*, declared that it was the duty of subjects to depose a Catholic queen, "and punish her to death with all the sort of her idolatrous priests." The same intolerance is taught in the Canons of Convocation of 1640; in the solemn League and Covenant; and in Jewell's Apology. And what shall we say of the oath taken by William and Mary as King and Queen of Scotland: "We swear to root out all heretics and enemies to the true worship of God, that shall be convicted by the true Kirk of God of the aforesaid crimes, out of our lands and empire of Scotland." I need say nothing of Protestant teaching and practice in Ireland. No wonder, indeed, that Frederic Seebohm should be obliged to acknowledge, in his *History of the Era of the Protestant Revolution*, that "there was one thing especially in which there seemed to be reaction rather than progress during the era, viz., in toleration." (Page 219.)

the evils of which it was the theatre, which are recorded in so many authentic documents; the secret assemblies; the leagues formed with foreign enemies; the attempts against the Government; the seditious threats, open revolts, conspiracies, and bloody wars; the plundering and sacking of towns; the deliberate massacres and atrocious sacrileges: suffice it to say, that from Francis I. to Louis XIV., during seven successive reigns, all these evils, and many others, with more or less violence, desolated the French monarchy. This is a point of history which, although it may be variously related, can neither be denied nor called in question."

4. As early as the reign of Francis I., many of the French courtiers had adopted the reformed tenets. In the religious wars which ravaged Europe in the first half of the sixteenth century, we frequently find the French monarch the ally of the Protestant German States. The purport indeed of such an alliance was a purely political one—to counterbalance the overwhelming influence of Catholic Spain; but it indirectly served to swell the numbers and to increase the authority of the French reformers. Soon after the accession of Charles IX., the Huguenot leaders reckoned themselves sufficiently powerful to attempt to supplant the Duke of Guise and the Catholic party at Court, and, under the guidance of Throckmorton, the English ambassador at Paris, they entered into a plot, known as the Conspiracy of Amboise, to seize the helm of State and take the government into their own hands. Owing to the energy of the Duke of Guise, their plans were frustrated. A far more serious attempt, however, was made in 1562; and once more it was the English ambassador that urged them to draw the sword. Their envoys negotiated a formal treaty with Elizabeth, and English troops, under the command of the Earl of Warwick, landed on the coasts of France, whilst another army of German mercenaries ravaged the fair plains of Normandy. Relying on this powerful aid, the Huguenots rose in arms, and, almost on

the same day, made themselves masters of eighteen cities and several towns.[1] We will refer just now to some of the terrible scenes of pillage and bloodshed which ensued; for the present, suffice it to remark, that the flame of civil war was kindled throughout all France. The Catholic troops, however, soon obtained a mastery in the battle-field, several victories crowned their arms, and the fall of Orleans, the last stronghold of the Huguenots, was hourly expected, when the Duke of Guise was treacherously assassinated in the Catholic camp. The Queen-mother availed herself of this opportunity to conciliate the contending parties, and conditions of peace, most favourable to the Huguenots, were accorded by the Crown.

There was one special feature in this Huguenot revolt which awakened the indignation of the French people. As the price of English support, the Huguenot leaders had surrendered Havre and Dieppe into the hands of Queen Elizabeth, and consented to admit an English garrison into Rouen. Such treasonable measures, indeed, excited the displeasure not only of France, but of all Catholic Europe, and were hailed with delight only by the German Lutherans and the Turks. They failed, however, to secure success for the traitors. Two-thirds of the English garrison were slain at the capture of Rouen; Dieppe was almost immediately abandoned as incapable of defence; and more than half of the Earl of Warwick's army being wasted by disease and the sword, in the hopeless defence of Havre, that city, too, after a short siege, was restored to the crown of France. This unsuccessful attempt of the Huguenots to recall a hated rival power to the French coasts, made their revolt doubly offensive to the nation: it was an outrage, at the same time, against patriotism and against religion.

[1] White (*Massacre*, page 202) gives the names of several of the cities and districts thus occupied by the Huguenots.

5. By the terms of the treaty, sanctioned by the Court, the Huguenots were allowed the free exercise of their reformed worship, and no penalty was imposed for their past treasons. This, however, was far from satisfying the restless ambition of their leaders. In 1567,[1] they again rose in revolt. "On the same day," writes Ranke, "the insurrection burst forth all over France. The writers of the period are obliged to go back to Mithridates, King of Pontus, to find an historical parallel for the secrecy with which this revolt was organized, and for the precision and rapidity with which it was carried into effect." (Ranke, *Histoire de France*, vol. i., page 259.) The signal of the war was a treacherous attempt to seize on the King and the Court in the neighbourhood of Meaux. The plot, however, was betrayed a moment before its execution, and the King, with difficulty, escaped to Paris.[2] All France was again in flames, and once more the English ambassador, Norris, is the instigator of the revolt, and the chief support of the rebels. Queen Elizabeth, indeed, wrote to the King, congratulating him on his providential escape; but her crafty minister, Cecil, accompanied her letter by a private despatch to Norris, instructing him "to comfort the insurgents, and exhort them to persevere."[3] The Catholic troops, however, were

[1] The Protestant Sismondi writes: "A la fin de Septembre 1567, les Huguenots se rendirent maîtres des villes de Montauban, Castres, Montpellier, Nimes, Viviers, Saint-Point, Uzès, Pont-Saint-Esprit, et Bagnolles; partout ils chassèrent des couvents et des églises les prêtres, les moines et les religieuses. Ils dépouillèrent les sanctuaires de leurs ornements, et quelquefois ils démolirent les édifices sacrés." (*Histoire des Français*, tom. xviii., page 16.)

[2] The King owed his safety to a select body of Swiss troops, with whom he marched to Paris. They were attacked on the way by Condé and 500 horse; but, without waiting to give battle, they continued their march, "standing fast awhile, and then retiring, still turning their head as doth the wild boar whom the hunters pursue." (La Noue., page 395; White, page 277.)

[3] See further details in Lingard, viii. 61. It was stated at the time, and was generally believed, that had the Huguenots succeeded they would have burnt Paris. For proofs, see J. Cretineau Joly, *Hist. relig. polit., &c., de la Comp. de Jesus*, vol. ii., page 85.

everywhere victorious; the Government again stepped in to negotiate terms of pacification, and favourable conditions, with full liberty of worship, were readily accorded to the Huguenots. All this only served to convince, more and more, the Huguenot leaders of the political advantages which the Government derived from their support, and to increase their defiant boldness.

6. A third time they rose in arms, in 1569. They had now increased their strength by the aid of German mercenaries, who were paid with English gold.[1] They were known as Reiters, and Davila describes them as devastating France like a frightful hurricane. "Fierce in demeanour, brutal in habits, as intractable as they were insolent, and a nuisance alike to friend and foe, they were insatiable pillagers, and their long train of waggons, filled with plunder, often caused irremediable delay in the march of the Huguenot army." (White, *Massacre*, page 289.) Some of these had been engaged by the Huguenots in the former wars, but now they came in increased numbers. Nevertheless, the decisive battles of Montcontour[2] and Jarnac broke the power of the Huguenot party, and crushed all their hopes for the present. They did not, however, cease to conspire, and though a general edict of pacification was published in 1570, they availed themselves of it only to renew their secret military organization, and to mature their plans for future struggles.

7. All this time the Huguenots were but one in ten of the French population; and the question was asked in every

1 Queen Elizabeth forwarded to Rochelle six pieces of artillery, with their ammunition. She also sent £50,000 in gold, with a promise of more. She required, however, a guarantee for repayment, and in the Cotton MSS. (Caligula, E. vi., fol. 90) there is an inventory of jewels and trinkets mortgaged to her by Joan of Navarre, Condé, and Coligny, on 12th June, 1569.

2 The battle of Montcontour, fought on 3rd Oct., 1569, was the most brilliant of the whole campaign. The Huguenots went into battle 18,000 strong, and before night it was a difficult matter to collect 1,000 of them to cover their retreat. (White, page 312.)

hamlet and town of France: Is this turbulent faction to be allowed thus continually to disturb our peace, to seek aid from the enemies of our nation, to make treaties, and to arm themselves for our destruction? Of what use are our victories in the field when the jealousy of the Court robs us of their fruit, and each overthrow of the Huguenots is only the signal for new favours to be lavished on them by the Queen-mother and the Government? As a consequence of the prolonged civil wars, the pursuits of agriculture had been almost entirely abandoned, and commerce was ruined. In Paris itself "the anarchy seems to have been complete, each man being a law to himself. Not even in the terrible revolution that closed the eighteenth century were the bonds of society more thoroughly relaxed." (White, page 232.) A few incidents will best serve to illustrate the state of popular feeling that prevailed at this time in Paris. On the 27th December, 1561, while the Huguenots were attending service in the Church of St. Marcellus, in Paris, the bells of the neighbouring parish church of St. Medard were rung to summon the Catholics to vespers. This was considered by the Huguenots to be a studied insult, and, accompanied by Beza, 1,500 of their number fully armed, headed by Audelot on horseback, burst into the Church of St. Medard, massacred fifty of the unoffending congregation, overturned the altar, carried away the sacred vestments, and trampled under foot the most Holy Sacrament. The next day the Huguenots assembled again in St. Marcellus' Church, in great numbers, to celebrate their triumph, but 4,000 citizens, unable to restrain their rage, attacked the church, dispersed the congregation, tore the pulpit to pieces, and burned the church to the ground. (Becchetti, *Istoria*, x. 338: White, *Massacre*, page 86.) When the news of the death of Condé reached the city, after the battle of Jarnac, in 1569, the Lent preacher declared it to be a divine judgment, and described the fallen leader of the Huguenots as "the chief of robbers, murderers, thieves, rebels, and heretics, in France: a prince degenerated from the virtues and religion of his ancestors, a man foresworn, guilty of treason against God and the King, a profaner of temples, a breaker of images, a destroyer of altars, a contemner of the sacraments, a disturber of the peace, a betrayer of his country, and a renegade Frenchman." (White, page 306.) Again, when the arrangements were being made for the marriage of the King's sister with Henry of Navarre, Joan of Navarre objected to its being celebrated in the capital, on account of the fanatical temper of the inhabitants; whilst, on the other hand, the Parisians were equally averse to it, fearing, says Claude Haton, "that they would be robbed and despoiled in their houses by the seditious Huguenots." (Claude Haton, *Memoires*, ii., page 663.) Throughout the marriage festivities the Huguenots were regarded as aliens—"aliens in language, costume, and religion." Both parties "were armed and equipped, as if about to enter upon a campaign." The Huguenots looked on the city as a volcano; yet "there were bigots and fanatics among them who seemed to court rather than avoid an explosion." (White, page 380.)

8. But it is time that I should give some instances of the Satanic cruelty which the Huguenots displayed towards the Catholics, and the Vandalism with which they raged against everything held sacred in the Catholic faith, wherever a momentary success placed the sword of authority in their hands. In the three wars of 1562, 1567, and 1569, no fewer than fifty cathedrals and 500 Catholic churches were plundered, the sacred vessels desecrated, the altars destroyed, the paintings and vestments torn to shreds or applied to profane uses. The Principality of Bearn was one of the first to adopt the Genevan tenets, and what was the result? All public acts of Catholic worship were interdicted, the clergy were exiled, and religious toleration was denied to the Catholic subjects. A decree was published in 1571,

banishing all superstition and idolatry from the territory, and commanding all to assist at the Calvinist sermons, under penalty of fine or imprisonment.[1] And yet it was in the name of religious liberty that such enactments were made. At Venez, a small town in Languedoc, more than a hundred Catholic prisoners were massacred in cold blood, and their bodies thrown into a well. (*Memoires de Jacques Gache*, page 17, *seqq.*) A plan was organized in Geneva by Balvin, Beza, and others, for the seizure of the city of Lyons, on the 5th September, 1561. The attempt was frustrated by the Catholics, who, however, exercised no violence towards the conspirators. In 1562, the treason of De Sault, the governor, gave possession of the city to the Huguenots. Then the most revolting scenes were witnessed. The destruction of everything sacred was decreed, and carried into execution with the greatest violence. "Never did the Goths rage with such fury against the city of Rome as was shown by these sectaries against the desolate city of Lyons;" thus writes De Rubys in his *Histoire véritable de la ville de Lyon*, published in 1640. All who refused to fight under the Protestant banner were despoiled of their property, and banished from the city. The life-size silver crucifix in the cathedral was thrown down by the Huguenot minister, Ruffi, who cried out, "Behold, the idol is cast down!" and then cut off the head, which he carried to his own house. The silver shrine, in which the body of St. Justus was preserved, was also broken open and carried off; the statues which adorned the *façade* and portico of the cathedral were demolished; the tombs were violated in search of treasure; the Church of St. Irenæus and the sanctuary of Notre Dâme de Fourvière were sacked; everywhere the relics of the saints were thrown into the fire or trampled under foot; and an order was published by the

[1] See "Déclaration pour servir de réglement pour la discipline des églises de Béarn," ap. Soulier, *Hist. du Calvinisme*, page 119.

commander, Baron des Adrets, that every citizen, under the severest penalties, should assist at the sermons of the reformed ministers, "since it is the will of God that idolatry should be banished from amongst us."[1]

This Baron d'Adrets was one of the most active of the Huguenot military leaders. He was, at the same time, pre-eminent among them for his cruelty. "He was, in regard to the Catholics," writes Feller, "what Nero was to the early Christians. He sought out and invented the most novel punishments, which he took pleasure in seeing inflicted on those who fell into his hands. This monster, wishing to make his children as cruel as himself, forced them to bathe in the blood of Catholics whom he had butchered." (Feller, *Dictionnaire Historique*, a. n.)

At Pamiers, in 1566, as Heylin informs us, the Huguenots fell on the clergy who were engaged in a procession of the Blessed Sacrament, on the festival of Corpus Christi, and massacred them. Similar outrages were witnessed at Montauban, Rodez, and Valence. In 1562, Languet, who was one of the leading Huguenots, wrote to the Elector of Saxony, that in Gascogne and the Lower Languedoc, as also in Provençe, and as far as the Pyrenees, within a range of forty miles, no Catholic priest dared to show himself. (Gandy, *Revue des Questions Historiques*, i. 30.) At Montpellier, the same year, 200 Catholics were put to death, the cathedral was pillaged, and Catholic worship was prohibited throughout the district. In 1569, the fanaticism of the Huguenot preachers was pushed to such extremes, that at Orthez, 3,000 Catholics were butchered; and in the neighbourhood of St. Sever, 200 priests, who had been arrested in various towns, were cast headlong from a precipice.

[1] "Discours des premiers troubles advenus a Lyon," par Gabriel de Saconay, praecenteur et Comte de l'Eglise de Lyon: printed in Lyons in 1569, in 12°. *Revue des Questions Hist.*, i. 34.

9. A few extracts, however, from Mr. White's *History*[1] of this period, which is derived almost exclusively from Huguenot sources, will best enable us to form an accurate idea of the outrages which were thus perpetrated throughout France, in the name of religion, by the Huguenot disciples of Calvin. Writing of the years 1561 and 1562, he says that the Huguenots "seized upon the churches, drove the monks from their convents, made bonfires of the crosses, images, and relics, and demanded an enlargement of their privileges. During the procession of the Fête Dieu at Lyons, 5th June, 1561, a Huguenot tried to snatch the Host out of the priest's hand. These indiscreet reformers were the dread of the moderate Beza:[2] 'I fear our friends more than our enemies,' he wrote." (Page 185.)

At Tours, everything most sacred was outraged: "For some weeks the town was in the hands of the Huguenots, who seized upon the churches, stole the plate, broke the images and ornaments, burnt the service books, desecrated the relics, and ordered every ecclesiastic to leave the place in twenty-four hours, under pain of imprisonment. Contemporary records describe the destruction of a Calvary of gold and azure, one of the wonders of the world, which sixty years before had cost the large sum of 10,000 ducats. The plunder of the churches served to keep up the war. That of St. Martin at Tours furnished Condé (the Huguenot leader) with 1,200,000 livres, without counting the jewels in the shrines. When the King's authority was restored in Tours,

[1] *The Massacre of St. Bartholomew: preceded by a History of the Religious Wars in the Reign of Charles IX.*, by Henry White, London, 1868. Mr. White, at every page, betrays his feelings of deep hostility against the Catholics, and adopts, most unfairly, the most atrocious tales and accusations against them, on the assertion of their Huguenot enemies. We are, on that account, the more justified in accepting his narrative of the atrocities committed by the Huguenots.

[2] "Nostros potius quam adversarios metuo," 4th Nov., 1561. (Baum's *Beza.*) In another letter to Calvin, the same Reformer wrote: "You will scarcely believe how intemperate our people are." (18th Jan., 1562.)

Mass was ordered to be sung in St. Martin's Church, but everything in it had been broken or destroyed, except the stalls in the choir and a few of the painted windows." (Page 216.)

At Rouen, "one Sunday in May, the Huguenots, in the exultation of their triumph, sacked and defaced the cathedral and thirty-six parish churches. They made such work, says Beza, 'that they left neither altar nor image, font nor benitier.'[1] That this was not the act of a lawless mob, nor of a sudden excitement, but of calmness and deliberation, is probable from what happened about the same time at Caen, in the same province, where the minister, Cousin, told the judges that 'this idolatry had been put up with too long, and that it must be trampled down.' And here the destroyers, after scattering the ashes of William the Conqueror, breaking organs, pictures, pulpits, and statues, to the estimated value of 100,000 crowns, had the impudence to ask the Town Council to pay them for their two days' work, which was done."[2] (Page 220.)

In the little town of Montbrison, in August, 1562, under the command of the notorious Baron des Adrets, "the slaughter was fearful: more than 800 men, women, and children were murdered; the streets were strewn with corpses, and the gutters looked as if it had rained blood," says a contemporary. All through the south of France, "at the first outbreak of hostilities, the Huguenots seized upon the churches, which they purified of all marks of idolatry, destroying the relics, and making a jest of the consecrated wafer. In some towns they entirely forbade the Catholic worship." At Lyons, whilst "liberty of conscience was

[1] Another writer of the time says: "Il a fait piller, ne laissant que les murailles et que les terres qui ne se pouvaient emporter." (*Canton d'Athis*, page 44.)

[2] This rests on the authority of De Bras de Bourgeville, a contemporary. (See *Memoires de l'Academie de Caen*, 1852.)

proclaimed, every convent was broken open, and the Mass was abolished. The Huguenots committed devastations that would have disgraced the Vandals. Churches were ravaged, tombs broken open, coffins stripped of their lead, and their gold and silver plates; the bells were broken up, and the Basilica of the Maccabees destroyed by gunpowder." (Page 242.)

At La Rochelle, "the people, excited by the violence of the preachers, rushed to the churches, threw down the altars, and burnt the images. Some priests who had been shut up in the lantern tower were stabbed, and thrown, half dead, into the sea. One Stephen Chamois, a Carmelite monk, had escaped from the city, but being recognised at Aunai, in Saintonge, he was called upon to abjure, and on his refusing to do so, was murdered on the spot." (Page 242.) (Arcere, *Histoire de la ville de Rochelle*, i., page 358. Vincent, *Recherches sur les commencements de Rochelle*.)

At Dieppe (the Rochelle of northern France), the Huguenots are found "pillaging and defacing churches, and melting down the sacred vessels, from which they collected 1,200 pounds of silver. In bands of 200 and 300 they made forays into the adjacent districts of Eu and Arques, from which they never returned empty-handed. We read of their dragging priests into Dieppe tied to their horses' tails, and flogging them at beat of drum in the market-place. Some were thrown into the sea in their sacerdotal robes; some were fastened to a cross, and dragged through the streets by ropes round their necks; and, to crown all, some were buried in the ground up to the shoulders, while the Huguenots, as if playing a game of nine-pins, flung huge wooden balls at their heads. A few weeks after the war broke out, the Protestants of Bayeux rose against the clergy, committing the customary devastations, besides violating the tombs, and throwing out the mouldering corpses. They gutted the bishop's palace, and made a bonfire of the chapter library, then the richest in all

France. The priests and others who opposed them were barbarously murdered, and tossed from the walls into the ditch. Once more, in March, 1565, the Huguenots gained the upper hand, when the troops under Coligny refused to be bound by the terms of the capitulation. Private houses were stripped of all the gold, silver, copper, and lead that could be found; priests who resisted were flogged, dragged up and down the streets by a rope at their necks, and then killed. Children were murdered in their mother's arms; one Thomas Noel, a lawyer, was hanged at his own window; and an unhappy woman had her face stained with the blood of her own son, who had been killed before her eyes. Here, too, more priests were buried up to the neck, and their heads made to serve as targets for the soldiers' bullets; others were disembowelled, and their bodies filled with straw—that they might burn the better. The priest of St. Ouen—we shudder as we record such horrors—was seized by four soldiers, who roasted him, cut him up, and threw his flesh to the dogs. It would have been well had these deeds of brutality been confined to Normandy, but they were repeated all over France. One Friar Viroleau died of the consequences of barbarous mutilation. Other priests or Catholic people were killed by hanging, speared to death, left to die of hunger, sawn in two, or burnt at a slow fire. All this happened in Angouleme. At Montbrun, a woman was burnt on her legs and feet with red hot tongs. At Chasseneuil, in the vicinity, a priest, one Louis Fayard, was shot to death after having been tortured by having his hands plunged in boiling oil, some of which had been poured into his mouth. The vicar of St. Auzanni, was mutilated, shut up in a chest, and burnt to death. In the parish of Rivieres, others had their tongues cut off, their feet burned, and their eyes torn out; they were hung up by the legs or thrown from the walls." (Page 248.) (Vitet, *Hist. Dieppe*, page 77; De Bras, *Antiquities de Caen*, page 170; *Archives*

Curieuses de France (Cimber and Danjou), tom. vi., ser. i page 299.)

Towards the close of 1565, the King and Court paid a vis to Joan, Queen of Navarre. She had "swept her dominior of every vestige of Romanism, and denied to her Catholi subjects that religious liberty which she claimed for he co-religionists in France. When returning through th province of Gascony, Charles, at every step, was reminde of the outrages offered to his religion. As he rode along b the side of the Queen of Navarre, who accompanied him t Blois, he pointed to the ruined monasteries, the broke crosses, the polluted churches; he showed her the mutilate images of the Virgin and the saints, the desecrated grave yards, the relics scattered to the winds of heaven." (Pag 265.)

"At Soissons the Huguenots pillaged the churches, demo lished the beautiful painted windows, broke the orgar melted the bells, stripped the lead off the roofs, plundere the shrines of their gold and jewels, burned the relics of th saints, and tore up the charters and title-deeds belonging t the clergy, Similar tumults occurred at Montauban an other towns." (Page 270.) (*Cimber*, vi. 309: "Discour des troubles," 5th June, 1566.)

At Nismes, in particular, the Catholics were repeatedl subjected to persecution. As early as 1562, "the municipa council decided that the cathedral, with some other churches should be made over to the Reformers, and further ordere the bells of the convents to be cast into cannon, the con vents to be let 'for the good of the State,' the relics an their shrines to be sold, and the non-conforming priests t leave the city." It was in 1567, however, on the 30th c September, that the terrible massacre occurred, which i known as the *Michelade*, on account of the pious people c Nismes being accustomed to celebrate the festival of S Michael the Archangel on the 29th September, and the tw following days. The whole of that terrible day the Catholics of the city were plundered and put to death by a merciless band of Huguenots. The bishop succeeded "in escaping from the mob, who, in their angry disappointment, sacked his palace, and killed the vicar-general. A number of Catholics, including the consul and his brother, had been shut up in the cellars of the episcopal residence. About an hour before midnight they were dragged out, and led into that gray old court-yard, where the imagination can still detect the traces of that cruel massacre. One by one the victims came forth: a few steps, and they fell pierced by sword or pike. Some struggled with their murderers, and tried to escape, but only prolonged their agony. By the dim light of a few torches between seventy and eighty of the principal citizens were butchered in cold blood, and their bodies, some only half dead, were thrown into the well in one corner of the yard, not far from an orange-tree, the leaves of which, says local tradition, were ever afterwards marked with the blood-stains of this massacre.[1] In the September of the following year, these brutal scenes of violence were renewed: the city was again plundered, and its streets were dyed with Catholic blood. The governor was shot, and thrown out of the window, and his corpse was torn in pieces by the lawless mob. In the country round Nismes, forty-eight unresisting Catholics were murdered; and at Alais, in the neighbourhood, the Huguenots massacred seven canons, two gray friars, and several other churchmen. . . Even the

[1] Le vicaire général, Jean Peberan, est livré aux insultes de la populace, traînê avec une grosse corde et précipité dans les puits; il avait voulu mourir à la place de l'évêque. Le massacre avait commencé à onze heures du soir; il dura toute la nuit et continua le lendemain. Ce jour-là, toutes les maisons des Catholiques sont recherchées; ceux qu'on arrête sont égorgés et jetés aux puits. Bien qu'il ait plus de sept toises de profondeur et quatre pieds de diametre, il est presque comblé de cadavres; l'eau, mêlée de sang, y surnage; des gémissements étouffés s'en exhalent; cent cinquante, suivant les uns, trois cents, suivant les autres, furent égorgés." (*Revue des Quest. Hist.*, i. 45.)

dead were not left in peace: in more than one instance the corpses were exhumed and treated with savage barbarity." (Page 285.) (Baragnon, *Histoire des Nimes*, tom. ii. See also Vaissette, *Histoire Gen. de Languedoc*, v., page 298; and Menard,[1] *Histoire de la ville de Nismes*, tom. v., page 16.)

In 1568 and 1569, the Huguenots, "in their fury, once more defiled the altars, destroyed the churches, and perpetrated a thousand atrocities. Briquemaut, one of their leaders, cheered them on to murder, wearing a string of priests' ears round his neck.[2] When the town of Orthez was stormed, so many of the inhabitants were put to death, without distinction of age or sex, that the river Gave was dammed up by the number of bodies thrown into it. The monasteries and nunneries were burnt, not one inmate escaping, the total slaughter being estimated at 3,000. When the citadel was taken, every ecclesiastic who was proved to have borne arms—and the proof was none of the strictest—was bound hand and foot, and tossed over the bridge into the river. At Aurillac they buried some Catholics alive up to the chin, and, after a series of filthy outrages, used their heads as targets for their muskets. Four hundred persons were put to death there, of whom 130 were heads of families." (Page 295.) (De Thou, vol. v., page 610.)

This recital of atrocities will, I am sure, suffice to explain how it was that the French populace, especially in the districts which were the theatres of such crimes, were so ready to engage in deeds of retaliation, and it will also prove that it was the aim of the Huguenots to exterminate, if

[1] This last-named writer states that most of the authorities in Nismes were secretly favourable to the Huguenots, and hence permitted them to rage with impunity against the Catholics.

[2] This fact of Briquemaut wearing a necklace of the ears of the priests whom he had massacred, is mentioned by all the contemporary writers. The same savage ornament was also worn by another Huguenot in 1562, but his name is not given. (White, page 248.)

possible, the Catholics of France. The Huguenot blood, shed on the feast of St. Bartholomew, 1572, was only as a drop in the ocean when compared with the torrents of the blood of Catholics shed by their relentless enemies in almost every city of France.

III.—It now only remains to make some comments on a few of the many questions which have arisen in connection with the St. Bartholomew massacre.

1. And first of all it will be asked, what sympathy was shown by the Government of England to their Huguenot friends in the terrible disaster which had thus befallen them? England, during the preceding years, had entered into secret treaties with the Huguenots, and they were publicly regarded as her allies. We would, therefore, expect that she would now avenge the St. Bartholomew outrage, or at least resent, as done to herself, the injury and insult offered to the Huguenot cause. Nothing, however, of all this occurred. A few days after the massacre, the King of France commissioned his ambassador in London, La Motte Fenelon, to explain to Queen Elizabeth the peculiar circumstances of the sad event; and, in obedience to these instructions, he set before her Majesty that his Sovereign, quite against the royal wishes, had been compelled to act with severity against Coligny and his adherents, on account of a wicked plot they had entered into against the throne, and that if some few innocent persons had suffered with the guilty, this was owing to circumstances which his Majesty was unable to control, and which occasioned him the most heartfelt grief. Elizabeth received the ambassador at Woodstock. The Court chronicler records that she was arrayed in the deepest mourning, and that all the lords and ladies who attended her were dressed in black. The whole sympathy, however, of England for the unfortunate dupes of her deceitful policy ended here. Amicable relations were almost immediately re-established, and the

friendship of the two Courts seemed more closely cemented than ever in the blood of the Huguenots. The English ambassador was instructed to proceed with the negotiations for the marriage of Queen Elizabeth with the Duke d'Alençon, brother of Charles IX., as if nothing had occurred to mar the harmony between their respective Courts; and when, a few months later, a daughter was born to the French King, Elizabeth consented to become godmother to the infant princess. She sent the Earl of Worcester on this occasion to present a font of gold as a baptismal gift, and to assist at the ceremony of baptism in her name. (Camden, page 275; De Thou, iii. 244; Castlenau, tom. xlvi. 55; Lingard, vi. 142.)

So completely, indeed, did Queen Elizabeth and the English Government seem to have overlooked the St. Bartholomew outrage, that the Huguenots regarded their proceedings as a studied insult offered to themselves. They pushed their resentment so far as to attack the English ambassador whilst sailing from England to France. One of the ships in his suite was taken and plundered, some of his attendants were slain, and he himself was for a time in jeopardy of his life. A little later, the Marshal de Retz was sent as a special envoy from Charles to the English Court, and the report was generally credited at the time that he received an express acknowledgment from the Queen that Coligny and his associates had deserved their fate.

2. And now a few words as to the question which was warmly debated in former times, whether the St. Bartholomew massacre formed part of a long premeditated scheme of the French Court, or was merely prompted by the difficulties which, in consequence of the failure of the attempt on the life of Coligny, had suddenly beset Catherine de Medici and her friends. There are some, indeed, who go so far as to affirm that the plan for the extirpation of the Huguenots was long before arranged by the King and his council; that the honours and caresses shown to Coligny, and even the

marriage of the Princess Marguerite, formed part of the scheme, the better to lull the suspicions of the intended victims, and to attract them to the capital. This opinion, however, rests on no historical grounds. Everything leads to the conclusion that Coligny had acquired a real mastery over the affections of Charles IX., and it is preposterous to suppose that that young monarch, so weak and vacillating, and impulsive, could have been such a master of dissimulation as to deceive Walsingham and the other foreign ambassadors, as well as his own courtiers, into the belief that he was favourable to the Huguenots, whilst in reality he meditated their destruction. There perhaps is somewhat more of probability in the opinion that Catherine de Medici had, for some months at least, planned in her own mind this plot for cutting off the leaders of the Huguenots; and possibly she had not forgotten the remarkable advice given to her by the Duke of Alva, who, at the conference of Bayonne, in 1565, as Henry of Navarre attests, put Tarquin's gesture into words, and counselled Catherine to rid herself of the obnoxious noblemen by the curious Spanish proverb that "one salmon's head is better than a hundred frogs." (Davila, lib. iii.; Mathieu, *Hist. de France*, i. 283; White, page 262.) Catherine, however, was not a person to readily suppose that the Spanish statesman was disinterested in his counsel, and that his advice was solely given to her in the interests of France. Whether or not, however, the Spanish proverb may have lingered in her mind, it is now generally supposed that, if any such plot existed, the Catholic leaders were likely to share in the fate of the Huguenots, and that had she been successful in the first attempt on the life of Coligny, the Duke of Guise would have been her next victim. But now, that that attempt had failed, she needed the strong arm of this brave nobleman to sustain the government against the Huguenots, and to this circumstance alone he owed his safety. Be this as it may, Catherine, a few days after the massacre, avowed that she had given orders for the death only of a half dozen of the Huguenot leaders, and that "she was responsible in conscience only for that number." (Ranke, *Hist. de la Papaute*, iii. 83.)

For us this is not a question of great moment, and we will readily leave it to be settled by the friends and admirers of Catherine de Medici, and of the Court of Charles IX. Whether the massacre was premeditated or not, it is manifest from the line of policy pursued by Catherine, and from the principles which guided the French Court, that the Catholic Church and the Holy See had no part in it, and are in no way responsible for its terrible excesses. Paris witnessed other bloody scenes in 1792 and 1793. Religion was not responsible for them. They were decreed by an atheistic policy in the name of the sovereign people. The St. Bartholomew massacre was the result of an equally irreligious intrigue, although it was,[1] nominally at least, carried into execution in the interests of the crown. It was the age of classic studies, and it is possible that, amid the peculiar difficulties which now beset her, Catherine may have recalled to mind the massacre so famous in Roman literature, when Scylla sought by one blow to rid himself of all his enemies, and, at his command, the streets of Rome one day flowed with the blood of 6,000 citizens. But, whether or not this vision flitted before the mind of Catherine, it is unquestionable that the Catholic Church had as little part in the Parisian crime as in that of Scylla; and an eloquent writer has well remarked, that were a Blanche of Castile, or a St. Louis on the throne of France in 1572, such a massacre would have been impossible.

3. The important question now presents itself: How was

[1] "The massacre of St. Bartholomew, in 1572, was the diabolical work of the Queen, Catherine de Medici, to maintain her political power." (Seebohm, *History of the Era of the Protestant Revolution*, page 211. Longman, 1874.)

the intelligence of the St. Bartholomew massacre received in Rome? The news, as conveyed to the Eternal City, was to the effect that a widespread conspiracy of the Huguenots had been discovered only a moment before their plans were matured; that their wicked designs had recoiled upon their own heads; and that the Huguenot power was now for ever broken in France. This intelligence was hailed with the greatest delight. The city bells rang out their merriest peals; a royal salute was given from the cannon of St. Angelo's; the Pontiff, with the Court and clergy, walked in procession from the Basilica of San Marco to the French Church of St. Louis, and the *Te Deum* was solemnly chanted in thanksgiving. In addition to all this, a gold medal was struck to commemorate the happy event, and the whole scene, by command of Pope Gregory XIII., was represented among the fresco decorations with which Vassari was then adorning the Sala Regia in the Vatican. All this, however, does not prove what the enemies of the Holy See contend, that the Sovereign Pontiff, or the citizens of Rome, gave expression to their joy for a cold-blooded massacre of the French Huguenots.

To fully appreciate the course pursued by the Roman Court, we must bear in mind the official intelligence relative to the massacre, which was conveyed by Charles IX. to his Holiness. A special agent was sent to Rome, and his instructions were in substance a mere repetition of the King's discourse in Parliament on the 26th of August, setting forth the conspiracy of Coligny and his associates, and how their wicked attempt had recoiled on their own heads. The French agent also brought with him a letter to the Pope from Louis de Bourbon, Duke of Montpensier, which attested that the Huguenots had conspired against the life of the King, the Queen-mother, the King's brothers, and all the princes and Catholic gentlemen of their suite, "to the end that Coligny might create a king of his own religion, and abolish every other religion in the kingdom: that, providentially, the conspiracy was discovered, and on the day they had designed to carry out their enterprise, execution fell upon them and their accomplices, so that all the chiefs of the sect, and several of their party, were slain."[1] The Nunzio, Salviati, sent at the same time a full account of the massacre, and transmitted with it the substance of the King's discourse in Parliament: "That his Majesty, thanks to Christ, detected a plot which Admiral Gaspar de Coligny had prepared against the royal authority, so that a terrible destruction and death threatened the whole family of the King; and, therefore, he inflicted on the Admiral and his followers the punishment which they deserved." (Theiner, i. 45.)

Indeed, this account was persistently repeated by the French envoys at every Court; and those who wished to maintain friendly relations with France, were, of necessity, obliged to accept it as an official statement of the facts and circumstances of the case. The Duke of Alva was at this time carrying on the siege of Mons, in the Netherlands. When he received the official despatch from Paris, he at once embodied it in a circular to all the governors of the provinces, declaring that "the Huguenots had resolved to murder the King and the royal family, and to seize on the government: that for this purpose Coligny had organized a body of 4,000 men in the faubourg St. Germain; but, the secret being betrayed, the King had anticipated their wicked designs, and thus secured the peace of the kingdom. Four hours later the storm would have fallen upon the King and the leaders of the Catholics of France."[2] The French

[1] This letter is published from the Vatican Archives, in continuation of the *Annals of Baronius*, by Theiner, vol. i., page 336.

[2] This document was discovered in 1842, in the State Archives of Mons, and was read by M. Gachard for the Academy of Sciences, in Brussels, on the 4th of June, 1842.

ambassador in Switzerland, M. de Bellievre, was also commissioned to lay before the Swiss Diet, then assembled in Baden, the motives which prompted him to such severity against the Huguenots. His discourse on the occasion is still extant. He declares that the execution ordered by the King was an act of justice, rendered imperative by the conduct of Coligny and his associates. "They had formed a plot," he said, "to introduce a dangerous tyranny into the kingdom. His Majesty, therefore, seeing the imminent danger to which his crown and life were exposed, took the advice of the princes and officers of state, and, with their counsel, proceeded to exercise strict justice against the leading conspirators." (MSS. National. St. Germain, 1247.)

We are not, however, without direct proof that the motive of the rejoicings in the Eternal City was the providential discovery and extinction of a dangerous conspiracy, which aimed at the lives and liberties of the Catholics of France. Soon after the news of the massacre had reached Rome, the famous Latinist, Muretus, was selected to deliver the usual sermon at one of the thanksgiving ceremonies, in presence of the Pope and the Papal Court, and his discourse has happily been preserved. A few of its sentences will suffice to set before us in its true light the whole matter of this solemn thanksgiving. "The Huguenots," he says, "did not hesitate to conspire against the life and liberty of that King, from whom, notwithstanding their atrocious deeds, they had received not only pardon, but kindness and affection. In which conspiracy, at the very time that they had marked out and decreed for carrying into effect their wicked design, the destruction which they had plotted against the King, and against almost all of the royal house and family, was turned upon the heads of the wicked traitors themselves. Oh! memorable the night which, by the execution of a few seditious men, thus freed the sovereign from imminent danger of murder, and the whole kingdom from the incessant alarms of civil war."[1]

With these words before us, the whole course pursued by the Sovereign Pontiff and the Roman people becomes clear and intelligible. Were the deluded conspirators Catholics instead of Huguenots, the same thanksgiving would have been offered up, that God had vouchsafed to strengthen the most Christian King, and to avert so great a calamity from his devoted Catholic nation. The Abbate di San Salvatore was at this time in Rome, as agent of Emanuel Filibert, Duke of Savoy. He writes to the Duke on the 5th of September, 1572, informing him that the official news of the massacre had that day reached Rome, and was received with unbounded delight by all, "on account of the interests of the King of France and of the kingdom and the Church being at stake." He adds, however—and his words abundantly prove that the rejoicings in the Eternal City were not the result of frenzy or savage exultation at the wilful shedding of innocent blood—that "far greater would have been the satisfaction of everyone if his Majesty could, with safety, have attained his purpose without dispensing with the formalities of law. Nevertheless, everyone returns thanks to God, being persuaded of the just intentions of his

[1] "Veriti non sunt adversus illius regis caput ac salutem conjurare, a quo, post tot atrocia facinora, non modo veniam consecuti erant, sed etiam benigne et amanter excepti. Qua conjuratione sub id ipsum tempus, quod patrando sceleri dicatum ac constitutum est, in illorum sceleratorum ac foedifragorum capita id quod ipsi in regem et in totam prope domum ac stirpem regiam machinabantur. O noctem illam memorabilem, quae paucorum seditiosorum interitu regem a praesenti caedis periculo, regnum a perpetua civilium bellorum formidine liberavit. . . . O diem denique illum plenum laetitiae et hilaritatis, quo tu, Beatissime Pater, hoc ad te nuncio allato, Deo immortali et divo Ludovico regi, cujus haec in ipso pervigilio evenerant, gratias acturus, indictas a te supplicationes pedestris obiisti. Quis optabilior ad te nuncius adferri poterat? aut nos ipsi quod felicius optare poteramus principium Pontificatus tui, quam ut primis illius mensibus tetram caliginem, quasi exorto sole discussam cerneremus." (*Opera Mureti*, tom. i., page 197, edit. Ruhnken.)

Majesty." (*Archivio Storico Italiano,* Appendix, tom. iii., page 169.)

It would be easy to add other testimonies to prove that such was, indeed, the opinion prevalent in Rome, and such the motive of the rejoicings and thanksgiving of the Papal Court. Early in the following century the celebrated Strada composed, in Rome, his *History of the War in Flanders.* Treating of the St. Bartholomew massacre, he styles it "a signal deed and a punishment deservedly incurred by a faction of conspirators against their sovereign."[1] Pagi, in his *Life of Gregory XIII.*, also writes that that Pontiff viewed the massacre as a necessary act of self-defence of the French Court, and therefore ordered the thanksgiving: "*actis publice Deo gratiis de periculo a Colinii conjuratione evitato.*" (*Brev. Gest. Rom. Pontif.*, vi. 729.)

There were not wanting, indeed, some special reasons why Rome should not regret that a just retribution had fallen on Coligny and his associates. It had been for centuries the anxious care of the Roman Pontiffs to combine the sovereigns of Europe in a holy league to check the advance of the Moslem armies. The leaders of the so-called Reformation pursued a different course. Luther even went so far as to avow his desire to enter into league with the Turks against the Catholic powers, that thus he might in some way weaken the influence of Rome, and he publicly preached that to fight against the Turks was to war against God.[2] True to this evil policy of the Reformers, Coligny presented to the King, in 1572, a memorial to dissuade him from attending to the counsels of Rome, and urging him to marshal

[1] "Insigne facinus sed meritum conjuratae in regem factioni supplicium." (Strada, *De Bello Belgico*, lib. vii., page 250.)

[2] Among the propositions which Luther refused to retract at the Diet of Worms, 1521, was the following, viz.: "Proeliari adversus Turcas est repugnare Deo." (*Opera Lutheri*, tom. ii., page 3; Audin, *Life of Luther*, page 174.)

his armies against Spain rather than against the Turks. (*De Thou*, tom. vi., page 34.) The Huguenot leaders wer also known to be in secret league with the banditti who a this time infested the several States of Italy. So numerou were these bands of freebooters, that their united strengt was supposed to be a match for an army of 30,000 men Their attacks were principally directed against the States o the Church, and their ravages often filled the citizens o Rome with alarm. By the destruction which now fell upo the Huguenots, the Italian bandits lost their chief support and being deprived of their war material and other resources the field soon became clear for their final overthrow.

Notwithstanding these various motives, the Sovereig Pontiff, Gregory XIII., when freely treating of the occurrenc with his private friends, was far from approving of the St Bartholomew massacre: he even burst into tears, and sai to those around him: "Alas! how can I be sure that som innocent souls may not have suffered with the guilty?" Maffei, the annalist of this Pontiff's reign, having stated tha Coligny's death was announced to His Holiness, as "ordere by the King, in defence of his own life and kingdom," further assures, that although Rome was thus freed from a sworn enemy, yet "the Pope showed a tempered joy, a when a diseased limb is cut off with pain from the body." (Maffei, *Annali*, lib. i., sec. 20.) Brantome's testimony i equally conclusive; he thus writes: "touching the joy an content the good and holy Pope showed concerning th massacre, I heard from a man of honour who was then i Rome, and who knew the matter well, that when the new was brought him he shed tears, not for joy, as men ordinaril

[1] The Calvinists continued for a long time to pursue the same policy Even under Louis XIV., their great preacher, Jurieu, declared that th Turks had received a divine mission to co-operate with the Reformers i the great work of the Gospel: "Pour travailler avec les Reformes a grand œuvre de Dieu."

[2] "Per sicurezza della sua persona e quiete del regno."

do in such cases, but through grief: and when some of those who were present remonstrated that he should weep and be sad on the news of the goodly execution of wicked men, enemies of God and of His Holiness, 'Ah!' he said, 'I weep at the course which the King has pursued, illegal and forbidden by God, to inflict punishment in such a manner, and I fear lest the like shall fall, and that before long, upon himself. I also weep because, among so many victims, as many innocent as guilty may have fallen.'" (Brantome, *Memoires de l'Amiral de Chatillon*, tom. viii., page 176.)

Twelve days after the news of the massacre had reached the Vatican, a partial Jubilec, with its special devotions and indulgences, was celebrated in the Eternal City. Lord Acton, and the enemies of the Holy See, assure us that this Jubilee was granted by the Pope that the faithful might return thanks to God "for the murder of the Huguenots," and implore courage and strength for Charles IX. to complete his good work "by exterminating all the heretics that yet remained in the kingdom." (Lord Acton's Letters to *The Times*, November, 1874.) You will deem it unnecessary for me to remark that no such motives were assigned by His Holiness for this Jubilee, and, indeed, no contemporary document, or other ancient record, has dared to impute such motives to the Pontiff. The whole statement rests on an artful interpretation of a passage in the Jubilee Bull, which invites the faithful "to return thanks for the happy victory of the King of France over his Huguenot enemies, and to pray that these most noxious heresies may be entirely banished from that kingdom, once so renowned for its religion and piety."[1] It needs no great acumen to understand how great a difference there exists between "extirpating the heretics" and "banishing heresy" from a Catholic kingdom: the latter alone, and not the former, was

[1] "Ad regnumantea religiosissimum a pestilentissimis haeresibus omnino expurgandum."

commended to the prayers of the Roman citizens. It is fortunate, however, in the interests of historic truth, that one authentic document has come down to us connected with this Jubilee, which of itself suffices to remove all doubts as to the purposes for which it was granted. This is the contemporary Diary of Francesco Mucanzio, Pontifical Master of Ceremonies (*Diaria Francisci Mucantii Caeremoniarum magistri.* MS. preserved in the Archives of the Gesú, Rome), who registered, day by day, the religious ceremonies as they were celebrated in Rome, in 1572. He informs us that on the 17th September, in that year, the Jubilee began, which was ordered by His Holiness "for the conversion of heretics, the success of the Christian armies against the Turks, and the election of a king for Poland.[1] Thus it was not to rejoice in the murder of the Huguenots that the Jubilee was celebrated, but to promote three great religious purposes dear to the heart of Pope Gregory XIII. The Turks, notwithstanding the overthrow at Lepanto, were at that moment menacing a new invasion of Europe; whilst the election of a king of Poland was to take place in a few weeks, and from it, too, depended in a manner, the fate of all Catholic Europe: no wonder, indeed, that the Pope should ask the faithful to redouble their fervent prayers in such a crisis of society as of the Church. Moreover, it was hoped that as the Huguenots relied on the arm of the flesh for their religious tenets, their conversion might result from their recent humilation, and, therefore, His Holiness makes this, too, one of the great intentions of the Jubilee, and urges the citizens to offer their prayers that God would look

[1] See *Revue des Questions Hist.*, 2[de] livrais. page 381. The Papal Medal, which was struck on this occasion, bears the inscription: "In perduellos iterumque nova molientes haereticos." (Bonanni, *Numismata Pontificia*, i. 336.) Thus it was not the murder of the heretics that was commemorated, but the triumph of the King over his rebel subjects. Capefigue mentions another medal struck at this time in France, with the French motto: "Charles IX. dompteur des rebelles." (Chap. xliv.)

down in mercy upon France, and restore its straying sons to the one true fold.

From all this it must be sufficiently manifest that it is a vile calumny against the Roman Pontiffs to assert that the Papal Court and the people of Rome rejoiced at the cold-blooded assassination of the French Huguenots.

4. There is one other matter which merits our attention before we close: it is the principle which guided the conduct, and subsequently became the plea of justification, of the French monarch, Charles IX. This was none other than the principle of assassination legalized by the command of the sovereign. At the present day, as in the ages of Faith, the bare mention of such a principle suffices to excite a thrill of horror, but it was far otherwise in the first century of the Reformed creed, when the influence of religion was weakened, and passion and frenzy obtained full mastery over men's minds.

It is not too much to say that that foul principle of assassination had become a recognised rule of the degenerate diplomacy and corrupt court life of the period of which we treat; a principle, moreover, of which the Huguenots of France and the Protestants of England had but little reason to complain. Indeed, as well in theory as in practice, it was adopted by the Huguenots themselves, and throughout all Europe none were found to reject the assassin's ministry save those who, not merely in fancy and in name, but in reality and in truth, were loyal children of the Catholic Church. But before I enter on this subject I wish to cite for you the words of Baron Hubner, who, in our own days, has been distinguished alike as historian and diplomatist. In his *Life of Sixtus the Fifth* he thus writes: "What would now-a-days be said of a government which would allow a man's life to be taken without having him previously tried? It would be universally condemned; or rather such a contingency is no longer possible. It was not always so. Even in the time of the Guises, the sovereign was looked upon as the supreme judge, who, it is true, had bequeathed his rights to competent tribunals, but who could dispense with their aid whenever the public safety, or that of his own person, seemed to require it. (Hubner, *Sixtus the Fifth*, i. 22. English edition. London, 1872.)

When the Duke of Guise, the leader of the French Catholics, had taken the city of Rouen, in 1562, a Huguenot gentleman attempted to stab him with a poignard, but was taken in the act. In excuse he pleaded that he made this attempt, not through any personal spite, but solely in the interests of his religion. "Well," replied the Duke, "I will show you that my religion is more generous than yours. You say that your religion bids you kill me, who have done you no harm; now mine commands me to pardon you, who have sought my life:" and so saying, he set him at liberty. Two months later this great Catholic leader was assassinated by another Huguenot, named Poltrot, who, before execution, avowed that he was employed to perpetrate this deed of blood by the Admiral Coligny,[1] and that the Calvinist preacher, Beza, had commanded and encouraged him in its execution. Sismondi is forced to admit this fact, but he seeks to exculpate the great Calvinist Reformer by the principles and maxims of the age.[2]

[1] Trognon, though an admirer of Coligny, writes that "la haute raison de Coligny était à ce point troublée par le fanatisme, qu'elle ne désavouait point la doctrine perverse du tyrannicide." (*Histoire de France*, tom. iii., page 280.) Martin makes a somewhat similar apology for Coligny: "Coligny n'avait pas suggéré le fait consommé, mais il croyait à la legitimité du tyrannicide inspiré par le ciel." (*Histoire de France*, ix. 154.) Lavallee, however, writes: "Coligny laissa comprendre qu'il connaissait les menaces de Poltrot, qu'il l'avait mis à même de les accomplir et qu'il n'en ressentait pas d'horreur." (*Histoire des Français*, i. 570; *Revue des Questions Hist.*, i. 35.)

[2] White, *Massacre*, page 228, contends that the statement of Poltrot in regard to Coligny was made in the hope of pardon; but admits "that Coligny assented, if he did not consent, to the crime." He adds: "This may diminish the lofty moral pedestal on which some writers have placed

The next Duke of Guise, who also was the life and soul of the Catholic party, met his death, in like manner, at the hands of an assassin. We have seen that in the terrible deeds of the St. Bartholomew massacre, the Duke of Anjou, brother of the King, took a leading part. He subsequently mounted the French throne as Henry III., and, jealous of the popularity of the Duke of Guise, and the success which everywhere attended his arms, caused him to be assassinated, together with his brother, the Cardinal de Guise. He even wrote to his ambassador in Rome to justify the horrid deed, declaring that it was "not only lawful but pious, seeing that it had for its object to insure the peace of the public by the death of a private individual." (Letter of Henry to the French ambassador, Pisany, December 24th, 1588.) Seven months later, Henry III. was himself assassinated, and Henry of Navarre, the hope of the Huguenots, became Sovereign of France.

Neither can it be said that the English reformed courtiers were strangers to the use of the secret dagger, and to the principle of assassination. When the youthful Reginald Poole, having completed his studies on the Continent, paid his first visit to his near kinsman, Henry VIII., and when the hum of flattery was heard around him on every side, and the highest dignities of the Church of England were marked out as already within his reach, Thomas Cromwell, taking him aside, presented to him a copy of the *Prince of Macchiavelli*, telling him that that precious work should be his guide and text-book if he aspired to be a true servant of his royal master.[1] Happy for Poole that he chose higher

the Protestant hero; but he was a man, and had all a man's failings. . . The murder was openly defended (by the Huguenots), Poltrot was compared to Judith, and ballads were sung in his praise." The *Histoire de l'Eglise Gallicane*, liv. xix., page 956, proves that Poltrot was the agent of the whole Huguenot body.

[1] This fact is mentioned by Cardinal Quirini in the preface to his noble edition of the Letters of Cardinal Poole.

and nobler principles! But yet Cromwell had stated the truth; for Macchiavelli's teaching was adopted as the rule of the English Court, and marked out the only high road to honours and emoluments in Church and State. I need not add, that the principle of assassination, when judged expedient by the royal authority, is broadly and openly justified in the pages of the unprincipled Florentine. Let us see, however, how his teaching was put into practice by the courtiers of Elizabeth at the period of which we treat.

A few days after the St. Bartholomew massacre, the English ambassador, Walsingham, wrote to Queen Elizabeth, suggesting that Mary Queen of Scots, now a prisoner in her hands, should be privately assassinated: "Certain unsound members," he says, "must be cut off; for violent diseases will have violent remedies." The Bishop of London, Edwin Sandys, added his prayer to Burleigh in the same strain: "Furthwith to cutte off the Scottish quene's heade: *ipsa est nostri fundi calamitas.*" (Ellis, *Original Letters*, 2nd series, iii. 25.) Nor did her Majesty lend an unwilling ear to these suggestions. She, without delay, sent her trusty agent, Killigrew, into Scotland, ostensibly to compose some differences that had arisen between the Regent and the Earl of Huntley; but in reality, as the State papers have placed beyond the reach of doubt, to make arrangements with the reformed leaders in Scotland for the assassination of her august prisoner, Mary Stuart.[1]

[1] "Of Marr, the Regent, it has been said, that he was too honest a man to pander to the jealousies or resentments of the English queen, and resolutely turned a deaf ear to the hints and suggestion of the envoy. Recent discoveries have, however, proved that, if at the first he affected to look upon the project as attended with difficulty and peril, he afterwards entered into it most cordially, and sought to drive a profitable bargain with Elizabeth." (Lingard, vi. 140.) Full details of this assassination policy of the English Court, in reference to the Queen of Scots, will be found in *The Letter-Books of Sir Amias Poulet*, edited by Rev. J. Morris, S. J. London, 1874.

The same principle held a prominent place in the policy of Elizabeth in regard to Ireland; and every student of our history is now familiar with the repeated efforts of assassination directed against Florence MacCarthy, Hugh O'Neil, and the other Irish chieftains. The State papers make strange revelations on this head. At one time we have an Englishman, in the pay of Sir Robert Cecyl, obtaining letters of introduction to the leading Jesuits in Ireland, and then, with their commendation, enrolling himself in the Order of St. Francis; and all this that he might "get an opportunity of poisoning Hugh O'Neil." Another time, with the sanction and approval of her Majesty's Council, an assassin receives £10 from the Lord President of Munster, and, being "furnished with a pistol out of the Queen's store, loaded by an experienced hand," sets out to murder John Fitz-Thomas, brother of the Earl of Desmond. Again, we have John Annyas set free from London Tower, and starting for Cork, with letters from her Majesty's ministers, to administer poison to Florence MacCarthy.[1] And so in innumerable other cases. Indeed, the history of the policy of the English Court towards Ireland, throughout the long reign of Elizabeth, may be traced in an endless series of such attempts at assassination and other legalized crimes of the deepest dye.

What a contrast is presented to us by the policy of the successor of St. Peter, who rules on the Seven Hills! Whilst Elizabeth was employing all her power against the Church of God, both at home and on the Continent, the agents of some great European powers suggested to the then reigning Pontiff, Sixtus V., that the hand of the assassin would, without trouble, rid the world of such a monster; but he

[1] Extracts from the State Papers and other contemporary records, to illustrate the examples given in the text, will be found in the *Life and Letters of Florence MacCarthy Mor*, by Daniel MacCarthy, pages 286-307. London, 1867.

indignantly spurned the suggestion: "He told Pisany," thus writes Baron Hubner, "that several times it had been proposed to him to assassinate her, and for a small sum; but that he had rejected such proposals, detesting and abhorring means of that kind." (Hubner, *Life of Sixtus V.*, vol. i., page 350.)

5. And here a few words may not be out of place as to a calumnious attack which has been rashly made against the memory of another great and holy Pope, St. Pius V. Lord Acton does not hesitate to write of that illustrious Pontiff: "Pius V., the only Pope who has been proclaimed a saint for many centuries, having deprived Elizabeth, commissioned an assassin to take her life." He was asked to assign his proofs for such an accusation, and, in his reply, he gives the case of Ridolfi as his only proof. Now, the whole case of Ridolfi has been a long time well known to English historians; and yet not one of them has ever dared to ground on it such a charge against the cherished memory of Pope St. Pius V. We are told that even Elizabeth esteemed the virtues of that sainted Pontiff, and, when he issued the sentence of excommunication against her, she stated that her only regret was, that it had proceeded from a Pope of such well-known piety as Pius V. (Bechetti, xii. 108.)

Ridolfi was an Italian merchant resident in London. The friends of Mary Stuart and the Duke of Norfolk chose him as their agent o solicit aid in men and arms from the Pope and from Philip II. of Spain. His chief commission, addressed to the Pope and the King of Spain, was signed by the Duke of Norfolk, a Protestant nobleman, then a prisoner in the Tower. It is published by Labanoff, and has not one syllable that even indirectly could be supposed to hint at the assassination of the Queen. Ridolfi was coldly received in Rome. (Lingard, vi. 128.) The Pontiff could not hold out a promise of the desired aid; but he wrote to Philip II., commending to his protection this mission of Ridolfi. The

King of Spain smiled at the idea of such a commission being addressed to him by one who was a prisoner in Elizabeth's hands, and summoned Ridolfi to explain in person, before his Council, what hopes could be entertained of success, and how far the friends of the Duke of Norfolk would be able, on their part, to co-operate with the troops of Spain. Ridolfi was so vague and extravagant in his statements, that Philip at once supposed him to be a secret agent of Elizabeth. It was on this occasion that Ridolfi spoke of a project, which had been suggested by some friends of the imprisoned nobleman, to seize on the person of the Queen, and to keep her as a hostage for the safety of Mary Stuart, and, if necessary, to put her to death. So manifest was it, however, that this formed no part of his commission, that, although the details of Ridolfi's interview with the Spanish Council were quickly conveyed to Elizabeth, yet, in the subsequent trials of the Duke of Norfolk and the Queen of Scots, and so many of her friends, no such commission was referred to, and no such project of assassination was laid to their charge. I will not detain you with further details on this subject. Suffice it to say, that in all the documents connected with Ridolfi, whether in the British Museum or at Simancas, there is not the slightest trace of any rumour or suspicion that the Pope had approved of a scheme of assassination—no hint is even given that Ridolfi was himself an intended assassin; and much less is there to be found the shadow of a suspicion that "St. Pius V. commissioned an assassin to take the life of Elizabeth."

6. There are many other points on which it would be interesting to dwell in connection with the St. Bartholomew massacre. But it is time that I should bring this tedious paper to a close; and I trust that enough has been said to convince you that that terrible deed of blood was not decreed by the Holy See, nor carried into execution in the interests of the Catholic Church. The punishment which

fell upon the Huguenots was a just retribution for their long career of conspiracies and assassinations; but it proceeded solely from the intrigues of the Court, and was conformable to the false maxims of Protestant and Macchiavellian policy which then prevailed.

And now, in conclusion, allow me to congratulate you on the ardour with which you have entered on the historical pursuits of your society, from which I trust that each one of you will derive the most abundant fruits. For three centuries, history in these countries has been little more than a conspiracy against truth. You will, therefore, need great caution in accepting the statements of English historians, even when their statements seem to be only remotely connected with the Catholic Church; but much more so when they openly assail those illustrious Pontiffs who steered the bark of Peter amid the shoals and quicksands of the heresies that arose in the sixteenth century. Listen not to their assertions until you have closely examined them in the light of authentic contemporary records; and even when supposed documents are presented to you, as sometimes happens, replete with calumnies against the Holy See, be still upon your guard; accept them not on the word of anyone, no matter how eminent may be his name, but test their genuineness, and apply to them the critical rules which must be our guide in historical research. Take one instance to justify this counsel which I have given you. There was a class of men in the Italian schools of the seventeenth century, who being enamoured of the latitudinarian maxims which sprang up in the reformed sects secretly bid adieu to morality and divine Faith, and became in their turn active propagandists of irreligion. One of the arts to which they had recourse in order to discredit the Holy See, which they instinctively recognised as the mainstay of religion and social order, was the following:—They invented a number of Papal briefs and official despatches, in which the style of the supposed authors was carefully imitated, and dates were attached corresponding to the matters of which they treated. In these documents, copies of which were industriously circulated in the various schools of Italy and Germany, lying tales were told which had no foundation except in the wicked fancy of these propagandists of impiety; and it is to such sources that we may trace most of the charges which are repeated at the present day against some of our greatest Pontiffs. It is on such documents that the enemies of the Holy See rely; and yet, as a German historian, to whom I have already more than once referred, describes them, "they present to us mere idle fables which bear the print of vulgar ignorance, and resemble the popular tales which are generally told in Germany at country fairs; but notwithstanding their absurdity, eminent authors have actually reproduced them." (Hubner, *Life of Sixtus V.*, vol. i., page 15.)

VIII.

RELIGION IN EDUCATION.

(*Address delivered in Wellington, New Zealand, on the occasion of the Solemn Blessing of St. Patrick's College, Sunday,* 21*st of February,* 1886.)

St. Patrick's College is to-day inaugurated with solemn religious ceremony, and with the blessing of Holy Church; and it is befitting that it should be so. Within its hallowed walls, religion shall go hand in hand with science, and the youth of New Zealand, with its bright genius and quick intellect, shall here be trained to the highest pursuits of secular learning. But, at the same time, the heart shall be moulded to virtue, and disciplined in the exercises of piety, and inspired with the heroism of Christian life. There is no work more noble, more important, more arduous than that which Christian education proposes to itself; there is none other on which, in so great a measure, the happiness and the destiny of individuals and of the State depend. It proposes to itself to develop, and adorn, and perfect every noblest faculty of man. If we look to the material universe around us, we see it arrayed in a thousand forms of loveliness; rich with exhaustless treasures; equipped with wondrous forces; armed with giant strength. And yet all this material universe has been created for man; all its wealth, and power, and beauty are subservient to his eternal

Church. She is the depository of Christian truth. She it is who for eighteen centuries has enlightened the world's darkness, and purified the world's corruption. She alone has preserved to man the blessings and consolations and strengthening graces of the Christian religion, and she has covered the earth with the fruits of civilization, learning, and holiness. Be not ashamed of the Catholic Church. She is the watchful guardian of the inspired writings. Every inquiring mind to-day must repeat what St. Augustine said of old: "If I receive the Gospel of Christ, it is through the authoritative teaching of the Catholic Church." She alone fulfils the prophet's words: "From the rising of the sun to the going down, My Name is great among the nations; and in every place there is sacrifice, and there is offered to My Name a clean oblation; for My Name is great among the nations, saith the Lord of Hosts." Amid the shifting scenes of empires and nations which the history of this world presents, she stands forth resplendent by her faith and works. Her devoted sons have never ceased to rank among the foremost in every ennobling pursuit of charity or science. In her pure atmosphere the truths of philosophy and the discoveries of the human mind have been preserved incorruptible and unshaken. If science and letters and the fine arts adorn the world to-day, the world is indebted for it to the Catholic Church. All the great languages of civilized nations have been matured under her fostering care—the French with its grace and delicacy, the Italian with its softness and sweetness, the Spanish with its stern dignity, the English and German with their strength and richness. The Catholic Church is "the city of the great King." (Psalm xlvii.) Around her divinely strengthened bulwarks the powers and the passions of this world have ever surged in vain. Wicked men, with words of blasphemy upon their lips, and with the hatred begotten of apostacy in their hearts, have never ceased to devise vain things against her;

but "He who sitteth in the heavens hath mocked them, the Lord hath derided them," and the promise made by God has been fulfilled in her: "No weapon forged against thee shall prosper, and every tongue that resisteth thee in judgment thou shalt condemn." (Isaiah liv.) It was said of old that nothing greater, nothing wiser, nothing more glorious than Imperial Rome, had ever arisen upon earth; and yet, like all other human things, Rome, with the accumulated glories of ancient civilization, was swept away, and so complete was its destruction that for a time the very ruins of the capital of the pagan world were absolutely deserted:—

"Quenched is the golden statue's ray;
The breath of heaven hath swept away
What toiling earth hath piled;
Scattering wise heart and crafty hand,
As breezes strew on ocean's strand
The fabrics of a child."

Amid the universal shipwreck the Catholic Church remained unharmed; she continued to be an ark of salvation, not for the conquered only, but also for the conquerors. Every human society contains within itself the seed of corruption and the germ of ultimate decay. The Catholic Church alone has the seal of immortality upon her brow. A special Providence ever guides her in her course. She has come from God, and it is her destiny to lead men to God. She is not identified with any form of human government. She witnesses the growth and decay of empires and kingdoms and republics, and amid all their changes and vicissitudes she remains unchanged. With all the boasted progress of science in modern times, and the advancement of learning, and the deifying of material power, is the Church broken down or weakened or decaying? No; never did she stand before the world arrayed in greater moral dignity than at the present time; and never was it more manifest that every discovery in the pursuit of truth can only serve to add radiance to her earthly crown, vigour to her strength, beauty to her comeliness. Be not ashamed of the Catholic Church. She alone displays to the world that peerless unity with which Christ endowed His Church. Her children are not tossed about by every wind of false doctrine. They hold the same doctrines of divine faith, and obey the same spiritual authority, on the Rocky Mountains and in Vienna, London and in Rome, in the depths of China and in Sydney. Like the sun in the firmament, she diffuses throughout the world the same rays of divine truth, and imparts the blessings of heaven to all who are gathered within her saving fold. She alone has been clothed with holiness, as with the golden garment of her betrothal, by her Divine Spouse. All the saints have been her children. Within her wide domain the heavenly waters of charity and mercy have never ceased to flow. Those who are outside her fold dig for themselves cisterns, but they are broken cisterns that cannot contain the life-giving waters of redemption. She alone leads us back to the Apostolic age, and unites the faithful of to-day with the Rock of Peter, upon which our Blessed Lord built His Church. For more than 1,800 years her Pontiffs have succeeded to Pontiffs, teaching with an authority derived not from earth but from heaven, fearlessly rebuking a sinful world, and inheriting the spiritual power and privileges of the first Vicar of Christ. She saw the commencement of all the governments and sects that now exist in the world. She shall see the end of them all. She was great and respected before the Saxon had set foot in Britain. She will be found flourishing in undiminished vigour when the sun shall have set on this greatest of the world's empires. She alone is truly Catholic. Armed with a divine commission, she teaches all nations. She goes forth "into the world, and preaches the Gospel" to every tribe and every tongue. The sun never sets on her widespread spiritual dominion. She is literally everywhere. At the present day she numbers more than 200,000,000, who receive the lessons of divine truth from her lips. You will meet with her not only in every civilized land, but at the remotest sources of the Amazon, the Mississippi, and the St. Lawrence; among the most savage tribes of South America; on the borders of the Caspian Sea; in the forests of India; on the burning sands of Africa; in Siberia and China and Japan; everywhere you will meet with her; everywhere you will find her teaching the truths of eternal life; everywhere leading souls to God; everywhere bearing imprinted upon her hallowed brow the seal of heaven as the bride of the Lamb.

Your society is Catholic, and I have told you not to be ashamed of the Catholic Church. But, again, your society is Hibernian, and I must add, be not ashamed of Ireland. That land of the west is fair, indeed, among the nations. Nature, spreading out her richest gifts with no stinted hand, has given to her noble harbours, majestic rivers, a genial soil. Erin's hills are green, her fields luxuriant, her climate mild. Her people are wise, her daughters are her pride, her sons are brave. Her music, so sad, yet so sweet, breathes a melody peculiarly its own. Love of country is the birthright of her children, a patriotism which time cannot chill, and which seems only to gain strength by the distance from the land which they love. Be not ashamed of Ireland. In the history of the Church there is, perhaps, no picture more beautiful than that which Ireland's early ages present. Her schools, her sanctuaries, her monasteries were the pride of Europe—the joy of Christendom. Pure as the refreshing waters of her holy wells was the faith and the Christian life of her children. The prophetic words of Isaiah were fulfilled in her: "The land that was desolate and impassable was glad, and the wilderness rejoiced and flourished like the lily; then did it bud forth and blossom, and rejoice with joy and praise." Her sons went forth, with a heroism which has never been surpassed, to renew in the airest countries of Europe that Christian civilization which iad been swept away by the barbarian invasions as by the empests of a raging sea. If the ruthless barbarian was changed into a Christian man; if the foundations were laid of that grand civilization which for centuries diffused over the airest regions of Europe the blessings of peace and piety, of rue charity and religion, it was mainly the work of Irishmen. Their names are to this day cherished in Germany and France, throughout Belgium and Switzerland. Churches enshrine their relics on the banks of the Danube and the Rhine. Pilgrims flock to their sanctuaries in the depths of the Black Forest, and in the silent recesses of he Alps. Even the slopes of the Apennines, and the olive groves of Taranto, and the vine-clad hills of Florence esound to the praises of the sainted missionaries from Erin. Nor was the sister island less indebted to her heroic ons. When the natives of Caledonia were as yet unenlightened by the rays of divine faith, it was St. Columba and his brother missionaries that gave them the rudiments of Christian civilization and religion. When the Saxons fell away from the teaching of St. Augustine of Canterbury, it was Aidan and his associates from the Island of Saints that enewed amongst them the light and life of divine truth and grace. Centuries rolled on, lawless bands of seafaring mail-clad marauders overran England and a great part of Northern Europe. They failed to conquer Ireland, for her ons have ever proved themselves as brave in the battle-field as they were heroic in their piety. Again, for three centuries, heresy left nothing undone to crush out the religious belief of her people. This was, indeed, a season of dreary winter, a blighting and withering winter, a winter of ruins, a winter of tempests, a winter of tears. And yet the faith did not die out. Other nations more favoured with the wealth and power of this world bent before the storm. But in Ireland it was not so. The same heroism that guarded her shores against the Danes guarded the hearts of he children against the assaults of heresy. The more violentl the tempest raged, the deeper did the sacred tree of divin faith strike its roots in the affections of her sons, and Eri won from Christendom a peerless aureola as the marty nation of Holy Church. Be not ashamed of Ireland. Th winter is already passed, the spring-time is come. Th sunshine and the smile of summer is already upon th green fields of Erin. Addressing you on the great Easte festival, may I not recall to mind that our Divine Lord la three days entombed in the sepulchre and arose agai glorious and immortal? So does the Church of Christ after being hidden in the recesses of the bogs and mountain of Ireland for three centuries, come forth in our days renewed in life and vigour and arrayed in the comeliness o her early years to partake of the glory and triumph of th Resurrection. This glorious victory is given to Ireland t reward the fidelity of her people. Look through the annal of the Church; you will find no other people more full Christian, more truly Catholic. Amid every trial thei fidelity to religion has been inviolate and unstained. He inheritance of sorrow only serves to enhance the merit o her spiritual triumphs. But if bright and peerless is thi aureola of Ireland's faith to-day, we must never forget tha we are indebted for it to the heroism with which our father sustained the unparalleled sorrows and sufferings of a prolonged martyrdom. But it is not the Church alone i Ireland that has arisen from the tomb. Her national spirit too, has been revived, and Ireland stands before the nation of Christendom to-day arrayed in a moral force agains which the enemies of justice struggle in vain, and assertin her national rights, in the calm, dispassionate accents o freedom, and demanding constitutional independence as he inalienable birthright. At no distant day the great statesman who now holds the helm of empire will, by grantin this legislative independence, add another to the unfading laurels which he has already won in dealing justice to the Irish people; and this legislative freedom will be the crowning triumph of the peaceable struggle for justice which Ireland's sons, through good report and evil report, have carried on for centuries. We hail with joy the rising sun of this new era of prosperity and peace; its rays shall soon bathe with glory the emerald gem of the western world, and, reflected upon many distant lands, shall bring consolation and gladness to the sea-divided sons of Ireland. And here I may be permitted to adopt the words with which the immortal leader of the Irish people (O'Connell) congratulated his countrymen on their first great victory of Emancipation:—"The men of Erin know that the only basis of liberty is religion; they have triumphed, because the voice they raised on behalf of their country had first raised itself in prayer to God. Songs of liberty may now make themselves heard throughout our country, whose sound will travel through hill and valley with voice of thunder, and be wafted along the course of the rivers and streams, proclaiming far and wide that Ireland at length is free." Go on, then, gentlemen, pursue with courage and perseverance and earnestness the course of beneficence on which you have entered. Let religion and virtue guide your steps. Fear not those enemies who here, as in the home countries, persistently heap obloquy on everything that is just and honourable and good. Combat them only by the weapons of forbearance and charity, for the golden words of St. John Chrysostom should never be forgotten: "Christians are not to overthrow error by the use of violence or constraint, but by persuasion. instruction, love, and charity."

VII.

CATHOLICS AND IRISHMEN.

(*Reply to an Address presented by the Hibernian Catholic Society, in Sydney, on Easter Sunday*, 1886.)

I REJOICE to be amongst you this afternoon, devoted as you are to works of beneficence and religion, and it affords me sincerest pleasure to receive from you this beautiful address, expressive of filial affection and replete with sentiments every way worthy of your society. At the present day an immense energy is displayed throughout the world in working out schemes of pleasure or industry or commerce by thousands of associations and societies and syndicates, with every variety of means and every variety of purpose. The Church rejoices when she, too, sees her sons linked together in hallowed associations, not wasting their energies on mere trifles of the passing hour, nor restricting them to purposes which cannot rise above this earth, but in a spirit of Christian philanthropy directing them to the highest aims, purified, elevated, ennobled, and sanctified by religion. Such is your Catholic Hibernian Society, and by continuing loyal to the spirit of its rules you will very soon find by experience that it will have contributed not a little to bring manifold blessings to your families, and to make yourselves such as the Church wishes you to be—thoroughly religious, honest, intelligent, earnest, and practical Christian men. Your society is Catholic. Be not ashamed of the Catholic destiny, and fade into insignificance compared with his exalted dignity. In man himself the perishable material frame is controlled by the immortal soul, which, with its imperial faculties of intellect and will, soars above all earthly things, and yearns to possess God, the Supreme Truth, the Sovereign Good. Christian education strengthens, purifies, and disciplines these noble faculties, that they may attain their end; and leads them to the source of truth and goodness, that they may attain their perfection by knowing, loving, and serving God, and may be eternally happy hereafter in the possession and enjoyment of His blessedness. It is an essentially imperfect education that proposes merely to develop one faculty of man. If we suppose the body to be educated at the expense of the intellect and will, the result must be, as too often we see in the world around us, something little better than a mere lump of animated clay. If the intellect is developed at the expense of the moral and religious sentiments, you impart power to man without the virtue which is necessary to wield it. On the other hand, educate only the moral faculty, and you deprive virtue of her noblest ally. Religion embraces all the faculties, and becomes interwoven with the whole education of man. Surely no one will deny that the sciences, like the other gifts of God, may be distorted to purposes of evil with which they have no connection, and for which they were never intended. Do we not every day see, in the works of poetry and fiction, that imagination and literature may minister to sensuality; and do we not find too often that even philosophical inquiry may be degraded into a weapon of infidelity to war against truth? Science does not even pretend to control the passions. It presents no guarantee for conscience or for sanctity. The profligate and the heartless criminal may be an adept in some particular science, and only becomes the more insidious, the more dangerous, by his accomplishment, and the attractiveness which it imparts.

And here I may be permitted to use the words of an illustrious writer of our own times: "Quarry the granite rock, or moor the vessel with a thread of silk, then may you hope, with such keen and delicate instruments as human knowledge and human reason, to contend against these giants, the passion and the pride of man." St. Paul tells us to put on the armour of God, that, guarded by the sword of the spirit, the helmet of salvation, the breastplate of justice, the shield of faith, we may combat against the principalities and rulers of the darkness, who wage war against Christ. The secularist school will have nothing of this. It cultivates the intellect, but decries the cultivation of the will; for it knows too well that the human will, when trained to piety and disciplined in the practice of virtue, becomes docile to God's holy law, and obedient to the teaching of the Gospel. But in true Christian education, every ennobling pursuit of man is quickened and sanctified by religion. The holy Sacraments impart to him sacramental grace. Faith, hope, and charity lend him their safe guidance and their strengthening influences. Science enlightened by faith, the laws inspired by charity, the arts purified with a divine beauty, invest society with divine beauty, impart true dignity to man, and lead him onward to his eternal destiny. Take away Christian faith from philosophy, Christian worship from the fine arts, Christian morality from the institutions of the Civil State—what will remain but paganism in its most repulsive form; that paganism which, in Imperial Rome, crushed out all liberty of conscience and all civil liberty, and which deified the imperial ruler till his mere will became the source of law, and despotism and the wildest passions became the only virtues. And in this great question of education may we not take a lesson from those who in our own day assail the Church, whose aim is the overthrow of social order and the destruction of all religion. It is no longer this or that doctrine of divine faith that they assail. The teaching of the Church has long ago been placed in too clear a light; and every attack that has been made against it has only served to bring its heavenly origin, its sublime perfection, into bolder relief. Nowadays, the enemy gathers all his strength to get hold of the Christian school Against this outer bulwark of truth he directs all his combined and persistent assaults. Must it not be our endeavour to leave nothing undone, that the fortress which is thus assailed may be made impregnable, and that the banner of truth, which provokes such enmity, and which hitherto under the Southern Cross has been unfurled in triumph, may never be lowered in defeat? It is not the first time in the history of the Church that her enemies have endeavoured to get hold of the education of Christian children. Julian the Apostate was the last of the Roman emperors to wage an open war against the Christian name. He made use of every engine that the imperial power could command, or that human philosophy could suggest, to achieve the triumph of paganism; but his main effort, and that on which he and his courtiers most relied for success, was the exile of the Christian teachers from the schools. His overthrow by an enemy whom he despised, and his death on the battle-field, baffled his designs. Towards the close of the last century, the infidels of Europe, in their combined deadly assault against religion, again took the school for their watchword, and made it their chief effort to get hold of the education of youth. In too many districts of France their efforts, alas! were crowned with success. D'Alembert, writing to Voltaire, had said: "Let your thoughts, above all things, be turned to the enlightenment of youth." Voltaire replies: "The light is spread to such a degree that the great convulsion must speedily spring to birth. Happy the young men of our age, who will witness grand things." What was the result? Very soon, under the name of liberty, we see the guillotine, and tyranny, and libertinism triumphant in France; whilst the profane adoration of the worst and vilest passions took the place of the worship of God. The same result would very soon ensue were we in these flourishing colonies to fling aside the traditions of our fathers, and banish Christian principles from our schools. However, it is not only in the interests of religion, but also in the interests of true science and human knowledge, that we protest against the secularist system being imposed upon us.

Let us see how the secularist system shall deal with history. History, indeed, records the achievements of man and the progress of our race; but it is no less a record of God's dealings with us. His providence ever guides us in our onward course; and, no matter what vain things we may devise, He pursues His own divine plans, and our free-will is made subservient to the fulfilment of His eternal design. When treating with the first century of our era, will the secularist omit all mention of our Blessed Lord? And yet the Redeemer is the one source of truth and of all the spiritual light which, for eighteen centuries, has brought blessings to men. Again, when treating of the Middle Ages, and when we see the Moslem empire at the zenith of its power, are we to forget that it threatened to bind Europe as well as Asia in the fetters of barbarism, and that it was reserved for the Sovereign Pontiffs to rally the Christian knights of Europe around the banner of the Cross, and to speed them on to victory in the cause of civilization? We glance at the clouds which overshadowed Europe in the thirteenth century. We see in many places the people oppressed, the nations in sorrow, the Church in tears. Heresy is triumphant; princes are in arms against religion; the very pillars of the house of God appear to be shaken. Are we to omit that, when the storm is at its height, one champion of the Cross was summoned from Castile; another came forth from Umbria; and that St. Dominick and St. Francis—not by the arms of this world, but by prayer and charity—combatted the many enemies of truth, and triumphed? In the sixteenth century, is no mention to be made of St. Francis Xavier? He laboured as an apostle at Goa, in Malacca, all through India and Japan; he established the faith in fifty-two kingdoms; he baptized, with his own hand, 1,000,000 of pagans. A true Christian hero, in ten years of missionary toil, he won more souls to Christ than were torn from the fold by all the assaults of heresy. We come to the next century. Seven civil wars have rendered desolate some of the fairest territories of France. Her cities are in ruin; her princes—at one time Huguenots, at another time Catholics—no longer follow the guidance of Christian principles; famine and pestilence, chastisements from Heaven, have swept over the land. One man is raised up by God to be the counsellor of princes and people—the father of the afflicted and the orphans. But the name of St. Vincent de Paul cannot appear in the pages of secularist history; and yet, even the infidels of the last century allotted him a prominent place in the Pantheon of the illustrious citizens of France. His name shall long be inscribed on the hearts of his countrymen, and it shall ever live in the manifold institutions of charity and beneficence of which he was the founder. So true it is that, in the matter of history, secularist education is only half education, with the best half left out.

Even the study of geography must be out of place in the secularist schools. Are we to cancel from its pages the names of Bethlehem and the Jordan, of Jerusalem and Rome? But the science of geography is not a mere list of the names of the rivers and cities, of mountains and plains. Geography has justly been styled the twin-sister of history; for it, too, must mark the growth of nations and trace the migration of the various races. For instance, it is not enough to say that Latium marks a territory of a few square miles in Central Italy. On that favoured land, palimpsest-like, has been written the history of the modern world. If it became the seat of universal empire, it was that it might prepare the way for the Gospel of Christ. There the Cross, appearing in the heavens, summoned Constantine to victory—the victory of Christian truth—the triumph of the Christian name. There the golden house of Nero has crumbled to dust; whilst the throne of the Vicar of Christ remains unmoved, and the sceptre of his spiritual rule extends to nations and peoples who were unknown to Imperial Rome.

What shall I say of the studies of antiquities, so prized at the present day? If we examine the hieroglyphics of the Egyptian monuments, we must not find there the facts that confirm the Scripture narrative; if we read the inscriptions of Assyria, we must close our eyes to the fulfilment of the prophecies which they record. But I would ask the antiquarian student, who accompanies me to the Arran Islands, off the Irish coast, or to Clonmacnoise, Tullaherin, and Glendalough, shall he be guided in his visit by the cold maxims of secularist education? Must he look with indifference at the stately round towers, the crumbling ruins, the scattered monuments of former days? Should he not rather go back in thought to the early ages of our faith, and commune in spirit with the great saints who adorned Ireland by their learning and sanctity, and won for her peerless fame as the Island of Saints and Sages? Will he not make inquiry as to the schools which attracted the holiest and the best from England and Gaul, and the remotest countries of the then-known world, hastening thither to satiate their thirst at the fountains of piety and knowledge; and will he not cherish the memory of the heroic men who, from these schools, as from spiritual hives, went forth, in countless swarms, as missionaries and apostles, to evangelize the newly-formed nations of Europe, and bring the glad tidings of Redemption to the cold regions of Greenland and Iceland, and preach the faith on the banks of the Rhine, or amid the vineyards and olive-groves of Fiesole and Taranto? And shall that student be forbidden to look from the ruins before which he stands, to the scene that Ireland even now presents? Three centuries of the most bitter persecution have not deadened the heroism of her piety; the same spirit of faith that lit up the sanctuaries of old still lives through the length and breadth of the land; the same love of knowledge, the same generous devotedness of our fathers; and once more the Church is arrayed in comeliness, and shows forth a vigour, freshness, and fruitfulness which only the true faith could inspire, and which has never been surpassed in the annals of Christendom.

The Catholic Church, whilst condemning the divorce of science from religion, which secularists so persistently insist upon, has ever proved herself the devoted advocate and patron of every branch of true knowledge. Even in the early ages of persecution, she had flourishing schools at Antioch and Alexandria, in Corinth and Rome. In these schools the Catholic youth was trained in the highest paths of science, and perfected in the heroism of the saints. We read in the Life of Origen that, whilst he was as yet in the years of childhood, on seeing some martyrs borne along to the scaffold by the Alexandrian mob, he rushed forth from school, and cried aloud, that he, too, was a Christian—so heroic was his desire to be witness to the faith, heedless of the terrors of martyrdom. A writer of the sixth century states that, from the first dawn of the faith, the classic authors had been studied in the Christian schools, "for the sake of grace of elocution and the culture of the mind." So great was the encouragement of literature by the Church in the eighth century, that a contemporary writer cries out: "The muses of Greece have abandoned their native home, and have migrated to Germany and Gaul." Almost all the great universities of the Middle Ages were founded by the Sovereign Pontiffs. In Italy, not only the greater cities, such as Rome, Naples, and Bologna, had their universities, but eleven other cities had similar institutions, through the fostering care of the Popes. Throughout the various countries of Europe, no fewer than sixty-five universities were thus established by the Church before the Reformation period. Nor were the schools of those days mere empty names. The University of Bologna, in the thirteenth century, had 10,000 scholars. A single college of the Bordeaux University had 2,000 students. Oxford, in Henry III.'s time, had 30,000 names on its honoured roll. Paris, perhaps, outstripped them all. Whatever branch of knowledge, whether of law or medicine, literature or science, was known to be taught in any other university, was at once introduced into its halls; and such was the concourse of students from all parts of Europe, that "it was difficult to find lodging in the city; and very often, as the annalists attest, the number of strangers exceeded that of the inhabitants."

I have referred to the University of Oxford. Perhaps there is no university in our days that can rival it in the marvellous beauty of its gardens, churches, colleges, and other noble edifices—

. . . "Majestic towers,
Lifting their varied shapes o'er verdant bowers."

In the pre-Reformation period, its motto, *Dominus illuminatio mea*, was its proudest boast, and at no time did it win for itself a brighter name than when it reckoned among its professors and chancellors such great and holy men as St. Edmund of Canterbury, St. Richard of Winchester, and St. Thomas of Hereford. On the other hand, its fair fame became dim and was almost lost at the Reformation period. An effort, indeed, was made to revive Greek studies there, but, like plants in an ungenial soil, they quickly drooped and perished. The annalist writes that most of its halls were shut up or let to laundresses: "Where Minerva formerly sat as regent, there was nothing during all the reign of King Edward but wretched solitariness, and nothing but a dead silence prevailed." The University of Cambridge was in no less a plight. Even Latimer writes that "it would pity a man's heart to hear what I hear of Cambridge;" and he adds, that there were at that time at least 10,000 fewer scholars in the kingdom than might be found twenty years before.

Nor can this surprise us, for the heresiarchs of those days strove might and main to suppress the higher studies throughout Europe. Luther declared that the high schools "were an invention of Satan, destined to obscure Christianity, if not to overthrow it completely;" and Wickliffe affirmed that "universities, places of study, and colleges, and degrees and masterships in the same, have been introduced by vain paganism, and are only of service to the Church, as the devil is." I need scarcely remark that in the pre-Reformation period religion and education went hand in hand. In those days, before religious unity was broken, when from the altars of united Christendom there went up to God one harmonious hymn of praise, the idea of education without religion was too monstrous even to enter into the minds of men. The golden rule of those ages of truth was laid down by one of our own great masters, when he taught that "no man can be the client of science who does not love justice and truth; but there is no truth or justice without the light of the knowledge of God." The Church has never ceased to encourage the pursuit of learning. May I not name the illustrious Benedictine Order, whose countless monasteries have been in the past, as they are at the present day, homes of piety and centres of higher studies? Even the infidel historian, Gibbon, did not hesitate to write that "a single Benedictine monastery has produced more valuable works than both universities, Oxford and Cambridge." Pope Leo X., writing to Henry VIII. of England, attests, "I have always loved learned men and literature. This attraction was born with me, and it has increased with years. For I always see that those who cultivate literature are most firmly attached to the dogmas of the faith, and form the glory of the Christian Church." The great Pontiff, Benedict XIV., not only encouraged by word and example the pursuits of science and literature in Rome and throughout Italy, but inculcated the same upon all the bishops of the Church, declaring that "there is nothing which so much contributes to the welfare of a State as the right education of youth."

In our own days, the illustrious Pope who guides the helm of Holy Church, has again, by word and by deed, inculcated the same great truth, and in no schools of Europe are the higher studies pursued with greater zeal and more complete success than in the academies formed by Leo XIII. It is in accordance with the traditions of our fathers, and in the spirit of the teaching of Holy Church, that your venerable prelate has instituted the great College of St. Patrick, and has spared no expense, that even its material buildings, its noble halls, its museums, its observatory, and all its surroundings should be worthy of the noble purpose for which it is intended. Its inauguration to-day is a source of ineffable consolation to him as it is a cause of rejoicing to us all. Each collegiate institution that is opened amongst us becomes at once a centre of truth, a new focus of intellectual light, a fountain of pure, refreshing waters, and, like this College of St. Patrick, is full of brightest hope and fairest promise, not for New Zealand alone, but for all our Australian colonies. It is a hardship that such grand institutions should be left to their own unaided resources, and receive no assistance from the

State, which is so largely benefitted by them. But I have no doubt that before many years all this shall be remedied, and the cause of truth and justice shall triumph. The Catholic body shall not cease to assert its rights with firmness, and, withal, with moderation—with firmness, because as free citizens we only ask for what of right belongs to us; with moderation, because, whilst unflinchingly asserting our own inalienable rights, we must persistently refuse to have hand or part in compassing the slightest violation of the rights of others. There are many, not of our fold, who, when they dispassionately consider the case, will espouse our cause. The advantages of religious education may, for a time, be questioned; its blessings may be, for a time, denied us; but, armed with the sword of charity, and combatting in the cause of justice and truth, our victory is secure; and it shall be our prayer that ere long the honoured motto of Oxford University may be emblazoned on the banner of this privileged colony—*Dominus illuminatio mea.*

IX.

IRELAND AND AUSTRALIA.

(*Address delivered at the City Hall, Dublin, October 4th,* 1888, *when the Honorary Freedom of the City was conferred.*)

My Lord Mayor, Aldermen, and gentlemen, I beg to assure you, that I deeply appreciate the singular honour which you have shown me by granting the honorary freedom of this ancient city, and I esteem the more the privileges which you have thus been pleased to confer, in that I feel assured that at no period of Ireland's history has the municipal body of Dublin more than at the present day been the representatives of the citizens—faithfully corresponding to their wishes, using every endeavour to promote local industry, meting out even justice to all, redressing, as far as in them lie, the long-standing grievances which sorely press upon this country, and asserting by every legitimate means the rights and the liberties of the people. You invite me as Cardinal to receive this civic honour at your hands. I cannot but recall to mind those venerated men who, by their exalted virtues, in our own days, and in the ranks of the Irish Episcopate, shed lustre on the Sacred Purple, and whose names shall ever remain embalmed in the hearts of their loving spiritual children. Nor can I forget that in days of old this purple was worn by many a champion of the nation's rights, from the bright summer day when a Cardinal, at the head of the barons of England, dictated at Runnymede the abiding charter of our freedom, to that scene of gloom at Tower Hill when the sainted Fisher, by the heroism of his love for religion and country, won the bright aureola of which the Sacred Purple is the emblem.

But, as I understand it, there are two special purposes for which you have been pleased to confer upon me the honorary freedom of this city. The one is, to emphasize in a public way the marvellous union which, binding together in indissoluble bonds the Irish priests and the Irish people, achieved great triumphs in the past, and is at the present day most conspicuous among yourselves and achieves new triumphs under the illustrious successor of St. Laurence O'Toole. The other is, that I happen to be amongst you a representative of distant colonies which are dear to you, and that you desire to make known to the Australians how you lovingly appreciate the earnestness and affection with which the sea-divided Gaels under the Southern Cross have never ceased to take the liveliest interest in the struggles and victories in the cause of liberty of this their dear old motherland.

During the past few weeks I have visited many hallowed scenes of Ireland's ancient glory; many others I would have wished to visit, for there is not one of them but has its lesson to strengthen and enlighten the earnest pilgrim who has at heart his nation's welfare. What shall I say of Glendalough, with its marvellous ruins and unrivalled scenery opening wide its bosom to the rays of the rising sun—of Clonmacnoise, with its towers and churches keeping watch over the lordly Shannon—of Derry, the home of many saints, which Columbkille so loved, and whose guardian angels he saluted as being numberless like the leaves of its forest trees—of Armagh, the centre of Ireland's enlightenment and Ireland's sanctity—of Cashel of the Kings—of Kilkenny, with its many shrines—of Lismore, with its sanctuaries and fertile plains? All these hallowed spots tell us of the golden ages of Ireland's faith, when religion went hand in hand with freedom, and when, as perhaps nowhere else in Christendom, the clergy and the people were linked together by the closest bonds which nationality and religion could entwine. Seven centuries of civil strife, social disorder, and religious persecution have failed to sever these sacred bonds. Priests and people suffered the same hardships, mounted the same scaffold, went into the same exile, wore the same chains. And at the present time we cannot fail to see around us on every side that the same union of clergy and people, triumphing over every obstacle, prepares for this dear old land bright and happy days of renewed prosperity and national glory. How many churches and schools and other monuments of religion, charity, and enlightenment, homes of learning and hives of industry, do we not see arising throughout the country, rivalling in fair proportions, and number, and splendour, the most famous monuments of her ages of faith? Magnificent cathedrals have sprung up as if by magic; schools, colleges, and seminaries have been multiplied; convents, the fountains of charity and the homes of Christian peace, are to be found in every diocese, diffusing around them the blessings of heavenly mercy.

When accompanying your illustrious Archbishop in visiting some of the institutions of this great city, I could not but be filled with astonishment at the number, and variety, and perfection of the manifold works to promote education and religion which are being everywhere carried on. I do not hesitate to say that in no city of Europe have nobler monuments of religion and charity been created, or more glorious triumphs achieved during the past fifty years, than here among yourselves. Whence comes all this? It is due to the unconquerable union of the Irish priests and the Irish people, and to the strength and vitality which such a union imparts. And, looking to the future, who can doubt that this union shall triumph over every obstacle, and lead onward this nation to enjoy the pleasant fruits of abiding victory? If Ireland is to-day oppressed, and suffers more, perhaps, than at many periods of her chequered history, may we not hope and confidently expect that this is the last sacrifice which, as has so often been verified in the history of nations, Providence permits a people to endure before ushering in the dawn of lasting prosperity, and the full enjoyment of national freedom?

But the other feature of to-day's ceremony is not without significance, whilst you confer the high honour of civic freedom on an Australian Bishop, to prove that you appreciate the union and sympathy of the sea-divided Gael in Australia with those of the motherland. I am happy to bear witness that the Australian colonies are rapidly developing in fairest proportions; and I have no doubt that, at no very distant day, they shall become a great nation, and a centre of civilization for the various races of the Eastern World. The loyalty of our colonists to the throne is proverbial. Indeed, none but a fool would be disloyal amongst us. The imperial flag is the symbol of our strength and unity—of justice, prosperity, and peace. It guards our commerce, protects our industry, and is the ægis of our liberties. There is but little room for discord, or dissension, or strife, or for those irreligious follies that so often embitter social relations in the home countries. Our citizens mutually respect each other's religious convictions, and all combine to develop the resources of our adopted home, and to diffuse throughout the length and breadth of the Australian colonies, every blessing that Christian civilization can impart. All the rights and liberties which are enjoyed in the home countries, are, to the fullest extent, enjoyed by our people. We make our own laws; and there is no external power to check the golden streams of prosperity which flow from industry and peace.

It has been well said, that the acorn has found a genial soil under the Australian sky, and has in a few years expanded into a vigorous tree, spreading far and wide a pleasant and protecting shade. I do not know that on the face of the globe to-day you will find a fairer or richer land than Australia. Within fifty years, our commerce has so developed that, at the present day, it is equal to the commerce of Great Britain when her present gracious Majesty ascended the throne. In this period, our gold-mines have given more than £270,000,000 sterling to the currency of Europe. The mines of copper, iron, and tin have been extensively worked. Our silver-mines are practically inexhaustible. In one of these the ore has been valued at £7,000,000 sterling. Pearl fisheries abound on our coasts. Wherever you may travel, you shall find abundant proof of the same industry and energy which characterize the home countries. You will see cities which yield in nothing to those of the Old World; farms, and vineyards, and crops of wild luxuriance, which rival and surpass those of the best cultivated lands at home; flocks and herds, cottages and comfortable houses enclosed in gardens, with overflowing abundance of fruit and flowers. If you ask me what is the secret of the loyalty of which our colonists have given abundant proof; of the vigour which they everywhere display; and of the industry, and prosperity, and harmony which prevail—I must reply, that we are indebted for it, under Heaven, to the fact that we shape our own destinies and make our own laws. We know our interests, and we endeavour to promote them. If we have local grievances, a spirit of justice is abroad, and we are sure to redress them. And I have pleasure in adding, that all parties throughout Australia take the deepest interest in the progress and welfare of Ireland. Not only in New South Wales, but in Victoria, Queensland, New Zealand, and the other colonies, the leading English and Protestant statesmen are no less earnest than their Irish and Catholic fellow-citizens in giving proof of their cordial union and practical sympathy with the Irish representatives who assert the legislative independence of their country; and I beg to assure you, my Lord Mayor and the other representatives of Ireland, that in every legitimate effort to redress the wrongs and to assert the freedom of this dear old land, you may rely with confidence on being sustained and strengthened by the public opinion, and by the material aid, of the free citizens of Australia.

And, whilst the Australians are thus one in heart and one in hand with their brothers of the dear mother country, we are not the less loyal to the empire of which we are proud to form part. In our sympathy with your struggles in the cause of liberty, we are impelled, not by hatred of England, but by love of Ireland. The freedom which we enjoy is the mainstay of the empire's strength; and we desire that Ireland should, to the fullest extent, enjoy the same freedom, without which the empire cannot stand. Throughout our remote colonies the imperial flag is honoured and respected to-day as, perhaps, no other flag has been honoured since the early days of imperial Rome. I am confident that, with a free and enlightened people, making their own laws, developing their own resources, guarding the fruits of their thrift and industry, promoting their own interests, asserting their rights, and exercising, with all, a legitimate influence in shaping the destinies of the empire, the imperial flag will nowhere be more respected and honoured, and nowhere more vigorously sustained, than in this your favoured land, by the generous and devoted sons of Erin.

THE FRUITS OF SELF-CULTURE.

(*Paper read at a Special Meeting of the Catholic Young Men's Association, Sydney, 1st December*, 1884.)

I PROPOSE to sketch for you this evening the advantages that accrue from cultivating the faculties with which nature may have endowed us. And it appears to me that this subject should be one of special interest to you, for nature has lavishly bestowed her richest gifts upon Australia's sons, gifts which uncultivated must remain sterile and fruitless, but when cherished and matured cannot fail to shed fragrance over life and to produce abundant and most happy fruits. But it is not my intention to lead you by any paths of abstruse logical rules or philosophical reasoning. I will endeavour to pursue my theme in accordance with the more familiar method of examples, setting before you some few instances of earnest and devoted men, who without the advantages which wealth and rank may bring, availed of the opportunities within their reach, and, cultivating their talents and disciplining the mind, lifted themselves up in the social scale, till they became ornaments of society and conferred blessings on their fellow-men.

It is to be regretted, indeed, that too many young men at the present day prefer a life of indolence to industry, and fritter away the years of ycuth and early manhood in idleness and vain pursuits. A thousand excuses are never wanting to justify them in such a course. Some will say: Oh! it is all the fault of a bad government. But they who thus speak appear to forget that it is not within the domain of government, no matter what its form or its perfection may be, to intrude itself at each one's fireside, even under the pretence to cultivate our individual talents, or to bring home to us the untold blessings of persevering industry and domestic peace. An old writer has well said that a government should be like the fence which the farmer constructs around his land. It should afford needful protection, and ward off intruders, and guard from injury; but something more than the fence is required to trim the flowers and reap the harvests, and ripen the fruits; on the owner himself it must in a great measure depend that the land which he has enclosed shall be a smiling garden rather than a desert waste.

But what are we to say of those who appear to fancy that if they were blessed with wealth and rank, their happiness would be complete? They forget that riches or dignity of themselves, do not bring contentment and peace. Even more than poverty, they stand in need of industry, energy and toil, and without noble sentiments, and self-discipline, and the training of the mind, wealth and titles are oftentimes little better than a burden.

> "Can gold calm passion, or make reason shine?
> Can we dig peace or wisdom from the mine?
> Nothing is meaner than a wretch of state.
> The happy only are the truly great."

You have probably heard of the rich Englishman who, in the last century, whilst enjoying a yachting tour fell into the hands of Turkish corsairs, and was led off to slavery in Algiers. He had been for a long time a martyr to gout; but during the two years that he was kept in slavery he was fed on bread and water, and forced to work every day, making bricks under the broiling sun of Africa. When he was at length ransomed he was found to be perfectly freed from the gout, and till the day of his death he never again suffered from its attacks. Lord Bacon calls riches "the baggage of virtue." If an army in battle-array be intent solely on its baggage, the victory will soon be lost. So, too, unless we have industry and make good use of riches, they can be but of little avail to us. There are not wanting those who make the proper use of wealth, great souls, who

> "Touch'd with warmth divine,
> Give gold a price, and teach its beams to shine;
> All hoarded treasures they repute a load,
> Nor think their wealth their own, till well bestowed."

But others, with no end of riches, never enjoy a day's happiness. Take, for instance, the nobleman with £50,000 a year, whose death-bed scene is described by Pope:

> "In the worst inn's worst room, with mat half hung,
> The floors of plaster, and the walls of dung:
> On once a flock bed, but repaired with straw,
> With tape-tied curtains never meant to draw;
> The 'George and Garter' dangling from that bed
> Where tawdry yellow strove with dirty red—
> Great Villiers lies.
> No wit to flatter; left of all his store;
> No fool to laugh at, which he valued more;
> There, victor of his health, of fortune, friends,
> And fame, this lord of useless thousands ends."

But to proceed to the subject of my lecture, I might cite for you many examples from the early classic period. Take, for instance, the history of Proæresius and his companion Hephæstion. They were of humble birth; but having heard at Antioch of the fame of the schools of Athens, they set out on foot and worked their way as best they could, till they reached the Grecian capital of letters, where they found themselves wholly destitute of even the ordinary necessaries of life. They had only one suit of clothes and one set of blankets. During the time that Hephæstion was engaged at school, his companion betook himself to the blankets, studying his lessons there and working at his exercises. When Hephæstion returned from school, they exchanged places; Proæresius put on the clothes and hurried off to class, whilst Hephæstion took possession of the blankets. What was the result of this persistent cultivation of their talents, and of this persevering industry? The result was that Hephæstion became one of the most distinguished grammarians of the age; and as for Proæresius, he made his way to be the leader of the Rhetoricians of Athens, and subsequently won immortal fame in Gaul and Rome. A bronze statue, as large as life, was erected to him in Rome, with the inscription, "The Queen of Cities to the Prince of Eloquence;" every honour was lavished upon him that the capital of the world could bestow, and he enjoyed his laurels till the ripe old age of ninety years.

But you will wish me rather to illustrate my subject by examples from later times, and perhaps it would be difficult to find a weightier or more appropriate example than that of the illustrious Sovereign Pontiff Pope Sixtus V.

About 100 miles below Ancona, on a crest of the Apennines, in one of the least frequented parts of that classic land, with the blue waters of the Adriatic spread out before it, and the highest mountains of Umbria towering in the distance, stands the castellated hamlet of Grottamare. There, Felice Peretti, the future Pope, was born, in 1521. His father was an humble gardener, who had to struggle all his life against the direst poverty, and the mother, in order to find bread for the children, was obliged to take service with a wealthy neighbour. The young Felice was himself for a time a swineherd on the neighbouring hills. It was only after a long and earnest appeal that the father permitted his child to go to school, for the family, he said, stood in need of his help. Very soon, by his attention to his lessons, the youth attracted the notice of a Franciscan friar, who used often to visit the school, and who was particularly struck by his earnestness, as well as by his talents and piety. At twelve years, through the influence of this good friend, he became an inmate of the neighbouring Franciscan monastery, at Montalto, and he brought with him to the cloister the love of discipline, and the devotedness to study which had characterized his earlier years. Promoted to the priesthood, he soon ranked among the most fervent preachers of the age. It was no small tribute to his eloquence and piety that, when he preached in Rome, all that were most distinguished in its schools and religious houses gathered around his pulpit, foremost among them being St. Ignatius of Loyola, St. Philip Neri, and Cardinal Ghislieri, afterwards Pope, and honoured on our altars as St. Pius V. At every stage of his eventful career he was remarkable for three things; that is, for his love of books, and of the fine arts, and of building. On the third day of the Conclave, after the death of Gregory XIII., Cardinal Peretti was proclaimed Pope, and took the name of Sixtus V. His Pontificate, though short—for it lasted only five years—was nevertheless one of the most brilliant that adorned the annals of the Church. It has been truly said of him, that he held in his firm hand the balance of European power. He saved religion in France, and with it saved the French monarchy. He dealt a death-blow to Lutheranism in Germany. He strove to consolidate the kingdom of Poland as a bulwark of civilization and of Europe against the Ottoman incursions and against the Russian power. He banished public crime from the Papal States, rooted out the lawless bands of banditti that made life and industry insecure, and reformed the whole administration of justice. The material aspect of the city of Rome was renewed with an unrivalled magnificence. The genius of Michael Angelo had devised the wondrous dome to crown the noblest church in Christendom. Twenty years had now elapsed since his death, and no one had dared to take in hand the task of erecting it. Public opinion was beginning to entertain a fixed idea that nothing short of a miracle could achieve this work. It was achieved, however, by the indomitable will of Sixtus V. He built the Vatican Library; and one of the most distinguished Italians of the present day has not hesitated to write of this great work, that "to it Italy owes the most splendid of her glories, and the preservation and recovery of the classic arts and culture, and not unfrequently her priority in all kinds of literature and science." Several quarters of the city were badly provided with water. He spanned the Campagna with an aqueduct, resting on tiers of arches, and extending over more than twenty miles, and brought an inexhaustible supply, which has ever since proved a blessing, especially to the poorer citizens. He erected the magnificent obelisk which adorns the piazza of St. Peter's. It had once stood in Nero's circus, but was cast down during the incursions of the Barbarians. Many times men had devised schemes for re-erecting it, but had given up their projects in despair. Even Michael Angelo declared such an undertaking to be impracticable. That was not the age of electricity and steam, yet Sixtus V. decreed that the work should be commenced. Very soon the salvos of cannon from St. Angelo's and the enthusiastic cheers of an immense concourse of people announced that the enterprise was happily accomplished. Thus every day new works were planned, streets were marked out, churches built, monuments erected. Of the Emperor Augustus it was said, that he found Rome a city of brick, and that he left it a city of marble. Something similar might be repeated of this great Pope. Shortly after the death of Sixtus V., a Benedictine abbot thus wrote from the Eternal City: "I am here after an absence of ten years, and do not recognise the city, so new does all appear to me to be: monuments, streets, piazzas, fountains, aqueducts, obelisks and other wonders, all the work of Sixtus V. If I were a poet, I would say that at the imperious sound of the trumpet of that magnanimous Pope, the wakened limbs of that half-buried and gigantic body which spreads over the Latin Campagna had been summoned to life, and that, thanks to the power of his fervent and exuberant spirit, a new Rome had arisen from the ashes of the old."

Such were the great deeds of the Sovereign Pontiff, whose early days were spent tending swine on the coast of the Adriatic.

Cardinal Wolsey, "one who though fashioned to much honour, was from an humble stock," was born in the market-town of Ipswich, in 1471. His talents and application to study won for him a place in the grammar school of Ipswich, and subsequently a scholarship in Magdalene College. Step by step he rapidly advanced, till we meet him installed Royal Chaplain, "exceeding wise, fair spoken, and persuading." As Archbishop of York, Lord Chancellor, confidential adviser of the King, and Cardinal, he guided the helm of state amid stormy seas, and had at his disposal every office of emolument in the kingdom. His household comprised about 800 persons, the chief offices being filled by barons and knights, and among his retainers were numbered the sons of the highest families, aspiring, under his patronage, to posts of civil or military preferment. But unerring wisdom has written the words, "Put not your trust in princes," and Wolsey was to be no exception to the rule. He had erected, at Hampton Court, the noblest palace in England,

"Close by those meads, for ever crowned with flowers,
Where Thames with pride surveys his rising towers,
There stands a structure of majestic fame,
Which from the neighbouring Hampton takes its name."

This palace, enriched with all its costliest furniture, he presented as a gift to Henry VIII. But Wolsey had refused to pronounce the divorce of the King from his lawful wife, Queen Catherine, and no gift could stay the monarch's rage. Arrested, the Cardinal expired a prisoner in the captor's hands; but in Shakespeare's words:—

> "His overthrow heaped happiness upon him;
> For then, and not till then, he felt himself,
> And found the blessedness of being little;
> And, to add greater honours to his age
> Than man could give him, he died fearing God."

I will now cite the example of one whose world-wide fame has added lustre to the Cardinalatial dignity in our own days: I mean Cardinal Mezzofanti, the greatest linguist that the world has ever known. He was born in Bologna, on the 17th of September, 1774. His father was a carpenter by trade. The young Mezzofanti, having learned the mere rudiments, began to work in his father's shop. It is said that close by the shop was a classical school, and the youth overhearing the lessons in Latin and Greek, and applying himself privately to study, soon began to acquire a thorough knowledge of these languages. A priest of the oratory in Bologna, seeing his talent, directed him in his studies. One day this good priest was called away whilst giving him some lesson, and on his return looked in vain for his little pupil. There was a chest of drawers in a corner of the room, and the young Mezzofanti getting into one of the drawers, and partially closing it, had fallen fast asleep. In due course, Mezzofanti was promoted to Holy Orders, and during the invasion of North Italy by the allied army under the Russian, General Suwarrow, he gave singular proofs of his linguistic powers. Among the wounded soldiers in the hospital of Bologna there were some from Poland, and Roumania, and Finland, and almost every other province of Russia or Austria. When summoned to the bedside of these sufferers, a few days sufficed for him to acquire a knowledge of each one's language, and even of the particular dialect which he spoke, so that he was able to impart to them all the consolations of religion. Lord Byron visited him in Bologna, in 1820, and pronounced him to be "a walking polyglot and a monster of languages." A distinguished Hungarian astronomer, writing from Bologna in the same year, says: "The annual eclipse of the sun was one curiosity, and Mezzofanti another." Pope Gregory XVI. invited him to Rome. His answer was characteristic: "Holy Father, people say that I can speak a great many languages. In no one of them, nor in them all, can I find words to express how deeply I feel this mark of your Holiness's regard." The highest honours were heaped upon him at the Roman Court, and in a few years he was promoted to the Cardinalate. He was said to have been thoroughly conversant with more than fifty languages, and he was in a particular manner quite at home in English. More than once, in familiar conversation, I myself have heard him speak in a most learned way about our national literature, and cite long passages from Moore and Milton and other classical writers. On one occasion, in 1847, I accompanied the late Archbishop of Tuam to some solemn ceremony at the Sistine Chapel in the Vatican. Whilst waiting in the vestibule, Cardinal Mezzofanti happened to be passing, and stopped to speak with the Archbishop. After a few sentences in Irish, the Cardinal continued the conversation in English, expressing his regret that he had not had leisure to devote more attention to the Celtic, a language that he prized so much. When the Archbishop addressed some complimentary words to him on his wonderful knowledge of so many languages, the Cardinal exclaimed: *Vox et praeterea nihil:* "I am a voice and nothing more." He was then old, and the words seemed most appropriate, for he was so remarkably thin and slender and weak that one would fancy the first breeze would carry him away. Two years later he died, and his remains were deposited at San Onofrio, where Tasso rests in peace.

But I must choose some instances from other walks of life. The celebrated Giotto holds a foremost place among the great restorers of painting in the fourteenth century. He was the son of a poor shepherd, and passed his early years tending the flocks in his native Tuscan valley of Vespignano. Even whilst thus engaged he endeavoured to cultivate his talent for drawing, and essayed to reproduce on some fragment of rock or slate the sheep and the trees and other forms of nature that he saw around him. One of his simple designs being brought under the notice of Cimabue, that great master invited him to his studio, and gave him lessons in the art of painting. Giotto soon outstripped all his compeers. There was this particular that gave perfection to his style of art, that he introduced into his paintings all that was beautiful in nature, whilst he exhibited at the same time an unrivalled ideal elevation and grandeur of character. Florence, Padua, Verona, Pisa, Naples, and Rome vied with each other in their efforts to be enriched with his works. We are told that Pope Boniface VIII. sent a messenger to visit the different studios throughout Italy to procure specimens of the artists' skill. When he came to Giotto, the famous painter in reply to his queries took a paper and pencil, and, resting his elbow on his side to form a sort of compass, with one turn of his hand drew a circle so perfect and exact that it was a marvel to behold. "Is this all that I am to get," asked the courtier. "That is enough and to spare," replied Giotto; "put it with the rest, and see will it be recognized." It is needless to add that it was recognized, and that some of the most remarkable of Giotto's masterpieces are those that, thanks to the Pontiff's patronage, adorn the halls of the Vatican. He was no less famed as an architect than as a painter. The matchless Campanile, or Bell-tower of Florence, so well described as a "serene height of mountain alabaster, coloured like a cloud and chased like a sea-shell," is, perhaps, the greatest monument of his architectural skill. It is encrusted with many coloured marbles, from the base to the summit, and no engraving or photograph can give an idea of the chaste elegance of the columns, and the tracery of the windows, which give lightness to the structure, and the finish and soft harmony of the whole building. Ruskin avows himself enchanted with this great monument of the fourteenth century, and treating of the "Seven Lamps of Architecture" declares that they are all combined, "and that in their highest possible relative degrees, only in one building of the world, the Campanile of Giotto at Florence." Such were the works of the Tuscan shepherd-boy. He was the cherished friend of all the literary men of the day, and his fame is enshrined in the writings of Dante and Petrarch. He died in the year 1336, at the age of sixty, and was interred in the Cathedral of Florence with all the pomp and ceremony befitting the obsequies of one whom all Italy honoured and revered.

Claude of Lorraine attained pre-eminence in landscape painting. He was a native of Lorraine, and served his time as a pastry-cook. His parents dying, a relative, who travelled as a lace-dealer, took the young Claude to Italy; but deserted him, quite penniless, in Rome. He was there employed as servant by a painter, for whom he cooked, and cleansed the brushes, and mixed the paints. He accompanied his master when sketching the scenery of the Sabine Hills, and, humble though his duties were, his observant mind neglected not a single one of the varied tints of light and shade, and the gems of nature that are scattered there. The waterfall at Tivoli, with the surrounding scenery, and the autumn sunset, seen from the slopes of Monte Catullo, left an indelible impression on his mind; and in after years he would seem to have taken them as his ideal in his greatest works. Robertson does not hesitate to say that, "for purity of atmosphere, sunny serenity of sky, and all-pervading sweetness, the landscapes of Claude are still without a rival." And Charles Blanc writes: "He is the only painter who could look in the face of the sun—who could paint atmosphere as necessary to the life of the landscape as to the respiration of man. Nicholas Poussin exaggerated nature as if she were insufficient of herself to fill his heart with grandeur; and Gaspar Poussin dramatized his landscapes by the introduction of storm and tempest; but the beautifully emotional nature of Claude lifts us into a land which is a paradise in its peace and brightness, and dream-like in its light and splendour." He was never ashamed of his humble origin; and, a little before his death, one of his friends, giving a sketch of his career, added: "If ever anyone from poor beginnings or scanty learning became so skilled in painting as to fill the world with his fame, this was surely our Claude, universally known by the name of his native place—Lorraine."

But I must take a few instances from the celebrated painters who flourished nearer home. William Hogarth, who is regarded as the greatest pictorial satirist of England, was born in 1697. His father was a school-master, who, quitting his native Westmoreland, went to London in search of fortune; but failed to ascend higher in the walks of life than reader at a printing-office. William's first employment was the engraving of arms and shop-bills; and, as he gave proof of skill in this branch of trade, he was employed in designing plates for book-sellers. At this time he is described as a little man, fond of wearing a sky-blue coat whenever he could get it; but seldom having a shilling in his pocket. He was, however, at all times busy, sketching every ludicrous scene that he happened to witness in the taverns and thoroughfares of London; and so faithfully did he reproduce nature, that, notwithstanding he was entirely self-taught, his first paintings secured the attention of the public, and he almost at a bound rose to fame. One of the most remarkable of his paintings is "The March to Finchley." The approach of the Pretender had stirred up the military ardour of the Londoners, and the guards were ordered to the front. The sky and the scenery of the painting are admirably executed; but the confusion of the motley group of grenadiers, boxers, chimney-sweeps, and pipers, and of the waggon-loads of women, babies, knapsacks, &c., baffles description. Hogarth desired to dedicate it to George II.; but his Hanoverian majesty replied: "I hate *bainting and boetry.* Neither the one nor the other ever did any good. Does the fellow mean to ridicule my guards? He deserves to be picketted for his insolence. Take his trumpery out of my sight." In 1747, Hogarth gave to the world his twelve Plates, alternating the results of Industry and Idleness, exemplified in the lives of two apprentices. One of them, pursuing good courses, is described rising gradually in the social scale, till he becomes an ornament of his country; the other, giving way to idleness, falls into wretchedness and ends in ruin. The last painting of Hogarth, by a singular coincidence, was called "*Finis*, or the End of All Things." On the left is a ruined tower, with a decayed dial-plate; at its base is a tombstone, sculptured with a skull, and leaning upon part of the shaft of a column is Time, breathing out *Finis*, his scythe and hour-glass are broken, and in one hand he holds his Will, in which he bequeathes all to Chaos. Close by, are an empty ragged purse, a commission of bankruptcy against poor Dame Nature, and a play-book opened at the last page. In the foreground are a broken bow, a broken crown, and a worn-out scrubbing-brush. On the right hand are a withered tree, an unroofed cottage, a cracked bell, a broken bottle, a whip without its lash, a defaced Ionic capital, a painter's broken palette, and other emblems of ruin. In the distance we see a man gibbetted in chains, and a ship foundering at sea; and, in the firmament, the moon is darkened by the death of Phœbus, who, with his lifeless coursers, lies extended on a cloud, his chariot-wheels broken, and his light put out. When this painting was completed, Hogarth cried out, "All is over," and he never again resumed his pencil.

William Turner, the most varied and the best landscape painter of the English school, was the son of a hairdresser in one of the back alleys of London. His first drawing is said to have been a lion, copied from an emblazoned coat-of-arms in the house of one of his father's customers. He had accompanied his father thither to take a lesson in hair-cutting; but the boy's attention was more engaged by the coat-of-arms and its rich colours than with the old man's skill in his art. His father was so pleased with the copy of the lion, that ever afterwards, when asked, as he often was, "Well, Turner, what is William to be?" he would reply, with a look of delight, "William is going to be a painter." As years rolled on, he was employed to colour prints; and when in this he gave proof of talent, he was engaged to add skies and foregrounds to architectural designs. He was thus encouraged to study nature, and was led on by degrees to perfection in the landscape art. "If he did not exhaust art or nature, he may be fairly said to have exhausted all that was then known of landscape art, and to have gone further than anyone else in the interpretation of nature." Others have drawn the appearance of clouds; but Turner would attempt to show how they were formed. Others have drawn rocks; but he, with a few deft lines, would teach their very structure and consistency. Others could hide things in a mist; but he would reveal things through mist. Others could make something like a rainbow; but he, almost without colour, shows it standing out, a bow of light arrested by vapour in mid-air, not flat upon a mountain, or printed on a cloud. Of "The Slave-ship," which is regarded as Turner's masterpiece, Mr. Ruskin writes: "I think the noblest sea that Turner has ever painted, and, if so, the noblest, certainly, ever painted by man, is that of 'The Slave-ship.' It is a sunset on the Adriatic after a prolonged storm; but the storm is partially lulled, and the torn and streaming rain-clouds are moving in scarlet lines to lose themselves in the hollow of the night. The whole surface of sea, included in the picture, is divided into two ridges of enormous swell—not high nor local; but a low, broad heaving of the whole ocean, like the lifting of its bosom by deep-drawn breath after the torture of the storm. Between these two ridges, the fire of the sunset falls along the trough of the sea, dyeing it with an awful but glorious light, the intense but lurid splendour of which burns like gold, and bathes like blood. Along this fiery path and valley, the tossing waves, by which the swell of the sea is restlessly divided, lift themselves in dark, indefinite, fantastic forms, each casting a faint and ghastly shadow behind it along the illumined foam. They do not rise everywhere; but three or four together in wild groups, fitfully and furiously, as the under-strength of the swell compels or permits them, leaving behind them treacherous spaces of level and whirling water; now lighted with green and lamp-like fire; now flashing back the gold of the declining sun; now fearfully dyed from above with the indistinguishable images of the burning clouds, which fall upon them in flakes of crimson and scarlet, and give to the reckless waves the added motion of their own fiery flying." The closing years of Turner marked a period of decay in his art, through the fault of an over-indulgence in drink. When heated with wine, he would seat himself to his work on the top of a flight of steps, astride a box. "There he sat, a shabby Bacchus, nodding like a mandarin at his picture, which he, with a pendulum motion, now touched with his brush, now receded from." At length, in 1845, his health, and with it in a great degree his mind, failed suddenly.

Canova, the founder of the modern school of sculpture in Italy, was the child of humble parents, living in a village of the Venetian territory. In childhood he displayed a taste for modelling, and was thus introduced to the patronage of a senator of Venice, who provided for his artistic training in a sculptor's studio. In his forty-fifth year, Canova was appointed chief curator of all the works of art in the Papal States. Napoleon was then at the zenith of his popularity, and Canova was called away to Paris, to furnish a model for a colossal statue of the idol of the French people. Napoleon, full of admiration for the artist's genius, pressed him to remain in Paris. "I could not live away from the treasures of Rome," Canova answered. "But," said Napoleon, "I will bring to Paris everything that is worth having in Rome." "You should bring Rome itself," was Canova's reply. Napoleon too literally endeavoured to carry out his threat. But when the idol of the French popularity was cast down, and peace restored, in 1815, Canova was the person deputed by the Papal Government to proceed to Paris to recover the works of art of which Rome had been so unjustly despoiled.

Two, at least, of the churches of Ireland are enriched with beautiful statues of the Blessed Virgin of the Immaculate Conception, one of the first religious subjects that won for the artist, Benzoni, a distinguished place among the sculptors of the present day. In my younger years I often visited his studio, and prominent there was a cast of a noble monument which he had presented as a gift to his native town in North Italy. It represented a venerable old man who grasped with one hand a young lad in tattered garments, and, lifting him up from his poor condition, pointed with the other to the artist's chisel and other various implements of art placed within his reach. And Benzoni took care to explain to the visitor that he himself was the poor lad thus rescued from poverty, and that he had executed this monument as a lasting memorial of his gratitude to his generous benefactor.

The great musical composer, Haydn, was the son of a struggling wheelwright. Almost from his childhood he sang in the cathedral choir of St. Stephen's at Vienna. In his sixteenth year, however, his voice broke, and unable to sing any longer in the choir he began to give lessons in instrumental music, and in this manner earned a maintenance. In his twenty-eighth year Prince Esterhazy placed him at the head of his private chapel. Whilst he held this post the Prince formed the design of dismissing his band. Haydn hearing of it composed the famous symphony, which is known as "Haydn's Farewell," in which one instrument after another becomes mute, and each musician, as soon as he has ceased to play, puts out his light, rolls up his music, and departs with his instrument. Esterhazy was so struck by this admirable composition that he changed his mind, and retained the band. Haydn spent the closing years of his life in the Imperial palace at Schönbrunn, situated in the most fashionable suburbs of Vienna. Full of gratitude to his Imperial benefactor, he not only every day, but many times each day, would perform on the piano, and sing in his feeble voice, "God save the Emperor." He was in his last illness when the French armies approached Vienna in 1809. A battery was erected close to the palace where he lodged. A few days later, as life was ebbing away, he had his piano moved to his bedside, and three times he sang as loudly as he could, "God save the Emperor:" this was his last effort, and the great musician a few hours later fell into his long sleep.

The life of George Kemp, architect of the beautiful Scott monument at Edinburgh, affords another instance of the success which is sure to attend industry and ability. He was the son of a herd, who pursued his calling on the southern slope of the Pentland hills. In his tenth year he was sent on a message to Roslyn, and the sight of its beautiful castle and chapel made a vivid impression on his mind. He served his time as a carpenter at Galashiels, and when travelling from place to place with his tools on his back took occasion to visit the noble ruins of Melrose, or Dryburg, or Jedburg, or some of the other monuments that abound in that neighbourhood. In order to cultivate his taste for architecture, he worked his way as a carpenter over the greater part of the north of England, availing himself of every opportunity to study and make sketches of its Gothic structures. On one occasion he travelled fifty miles on foot that he might visit the magnificent cathedral of York. Anxious to study the grand mediæval monuments of France, he proceeded to the Continent. His skill as a mechanic, and especially his knowledge of mill-work, readily secured him employment wherever he went. He usually chose for his work the neighbourhood of some fine old Gothic structure, and beneath its shadow he occupied his leisure hours. When the committee of the national monument, to be erected to Sir Walter Scott, offered a prize for the best design, some of the greatest names in classical architecture entered the lists of competition; but the design presented by George Kemp won the prize, and was unanimously selected.

None better understood the advantages that accrue from this discipline of labour than Pugin, whose name shall ever remain identified with the revival of ecclesiastical architecture in England. Having learned in his father's office all that could be taught him there, he hired himself as a common carpenter at one of the London theatres, that he might acquire a familiarity with work, whilst at the same time he continued to cultivate his architectural taste. At times he worked a sailing ship between London and the Continental ports, making drawings of the great ecclesiastical buildings wherever he went. He also made repeated journeys to study the mediæval cathedrals of France and Germany. Thus he indefatigably laboured till he attained that pre-eminence which has been most justly accorded him.

I might take very many examples to illustrate my subject from the lives of our English poets. Such, for instance, was Robert Burns, the great lyric poet of Scotland. His father was a nursery gardener, who had to struggle all his life with poverty and misfortune, but who nevertheless made every exertion to keep his children to school. As a boy, Robert was dull, and was only remarkable for being very much given to athletic sports. He studied hard, however, and in his sixteenth year began to write some poems in the Scottish dialect. Till his twenty-fifth year he cultivated a small farm, but his labour not proving successful he resolved to quit his native land and to emigrate to Jamaica. In order to procure sufficient money to pay his passage, he published a small volume of poems. His genius was at once recognised. He very soon gave up all thoughts of Jamaica, and found himself in Edinburgh associated with all that was eminent in letters, rank, and fashion. He experienced, however, the fickleness of patronage and applause, and was only in his thirty-seventh year when, towards the close of the last century, he died in the greatest wretchedness. His poems were a precious inheritance to his country; they were the first awakening of the spirit of true poetry in Great Britain after a long slumber, and the popularity which they at once acquired has continued unabated wherever the English language is spoken.

What shall I say of Shakespeare, the chief literary glory of England? His father was a glover in the town of Stratford-on-Avon, in Warwickshire, and appears also to have held a small farm. Several losses, however, brought the family to ruin; and our poet, at the early age of fourteen years, was withdrawn from school, and forced to seek a livelihood as best he could. We meet with him at one time as a butcher's assistant; at another, as a schoolmaster; and again, as a prompter's attendant in a London theatre. But all this time he silently cultivated his powers as a dramatist, and, step by step, he won his way to the very foremost rank among the writers for the stage. England is still proud of his genius, and reckons him among her greatest sons, fully endorsing the lofty eulogy pronounced by Dryden: "He was the man who, of all modern and perhaps ancient poets, had the largest and most comprehensive soul."

Some of these men may not have been everything that we would wish them to be. They may have strayed away at times into the devious ways of extravagance and folly, or perhaps of vice. But it is not in their faults that we are to follow them. We must only the more particularly admire and emulate their energy in overcoming the difficulties that strewed their path, and their care and industry in cultivating the talents which nature gave them. We do not judge of the sea by the scum which it casts upon the strand, nor do we admire its seething foam when it is lashed to fury by the tempest. But all this does not lessen the pleasure with which we listen to the harmony of its waves, or the delight with which we look out upon its boundless expanse when its tranquil waters reflect the beauty of the firmament, and mirror, to the thoughtful mind, the glory of the Creator.

But to return to our subject, it may interest you to have an example of one who, for a quarter of a century, was justly ranked among the leaders of the Catholic Press of France. Louis Veuillot died in Paris in the month of April last year. His family were humble peasants in the Department of Loiret. His father, a journeyman cooper, came to Paris, in search of employment, when Louis was only five years old, and, after a time, opened a small shop. Louis, in one of his works, relates that, whilst he was a child, he felt indignant at the tone of insolence and superiority with which rich infidel customers used to give their orders in the poor shop of his father. "Why should this be," he used to ask; "for my father is good, and brave, and strong, and has never wronged anyone; whilst these insolent men are mean, and dishonest, and immoral? My heart," he adds, "used to leap with indignation at this sight, and with longing to put down, humiliate, and crush their insolence." And, in after-life, he did crush it with a vengeance. Louis was, at this time, ignorant of religion; and, as he grew up, ranged himself among the socialists and infidels. In 1838, however, whilst visiting Rome, the light of truth shone upon him, and he was led to the bosom of the Catholic Church. Thenceforward, he waged an unceasing war against the infidelity, and socialism, and false liberalism of his native land, with a vigour and brilliancy without a parallel in the annals of journalism. Montalambert and his school would fight the adversaries of truth only with gilt rapier and crusader's lance; but Louis Veuillot would wield the battle-axe with giant force, and fell his opponent with the first weapon at hand, whatever it might be. The secret of his many triumphs lay in this, that he never parleyed with error, and never compromised the principles of truth. He never bowed to injustice; never flattered the passions of the great; never flinched before tyranny; and, so far as within him lay, never failed to tear the mask from hypocrisy. With all this, in private life, he was affectionate, and affable, and genial, and he was untiring in works of piety and charity. The *Imitation of Christ* was his favourite book; and to it he refers in the opening verse of the sweet little poem which he composed:—

"Let my pen be at my side;
At my feet this book be hid;
And the Crucifix, my pride,
On my heart—then close the lid."

The astronomer, Copernicus, who has given his name to the scientific solar system now accepted by the learned world, was the son of a Polish baker. He had a natural bent towards mathematics, and he cultivated this study with passion through all its branches. That he might improve his knowledge of astronomy, he proceeded to Rome, and taught mathematics there for several years. In recognition of his singular merit, he was promoted to a rich benefice in Germany, the revenue of which supplied him with abundant means for his life-long astronomical researches. His working-day he divided into three parts: one, devoted to the duties of his benefice; another, to giving medical advice gratuitously to the poor; and the third, to study. His great work, *De revolutionibus orbium*, which has immortalized his name, was published in 1543, in his seventieth year. It was only a few hours before his death that the first complete copy of this work was presented to him.

The career of Herschel, one of the most famous astronomers of the present century, was still more remarkable. He was a native of Saxony; and, associating himself with a strolling German band, went about from town to town in England to earn his bread. Being enrolled in the band of the Durham militia, whilst the regiment was stationed at Doncaster, he got access to some scientific works, which he perused with avidity. He was subsequently organist in Bath, and applied himself during his leisure hours to the construction of telescopes. Step by step he perfected himself in the study of astronomy. After long and painful labour, he completed a five-foot reflector, by which he was able to observe the ring and satellites of Saturn. Not satisfied with this triumph, he proceeded to make other instruments, in succession, of seven, ten, and even twenty feet. As an instance of his untiring perseverance, we are told that, when constructing the seven-foot reflector, he made no fewer than 200 specula before he could give to his work that perfection which he sought. Whilst gauging the heavens with his telescopes, he patiently earned his bread by performing on the violin and other instruments at the public concerts. So eager was he in his astronomical studies, that he would steal away from the concert-room during an interval of the performance, give a little turn at his telescope, and then contentedly return to his place in the band. At length he discovered a new planet, to which he gave the name of *Georgium Sidus*, and was at once lifted up from obscurity to fame. He was appointed Astronomer Royal, with a salary of £400 a year; other honours followed in quick succession; but, in prosperity as in adversity, he was indefatigable in his labours till his death, in 1822, at the age of eighty-four years.

Cuvier was a native of Würtemburg. When a boy, he was attracted to the study of natural history by the sight of a volume of Buffon, which accidentally fell in his way. He read with delight the *System of Nature* of Linnæus, which he got as a prize at school. Owing to the straitened circumstances of his parents, he, in his eighteenth year, took the situation of tutor in a family residing on the coast, near Fécamp, in Normandy. Here he was brought face to face with the wonders of the sea. Strolling along the shore one day, he observed a stranded cuttle-fish. This he brought home and carefully dissected; and thus began the study of the molluscs, which he pursued for several years, till it won for him an eminent place in the scientific world. He never relaxed his industry; and, though a foreigner by birth, he attained the honourable post of Chancellor of the University of Paris, and became a Peer of France.

No less remarkable in the pursuits of science was Faraday, whom Chambers justly styles "one of the most distinguished chemists and natural philosophers of the present century." He was particularly successful in his researches regarding electricity and magnetism, and opened the way to those practical wonderful discoveries which have marked the progress of science in our own days. And yet he was the son of a journeyman blacksmith, who lived in rooms over a coach-house near Manchester-square in London. His education was limited to the rudiments of reading, writing, and arithmetic, at an ordinary poor school. At the age of thirteen he was employed as an errand-boy by a fourth-rate London bookseller. In after life he used to display a special kindness for the newspaper boys, and he would say: "I once carried newspapers myself." In 1805, being fourteen years of age, he served as an apprentice to the bookbinding trade; and here it would seem that there could be no escape from the poet's words being verified in his career:—

> "Full many a flower is born to blush unseen,
> And waste its sweetness on the desert air."

But the youthful Faraday utilized his time, and, when he had done the work allotted him, applied himself to derive information from the books which were passing through his hands. Works treating of chemistry and electricity were his delight. Whenever he could, he attended the evening lectures given by Mr. Tatum, on Natural Philosophy, the fee of 1*s*., for entrance, being paid by his brother, who was a blacksmith. From the knowledge which he thus acquired, he was enabled, on the termination of his apprenticeship, to secure the post of assistant in the chemical laboratory of the Royal Institution, with a salary of £1 5*s*. a-week, and with two rooms at the top of the house. Here, humble as his employment was, he was in constant intercourse with Sir Humphrey Davy, the greatest chemist of the day; and, to use his own words, his daily manual work was "an inexhaustible mine of knowledge and improvement." Step by step, by his industry and untiring spirit of observation, he advanced in the paths of science, till we find him Lecturer at the Royal Academy of Woolwich, the correspondent of

Humboldt and Arago, honoured by the universities and scientific academies, and with a house in Hampton Court allotted him by the Queen, receiving a pension from the State in recognition of his public services. With all that, he was most disinterested and ever ready to give a helping hand to those who were in need. The words which he made use of in one of his early lectures mark out his own course through life: "It is not he who has soared above his fellow-creatures in power—it is not he who can command most readily the pampering couch or the costly luxury; but it is he who has done most good to his fellows—he who has directed them in the weak moment, aided them in the moment of necessity, and enlightened them in their ignorance—that leads the ranks of mankind."

Here I may remark, that efforts have been made at times to stir up prejudice against the study of natural philosophy, on the plea that it leads to the shipwreck of Divine faith. But, I may assure you, my friends, that such a statement is a mere fallacy, and proceeds solely from the ignorance or the sophistry of weak and half-instructed minds. True science cannot lead away from God; for all truth must lead to Him. Divine Revelation has come to us from God; and it is the same Creator who has spread out the book of nature before us, to be studied by the rational soul. Like the clouds that obscure the sun, a little learning and imperfect science may, for a time, hide Divine knowledge from us; but mature study and perfect science will be sure to lead back to God. To the irreligious soul, already defiant of the Creator's wisdom, science may be a peril; but to the child of faith, the study of nature and the pursuits of science serve only to reveal more and more the wondrous perfections of God, and, full of gratitude and joy, he will repeat:—

"Teach me so Thy works to read,
That my faith, new strength accruing,
May from world to world proceed,
Wisdom's faithful search pursuing.

Through the creatures Thou hast made
  Show the brightness of Thy glory;
Be eternal truth displayed
  In their substance transitory,
'Till green earth and ocean hoary,
  Massy rock and tender blade,
Tell the same unending story:
  We are truth in form arrayed."

But whilst we range from country to country in search of examples to illustrate our subject, shall we cull no flowers from the far off Island of the West, so dear to us all? It would be passing strange indeed if none such examples were to be found among a people so richly endowed with talents and so devoted to the paths of industry. But here the difficulty arises, not so much from the want of brilliant examples as from their number and variety, for it is no easy task to know which to select from the many that present themselves. I shall take only two or three, and the instances which I shall choose will have this advantage that they are already familiar to you all.

Eugene O'Curry was one of those earnest men who in our own time have spent their lives in laying deep and broad the foundations on which the solid structure of genuine history of Ireland may one day be raised. He was the son of Owen Mor O'Curry, a struggling farmer of Carrigaholt, in the south-west of the County Clare. Owen Mor had a thorough knowledge of the traditions of the country, and possessed several Irish MSS., which, as precious heirlooms, were handed down for generations in the family, and he dearly loved his native tongue. He was much respected by all his neighbours, nor was it forgotten that his father, during the terrible famine of 1742, proved himself a devoted friend to the sufferers, feeding the starving poor, visiting the fever-stricken families, and when the churchyards could not contain the dead, giving up a part of his own farm that it might be consecrated as a cemetery. In better times it was his delight to gather his neighbours around the fireside on winter nights and there entertain them by readings in Irish, and by songs, and before the party broke up he always made sure to sing for them a venerable old Irish hymn to the Blessed Virgin. There was but little of the schoolmaster at Carrigaholt in the early days of our Eugene, and he appears to have learned little more than to read and write the Irish well. The farmers' sons of the district, however, in the winter's nights formed among themselves a class of mutual improvement, teaching one another arithmetic, geography, and other branches useful for them. The country abounded in holy ruins, and many was the excursion which in the summer evenings young O'Curry made to Iniscattery or Holy Island, lying out in the Shannon a few miles from his native place. St. Kieran of Ossory had sanctified that spot, and St. Senanus had chosen it for his hallowed home. Its chapels and its sanctuaries were endeared to the faithful people of Carrigaholt, and Eugene endeavoured, as best he could, to collect from the neighbours every tradition connected with its ruins. But, as he himself declared in after times, "it was not till after my father's death that I fully awoke to the passion for gathering together the old fragments of our history. I knew he was a link between our day and a time when all was broken, scattered, hidden. When I called to mind the knowledge he possessed of every old ruin, manuscript, legend, and tradition in Thomond, I was filled with consternation to think that all was for ever gone and no record left." Thenceforth every moment he could spare from his daily toil was given up to the study of the antiquities and traditions of his country. The small farm not sufficing to support the family, Eugene obtained an appointment as warder in the Limerick asylum. The resident physician there became acquainted with his passion for study, and his wonderful knowledge of the Irish language;

and thus, when the Ordnance Survey of Ireland was set on foot, and practical Irish scholars were sought out to translate the ancient documents and to record the traditions of the various localities, O'Curry was at once employed on this field of congenial labour. He found here full scope for his special talents, and he threw himself with all his giant energy into his task, which was indeed a labour of love for him. His merit was soon universally recognized, and from the year 1834, when he was associated to the Ordnance Survey, till his death in July, 1862, he may be said to have taken a leading part in every national movement having for its object to illustrate the history of our country. His whole time was spent in examining the various and scattered collections of Irish MSS., translating the oldest texts, and recording the fast-fading traditions of our people. In 1853 he was employed under the Brehon Law Commission to transcribe and translate those ancient laws. It was towards the close of that year that I was introduced to him in the little room at Trinity College, where he and O'Donovan were busily engaged making transcripts of the oldest texts of the Brehon laws. I was a very young priest, and, unfortunately, quite a stranger as yet to Irish history, whilst he was the very foremost of living Celtic scholars and palæographers. Nevertheless, he was unassuming as a child, and most kind and considerate in answering the questions which my curiosity and inexperience proposed to him. He was full of enthusiasm whilst explaining the relative value of the ancient MSS. piled up before him, but his voice became slow and mournful when he spoke of the prevalent neglect of Celtic studies, and the sad indifference of so many to the genuine history of Ireland. When the Catholic University was established, the chair of Irish History and Archæology was assigned to O'Curry. This gave him the prominence which was his due, and the lectures which he delivered are the most important contribution of this studious age to our early history. Partly for this reason, and partly for the sterling love of religion and country, of which at all times he gave abundant proof, the name of Eugene O'Curry is, perhaps, the one among the modern writers on Irish history the most universally revered at home and abroad wherever the sons of St. Patrick are to be found. The illustrious D'Arcy M'Gee in a soul-stirring poem, written far away on the American continent, thus proclaims the universal regret at his being too soon taken from us:

> "Who are his mourners? By the hearth
> His presence kindled, sad they sit—
> They dwell throughout the living earth
> In homes his presence never lit;
> Where'er a Gaelic brother dwells,
> There Heaven has heard for him a pray'r;
> Where'er an Irish maiden tells
> Her votive beads, his soul has share.
> Where far or near, be it west or east,
> Glistens the Soggarth's sacred stole,
> There from the true, unprompted priest
> Shall rise a requiem for his soul.
> Such orisons like clouds shall rise
> From every realm beneath the sun;
> For where are now the shores or skies
> The Irish Soggarth has not won!"

The same eloquent writer thus sketches the merits of O'Curry: "Ideas of greatness may and do differ. But if the highest moral purposes, sustained by the highest moral courage, constitute grounds and a standard; if the rarest union of patient labour and sleepless enthusiasm have any claim to be so considered; if a continuous career of recovery and discovery, in a long abandoned domain of learned inquiry, may be called proofs of greatness: then, assuredly, when Ireland counts her famous sons of this age, that indomitable academician's name will be pronounced among the very first of her magnates."

Charles Bianconi, though a native of Italy, was quite a young boy when he was brought to Ireland by a certain

Faroni, and employed hawking cheap pictures about the country. In a short notice of his early career, sketched by himself in after times, he writes: "I shall never forget the ludicrous figure I cut in going into the street with these things in my hand, saying 'buy! buy!' to every person I met, and, when questioned as to the price, I was unable to reply except by counting on my fingers the number of pence I wanted." When his master quitted Ireland, after a year and a-half's stay, young Bianconi continued his work on his own account: "I at once got a box," he says, "made to contain large-framed prints. It was two feet long by one foot wide, and eighteen inches deep. This I filled with an assortment of prints from the largest to the smallest size. With this pack on my back, which weighed over 100 pounds, I have frequently walked twenty or thirty miles in the day. I was then seventeen years old, and I knew neither discouragement nor fatigue, for I felt that I had set to work to become somebody." The great work carried out in after life by this energetic man was the establishment of public conveyances between the towns chiefly in the south and west of Ireland. We may form an idea of the vast extent of this enterprise and the employment given, when we remember that in the year 1864, when he gave up the work to younger hands, it realized an annual income of £40,000. He was at all times kind and considerate and charitable, and was constantly doing good, such as paying for the education of orphan girls, or providing for the helpless relatives of those who died or were disabled in his service. But to the day of his death he was sharp in his accounts. Arriving at a London railway station he secured the only cab to be found there. He gave a seat in it to the millionaire Rothschild, but on landing him at his house made him pay the fare. Before the British Association, in 1857, he made the important statement which reflects such credit on the Irish people: "My conveyances, many of them carrying very important mails, have been travelling during all hours of the day and night, often in lonely and unfrequented places; and during the long period of forty-two years that my establishment is now in existence, the slightest injury has never been done by the people to my property, or that entrusted to my care."

I have already, I fear, detained you too long; and yet I cannot bring this lecture to a close without recording the name of Father Thomas Burke, of the Order of St. Dominick. Born in Galway, he had, from his early years, nothing save his piety and talents to commend him. Eloquence was, in a measure, natural to him; but, nevertheless, he studied and laboured, as few others could study or labour, to perfect himself more and more, and make his eloquence worthy of the noble themes of charity and religion, the interests of which he was, more than any man of the day, called upon to plead. Few lives can show a more fruitful record, or were more unselfishly devoted to the highest and noblest of causes—the building up of religion, and the succour of the widow, the orphan, and the indigent. At home and abroad he shall long be remembered as an ornament of his country, and his name shall be cherished by a grateful race. There is one thing which by word and example he never failed to teach his countrymen. It is this, that no matter what laurels they might win, or what high post of honour they might attain, they should love old Ireland, and cherish, fresh and unfading, a true filial devotion for their native land. Hear how, on the eve of St. Patrick's festival, far away beyond the Atlantic, after rebutting the false charges that had been made against Ireland, he apostrophizes his motherland: "O glory of earth and heaven! to-day thy great Apostle looks down upon thee from his high seat of bliss, and his heart rejoices. To-day the angels of God rejoice over thee; for the light of sanctity which still beams upon thee. To-day thy troops of virgin-martyr saints speak thy praises in the high courts of heaven. And I, O mother! far away from thy green bosom, hail thee from afar—as the prophet of old beholding the fair plains of the Promised Land—and proclaim this day that there is no land so fair, no spot on earth to be compared to thee, no island rising out of the wave so beautiful; that neither the sun, nor the moon, nor the stars of heaven, shine down upon anything so lovely as thou art, O Erin!" And again, looking forward to the future of the Irish race on the American Continent, he cries out: "Oh! how grand it is, as I see it to-day, this future of my race! Eight millions of people in America of Irish birth, and 18,000,000 of Irish blood! In thirty years there must be 50,000,000 born in this great country, spreading itself out in all things; rich, beyond all other nations, in minerals, rivers, harbours. Think of the magnificent element of 50,000,000 of Irishmen filling the public offices, and guiding the destinies of this country; and all bearing the distinctive marks of Irish character—an ornament and a pride to the land that adopted them by their Catholic temperance and purity. A power in this land will they be assuredly to guide and influence her actions, to draw the sword in the moment of danger, and to strike such blows in the cause of God and truth, as have never yet rung on the shield of injustice; a power in Ireland, before which the generous heart of America will be sure to bow in homage; a power that will not prevent you from being the best American citizens, while you will not lose the vision of Ireland, and of the debt you owe her. Then, and not till then, every enemy of Ireland will stand paralyzed to injure her; because the great phantom of Ireland in America will cause them to recoil, and force them to respect the dear, old, venerated, and beloved island."

As it is a rule not to speak of living men, I will take but one example from this our own fairest adopted land. Sir John O'Shannassy, who attained the highest posts of honour in the sister colony of Victoria, was born in the town of Tipperary, in the year 1818. His father was very poor, but sent his son, who showed signs of talent and proficiency, regularly to school. Owing to the death of his father, the young lad was, at an early age, thrown on his own resources, and opened a stationer's shop at Thurles. He soon, however, emigrated to Australia; and, settling at Port Philip, by his industry, ability, and energy, became, in a few years, the foremost man in the colony. Melbourne was but a hamlet when he landed there. He lived to see it become, and in no small part through his own exertions, one of the greatest and most flourishing cities of the empire. The colony was at first but a dependency of New South Wales: he was among the most prominent agitators for its independence. Their efforts were crowned with success in 1851; and thenceforward he was to be found in the front rank of all the changes of government that ensued. The men who fought the anti-transportation battle in Victoria, and who framed the constitution of the colony, did their task faithfully and well. They were brave, and they were intelligent. They kept the colony a home for free men, and they secured for it free institutions. They could say:—

> "With aching hands and toiling feet,
>   We dig and heap, lay stone on stone;
> We bear the burden and the heat
>   Of the long day, and wish 'twere done:
> Not till the hours of light return
> All we have built can man discern."

Not even his political opponents have denied to Sir John O'Shannassy a foremost place in that memorable band. When the gold rush took place, and oppressive regulations were made by the government, he became the advocate of the rights of the miners, and secured their recognition. The land had to be unlocked; and he worked untiringly to give the people due facilities for obtaining homesteads. If railways were developed, and a Local Government Act secured, it was mainly through the exertions of O'Shannassy. Three times he was prime minister; and if in his latter years this post of honour was denied him, this was due to his loyalty to the dictates of conscience, for he refused to lend the countenance of his name to any scheme, no matter how plausible, of infidel education. I had the pleasure of meeting him when he visited Ireland, towards the close of 1866. He was a man of colossal strength and colossal mind. In conversation he repeatedly expressed his gratification at the progress which his country had made whilst he was carving out his fortune in a more favoured land, and he was full of wonder and admiration at the institutions which he saw springing up on every side. In one of the convent national schools which he visited, he asked a little girl, very poor, but very bright and intelligent, to read her lesson; and she read it admirably for him. He then asked her what was her name; she replied, "Mary O'Shannassy." He did not attempt to hide his emotion; and he afterwards remarked, that he himself was at one time as poor as that little child. Addressing you, my friends, I must not omit that he took a prominent part in organizing the Victorian Catholic Literary Society, and was a constant patron of its lectures and re-unions. He was honoured with a special mark of favour by the Sovereign Pontiff a little before his death, in the month of May, last year. In addition to his many other merits, he was disinterested. He was entitled to a large pension from the Colonial Government, but never touched a penny of it. A few days after the demise of this illustrious Irishman, a political opponent, sketching his long and arduous services, declared that death had removed "the striking figure of one of the strongest of the men who built up Victoria."

These examples will suffice, I trust, to show how glorious are the triumphs, how fruitful the results achieved, in every country and in every walk of life, by persevering industry and self-culture. The young men of your Literary Society, availing themselves of the opportunities within their reach, may reap the same fruits. But even should their energy and toil not lead to the same material success, they shall at least have this to console them, that they have made the proper use of the noblest faculties with which the Creator has endowed them. Too often the talents received from nature are allowed to perish "like seeds upon the desert sand." And yet they are a sacred trust, a precious treasure placed in our hands, that we may cultivate, and perfect, and adorn them; and

> "As the form and pressure may be given,
> They wither upon earth, or ripen there for heaven."

BROWNE AND NOLAN, PRINTERS, DUBLIN.